STUDENT STUDY GUIDE
TO ACCOMPANY

SOCIAL WORK RESEARCH & EVALUATION

Quantitative and Qualitative Approaches

FIFTH EDITION

YVONNE A. UNRAU
JUDY L. KRYSIK
RICHARD M. GRINNELL, JR.

F.E. Peacock Publishers, Inc.
Itasca, Illinois

Printed in the United States of America.
ISBN: 0-87581-408-5
1 2 3 4 5 6 7 8 9 10
97 98 99

Contents

Introduction

THIS STUDY GUIDE is to be used as an inexpensive supplement to Grinnell's fifth edition of *Social Work Research and Evaluation: Quantitative and Qualitative Approaches* (F.E. Peacock Publishers, 1997). As in the Grinnell text, its major goal is to aid your understanding of basic research methodology and its applications to social work problems.

ORGANIZATION

To accomplish this goal, the *Guide* is organized into three basic parts: (1) exercises, (2) sample research studies, and (3) glossary.

Part I: Exercises

Part I contains 25 exercises that correspond directly to the 25 chapters in the Grinnell text. The exercises are intended to provide you with the opportunity to apply the basic concepts presented in the text to actual social work research studies contained in Part II.

To complement a variety of students' learning styles, three types of exercises are provided (i.e., self-study, group, and library). The self-study exercises require an individual, in-depth examination of each chapter. The group exercises facilitate class and group discussion. The library exercises encourage exploration of additional literature in an effort to strengthen your information retrieval skills.

The exercises are presented at varying levels of abstraction and require your creative and thoughtful input. For each set of exercises, you will be required to refer to a sample research study contained in Part II in the *Guide.*

Part II: Sample Research Studies

Part II contains eleven (A–K) real-life social work research studies that provide concrete examples of how the research concepts described in the Grinnell text can be used in actual social work research studies.

Part III: Glossary

The last part of the *Guide* defines over 600 terms that are commonly found in the professional social work literature. Many of these terms are used in the Grinnell text.

THE *GUIDE* CAN BE EASILY MODIFIED

In an effort to acknowledge individual preferences of research instructors and students alike, this *Guide* can be modified in three ways:

1. Additional exercises (self-study, group, and library) can be formulated in addition to the ones that are currently contained in Part I.
2. Additional sample research studies can be used to supplement the ones that are currently contained in Part II.
3. A different sample research study can be used rather than the one that is presently required for an individual chapter. For example, it may be preferable for students to read Research Study J to correspond with Chapter 1 rather than Research Study G, which is now required in this *Guide.*

All in all, the flexibility of this *Guide* is limited to the imagination of the research instructor and/or student. Your creative use of this *Guide* is encouraged.

RECOMMENDED PROCEDURE TO COMPLETE THE EXERCISES

You will get the most benefit from this *Guide* if you follow a five-step procedure:

1. Read the set of exercises that corresponds to the specific chapter in the text. As you read the exercises make a preliminary mental note of the key terms, concepts, and themes. Highlight these by underlining them in the exercises.
2. Note the sample research study that you will have to read in order to complete the assigned exercises. If a different research study is assigned by your instructor, make sure to obtain a copy before completing the exercises.
3. Read the assigned chapter in the text, paying particular attention to the terms and concepts you previously identified when you perused the exercises in Step 1.
4. Read the sample research study referred to in the exercises or assigned by your research instructor. Pay special attention to the corresponding terms and concepts contained in the study.
5. Answer each question by combining your understanding of the material in the chapter and its application demonstrated in the research study.

ACKNOWLEDGMENTS

Research Study B: Flowers, J.V., & Booarem, C.D. (1990). Four studies toward an empirical foundation for group therapy. *Advances in Group Work Research, 5,* 105-121. (Used with permission, Haworth Press)

Research Study C: Stephens, M.W., Grinnell, R.M., Jr., & Krysik, J.L. (1988). Victims of child sexual abuse: A research note. *Journal of Child Care, 3,* 65-76. (Used with permission, University of Calgary Press)

Research Study D: Moran, J.R. (1990). Social work education and students' humanistic attitudes. *Journal of Social Work Education, 25,* 13-19. (Used with permission, Council on Social Work Education)

Research Study E: LeCroy, C.W., & Goodwin, C.C. (1988). New directions in teaching social work methods: A content analysis. *Journal of Social Work Education, 24,* 43-49. (Used with permission, Council on Social Work Education)

Research Studies A, F–K: Used with permission from the authors.

Some of the statistical terms contained in the Glossary have been adapted and modified from: Robert W. Weinbach and Richard M. Grinnell, Jr. (1998). *Statistics for Social Workers* (4th ed.). White Plains, New York: Longman.

A FINAL WORD

The field of research in our profession is continuing to grow and develop. We believe this *Guide* will contribute to that growth. A sixth edition is anticipated, and suggestions for it are more than welcome. Please send your comments directly to:

Richard M. Grinnell, Jr.
Box 221
Bragg Creek, Alberta TOL OKO
CANADA

NOVEMBER, 1996 RICHARD M. GRINNELL, JR.

PART I

Exercises

This chapter utilizes Study F

Chapter 1

The Generation of Knowledge

CHAPTER OUTLINE

SELF-STUDY EXERCISES

1. Before you entered your social work program and before you read the chapter, how did you think our profession obtained its knowledge base?
2. After reading the chapter, discuss in detail the five ways our profession obtains its knowledge base. Compare and contrast your answer to your response in Question 1. Do you feel Study F contributed to our knowledge base? If so, why? If not, why not?
3. List and discuss the four reasons why we should never exclusively rely on our intuitions when making practice decisions. When is it necessary to make practice decisions based solely on intuition? Explain and discuss in detail using a social work example in your discussion.
4. What is "the research method?" How is this "method of knowing" more "objective" than the other four ways of knowing? What method of knowing did Study F use? Discuss in detail. Discuss how the authors of Study F could have used the other four ways of knowing to address the same research question. Be specific in your answer. Provide specific hypothetical examples in your discussion.
5. List and discuss in detail the four basic steps that the research method uses to obtain knowledge in our profession. Provide a social work example throughout your response. In relation to Study F, discuss how the authors must have used the basic steps contained within the research method.
6. List and briefly discuss the two complementry research approaches that are used within the research method way of knowing. Discuss in detail how Study F could have used the other research approach to answer the same research question. Do not read Chapters 4–6 to answer this question.
7. Define the word *research* in your own words. How does your definition differ from the one provided in the chapter? What are the similarities and the differences between the two definitions? Discuss in detail.
8. Discuss some of the factors that motivate social workers to do research studies. What do you feel the motivations of the authors of Study F were when they decided to do their study? Explain in detail.
9. List and discuss the two main goals of social work research studies. Provide a social work example in your discussion. Was study F a pure or an applied research study? Justify your response.
10. What is the general research problem area in Study F? Why is it important to clearly define the problem area before embarking on a research study?
11. In your opinion, what other related research question could have been the focus of Study F? What factors motivated the development of *your* research question? Discuss in detail.
12. What role do you believe applied research plays in the social work profession? Discuss the similarities and the differences between applied and pure research using Study F as an example.

13. List and discuss in detail the three research roles social workers can take to generate knowledge for our profession. Relate your discussion to Study F.
14. Discuss how the integration of social work practice with social work research (social work practitioner/researcher) could enhance the development of our profession. Use the points as outlined in the chapter to justify your discussion and relate your response to Study F.
15. In your opinion, were the three social work research roles as outlined in the chapter integrated in Study F? Why, or why not? Use the points as outlined in the chapter to justify your discussion.

GROUP EXERCISES

1. In groups of four, discuss the possible problems you feel could surface between social work researchers and social work practitioners. Discuss how the research method of knowing—*one* of the five ways of knowing—can be used to highlight the similarities rather than the differences between the two. How can the integration of the three research roles assist in diminishing potential problems? What other solutions can your group suggest to bridge the gap? Present your findings, in point form, to your entire class.
2. In groups of four, agree on one social work–related problem area (and a specific research question) and briefly discuss how each one of the five ways of knowing could be used to answer the research question. Discuss the factors that motivated your study. What is the overall goal of your study? Present your findings to the entire class.
3. *A Hard Question.* At this very beginning point in your social work research course, and after reading the Appendix, in groups of four, discuss the various cultural factors that you feel need to be taken into account when doing any social work research study. Do you feel any of these factors are different for doing a qualitative study verses a quantitative one? an applied study verses a pure one? Do you feel any of these factors are related to the motivation of social work researchers selecting research topics (e.g., Figures 1.1, 1.2)? Do you feel any of these factors influence any of three research roles as outlined in the chapter? Discuss in detail and provide one common social work example in your discussion. Report back to the entire class what your group found. Do not read Chapters 4–6 to answer this question.
4. *A Very Hard Question.* At this very beginning point in your social work course, and in groups of four, design a qualitative research study that proposes to answer a social work–related research question of your choice. With the same research question, design a quantitative research study. Compare the advantages and disadvantages of using both research approaches in answering your research question. Describe in detail how you could incorporate both research approaches, quantitative and qualitative, in a single research study

that answered the same research question. Present your results to the entire class. Do not read Chapters 4–6 to answer this question.

5. *A Very Very Hard Question*. With the results of Question 4 in mind, and in groups of four, discuss in detail how you would incorporate an "applied research component" and a "pure research component" in your qualitative study and in your quantitative study. Present your results to the entire class.

LIBRARY EXERCISES

1. At your university library, find out where the professional social work journals are located. What is the easiest way to locate a particular social work journal? List the titles of three social work journals, their call numbers, and library locations.
2. Select a research article from one of the journals you listed for the above exercise. After reading the article, answer the following two questions: (a) What problem(s) do you feel motivated this particular research study? (b) Was the goal of the study pure or applied? Explain in detail. In your opinion, did the study's findings contribute to our knowledge base? Why, or why not?

NOTES ON CHAPTER 1

This chapter utilizes Study J

Chapter 2

Research Contexts

CHAPTER OUTLINE

SELF-STUDY EXERCISES

1. List and discuss in detail the six factors that affect social work research studies. Provide a social work example throughout your entire discussion.

2. Discuss how the six factors mentioned above are highly interrelated with one another. After reading Study J, discuss how each one of these factors my have affected the research study.
3. Explain why social work research studies, such as Study J, must follow strict ethical guidelines. Would you have done anything differently to ensure that Study J was more ethically carried out? Why or why not?
4. In your opinion, how did the authors of Study J safeguard against possible concerns with violation of client rights? Discuss in detail.
5. Why was it necessary that the clients who participated in Study J participated on a voluntary basis? What, in your opinion, would have been the consequences of nonvoluntary participation? Justify your answer.
6. In your opinion, were the clients used in Study J competent to provide informed consent? Justify your answer.
7. In your opinion, how much and what kind of information would you consider adequate for obtaining a client's consent in Study J? What do you believe were the most important points to explain to these clients before embarking on the study? Justify your answer.
8. What were, in your opinion, the possibilities for coercing or rewarding the clients in Study J to participate? Discuss in detail.
9. Do you believe that the research approach used in Study J could harm the clients in any way? Justify your answer.
10. Do you believe that there was an appropriate balance between the provision of information and the disclosure of the study's purpose as outlined in Study J? Discuss in detail. How could the participants' knowledge of the study's purpose have influenced the outcome in Study J? Discuss in detail.
11. Do you believe that the issues of confidentiality in Study J were considered in the disclosure of the study's results? Why or why not?

GROUP EXERCISES

1. In groups of four, discuss the importance of ethics in social work. How do ethical considerations affect social work research? Discuss the dangers of conducting research in an unethical manner. As a class, discuss the six ethical guidelines for research as outlined in the chapter and any problems that might arise from adhering to or ignoring these guidelines.
2. In groups of four, create a hypothetical research study that would require the participation of social work clients. Decide on the study's purpose and the research methodology. Discuss how you would protect the participants from harm, ensure confidentiality, provide adequate information about the study, and encourage voluntary participation. Draft an informed consent statement that would address your ethical concerns. Read the statement to the class.

3. In groups of four, read and discuss the contents of Box 2.1. Have each member of the group answer the questions contained in the last paragraph. Present your results to the entire class.
4. In groups of four, read and discuss the contents of Box 2.2. Have each member of the group answer the questions contained in the last paragraph. Present your results to the entire class.
5. In groups of four, read and discuss the contents of Box 2.3. As a group, discuss how bias and insensitivity regarding gender and culture can hinder the methodological quality of a research study. Present your results to the entire class.
6. *A Hard Question.* At this very beginning point in your social work research course, and after reading the Appendix, in groups of four, discuss the various cultural factors that you feel need to be taken into account when writing a consent form such as the one presented in Figure 2.1. Do you feel any of these factors are different for doing a qualitative study verses a quantitative one; an applied study verses a pure one? Discuss in detail and provide one common social work example in your discussion. Report back to the entire class what your group found. Do not read Chapters 4–6 to answer this question.
7. *A Very Hard Question.* At this very beginning point in your social work course, and in groups of four, design a qualitative research study that proposes to answer a social work–related research question of your choice. With the same research question, design a quantitative research study. Compare the advantages and disadvantages of using both research approaches when it comes to gaining the permission for someone to become a research participant. Present your results to the entire class. Do not read Chapters 4–6 to answer this question.
8. *A Very Very Hard Question.* In groups of four, discuss in detail how you would go about gaining a client's permission to participate in an "applied" research study and in a "pure" research study. What are the main differences between getting a client to participate in a "pure" study verses an "applied" study? After reading the Appendix, discuss any cultural differences that need to be taken into account when gaining a client's consent to participate in a "pure" research study and in an "applied" one. Present your results to the entire class.

LIBRARY EXERCISES

1. At your university library, search the key words of *ethics* and *social work* on any computerized information retrieval system. Prepare a brief statement of the number and types of references you located.
2. At your university library, locate a social work–related research article. Discuss the author's research methodology in terms of its compliance with the

ethical guidelines as outlined in the chapter. On the basis of your readings, answer the following five questions: (a) How were the possible sources of physical and mental harm to the participants minimized? (b) What information was provided to the participants to ensure their informed and voluntary consent? (c) How was the competence of the participants ensured? (d) How was the confidentiality of information ensured? (e) What were the ethical strengths and weaknesses of the study's methodology? Discuss each one in detail.

NOTES ON CHAPTER 2

This chapter utilizes Study D

Chapter 3

Research Problems and Questions

CHAPTER OUTLINE

SELF-STUDY EXERCISES

1. What is the general research problem area in Study D? In your opinion, does it have all of the four necessary criterion for a good research problem as

outlined in the chapter? Discuss each criterion in reference to Study D in detail.

2. What factors do you believe may have motivated the selection of the general research problem in Study D? Would you have chosen to study the same research problem? Why or why not?
3. What is the specific research question in Study D? In your opinion, is it appropriately derived from the study's general research problem? Would you have formulated the same research question? Why or why not?
4. Do you believe the author of Study D used a procedure similar to the one as outlined in the chapter to derive the research question from the research problem? Why or why not? What procedure would you have taken to derive the research question from the research problem? How would your procedure differ from the one used by the author of Study D? Discuss in detail.
5. Was the research problem in Study D exploratory, descriptive, or explanatory? Explain your answer in detail. How could the author, investigating the same problem area, have conducted a similar study at the other two knowledge levels? Use Figure 3.1 as a guide.
6. Was Study D an applied research study or a pure research study? Explain your response in detail.
7. After rereading Boxes 3.1 and 3.2, discuss the various factors that may have lead the author of Study D to become interested in the study's general problem area.
8. Reread Box 3.3. Respond to the questions at the end of the box. Discuss the possible factors (as outlined in this chapter) that may have lead the researchers to select the research problem as outlined in Box 3.3. After rereading Chapter 2 on ethics, and pages 58–59 in this chapter, was the study in Box 3.3 ethical? Why or why not? Explain in detail.
9. Take the general problem area of homelessness. Construct a potential research question using this general problem area at the exploratory level, at the descriptive level, and at the explanatory level. Make sure your research problems meet the four criteria as outlined in the chapter.
10. Discuss the factors that are involved in selecting an "applied" research question verses the factors that are involved in selecting a "pure" research question. Discuss in detail. Discuss how one single research study answering one single research question can generate "applied" *and* "pure" knowledge. Provide a social work example.

GROUP EXERCISES

1. In groups of four, choose a social work–related problem area. Derive an exploratory, a descriptive, and an explanatory research question from the

general problem area. Does each research problem have relevancy, researchability, feasibility, and ethical acceptability? Why or why not? Discuss the differences and the similarities among these four criteria in relation to the three research questions. Present your findings to the class.

2. In groups of four, create a hypothetical *exploratory* research study that would require the participation of social work clients. Decide on the study's purpose (pure or applied) and the research methodology. Discuss how you would protect the participants from harm, ensure confidentiality, provide adequate information about the study, and encourage voluntary participation. Draft an informed consent statement that would address your ethical concerns. Read the statement to the class.
3. In groups of four, create a hypothetical *descriptive* research study that would require the participation of social work clients. Decide on the study's purpose (pure or applied) and the research methodology. Discuss how you would protect the participants from harm, ensure confidentiality, provide adequate information about the study, and encourage voluntary participation. Draft an informed consent statement that would address your ethical concerns. Read the statement to the class.
4. In groups of four, create a hypothetical *explanatory* research study that would require the participation of social work clients. Decide on the study's purpose (pure or applied) and the research methodology. Discuss how you would protect the participants from harm, ensure confidentiality, provide adequate information about the study, and encourage voluntary participation. Draft an informed consent statement that would address your ethical concerns. Read the statement to the class.
5. After hearing the responses to the above four group exercises, why do you think it is easier to do an exploratory study over a descriptive one, or a descriptive one over an explanatory one? Discuss in detail.
6. In groups of four, read and discuss the contents of Box 3.3. Have each member of the group answer the questions contained at the end of the box. Present your results to the rest of your class.
7. *A Very Hard Question.* At this very beginning point in your social work research course, and after reading the Appendix, in groups of four, discuss the various cultural factors that you feel need to be taken into account when formulating an *exploratory* research question. Do you feel any of these factors are different for formulating a qualitative research question verses a quantitative research question? an applied study verses a pure one? Discuss in detail and provide one common social work example in your Discussion. Report back to the entire class what your group found. Do not read Chapters 4–6 to answer this question. Repeat this group exercise using *descriptive* research questions and *explanatory* research questions.
8. *A Very Very Hard Question.* At this very beginning point in your social work course, and in groups of four, design one single *qualitative* research study that proposes to answer three types of social work–related research questions of

your choice, exploratory, descriptive, and explanatory. With the same research questions, design a *quantitative* research study. Compare the advantages and disadvantages of using both research approaches when it comes to formulating specific research questions from general problem areas. Do not read Chapters 4–6 to answer this question.

LIBRARY EXERCISE

1. At your university library, locate a research article on a social work–related topic of your choice. Answer the following six questions in detail: (a) What is the general problem area? (b) What is the specific research question? (c) Was the study exploratory, descriptive, or explanatory? (d) Was the study carried out in an ethical manner? (e) Did the study have relevancy, researchability, feasibility, and ethical acceptability? (f) Was the study pure or applied?

NOTES ON CHAPTER 3

This chapter utilizes Study I

Chapter **4**

Quantitative Approaches to the Generation of Knowledge

CHAPTER OUTLINE

SELF-STUDY EXERCISES

1. In your own words, discuss what is meant by the quantitative research approach to knowledge generation. In your opinion, what might the implications have been for the results in Study I if a quantitative research approach had *not* used?
2. After rereading Box 4.1, what are the limitations of defining *quantitative* by the hypothetico-deductive method? Do you believe that Study I possessed any of these limitations? Explain in detail.
3. Discuss the four functions of quantitative research studies. What, in your opinion, was the function(s) of Study I?
4. Discuss the five characteristics of quantitative research studies as opposed to the characteristics of obtaining knowledge via tradition, authority, intuition, and practice wisdom methods.
5. Discuss the process of selecting problem areas and formulating research questions within quantitative studies. After rereading Box 4.2, what alternative hypothesis might have been formulated in Study I?
6. Discuss the differences between duplication and replication. Use one common example throughout your discussion.
7. Discuss all of the steps of doing a quantitative research study. Use an example throughout your entire response.

8. What are the concepts and variables contained in Study I?
9. In what other manner could the variables have been conceptualized and operationalized in Study I? Discuss in detail.
10. Discuss the sequencing of steps in the quantitative research process. List, in your opinion, the sequence of steps that were utilized in Study I. Do you believe that the flexibility of the steps played an important role in carrying out Study I? Discuss in detail.
11. Discuss the ethical considerations associated with quantitative research studies such as Study I. What were, in your opinion, the ethical limitations associated with the authors' choice of the quantitative research approach? Justify your answer.
12. Discuss the advantages and disadvantages of the quantitative research approach to knowledge generation. Use one common example throughout your discussion.

GROUP EXERCISES

1. In groups of four, assign one of the four classifications of quantitatively based research studies as outlined in the chapter to each group member. Have each group member develop a brief statement on the purpose of each type. Share your statements with the group. Discuss the differences and the similarities among the four classifications. Present your findings to the entire class.
2. In groups of four, choose one (of the four) classification of quantitatively based research studies discussed in the above exercise. Using all the steps as outlined in the chapter, construct a step-by-step procedure for conducting a quantitative research study for the classification selected. Would the steps follow one another in a strict order for each of the four classifications? Why or why not? Present your findings to the entire class.
3. Review Figure 4.2. In groups of four, construct other research questions that could have been explored from the research problems. Present your findings to the entire class.
4. Review Figure 4.2. In groups of four, construct other research hypotheses that could have been explored from the research questions. Present your findings to the entire class.
5. *A Hard Question.* At this very beginning point in your social work research course, and after reading the Appendix, in groups of four, discuss the various cultural factors that you feel need to be taken into account when doing a quantitative social work research study. Do you feel any of these factors are different for doing an "applied" study verses a "pure" one? Discuss in detail and provide one common social work example in your discussion. Report back to the entire class what your group found.

6. *A Very Hard Question.* At this very beginning point in your social work course, and in groups of four, design a quantitative research study that proposes to answer a social work–related research question of your choice. Describe in detail how you could incorporate both an "applied" research component and a "pure" research component in the same quantitative study. Present your results to the entire class.
7. *A Very Hard Question.* At this very beginning point in your social work course, and in groups of four, design a quantitative research study that proposes to answer a social work–related research question of your choice. With the same research question, design a qualitative research study. Compare the advantages and disadvantages of using both research approaches in answering your research question. Describe in detail how you could incorporate both research approaches, quantitative and qualitative, in a single research study that answered the same research question. Present your results to the entire class. Do not read Chapters 5–6 to answer this question.
8. *A Very Very Hard Question.* With the results of Question 7 in mind, and in groups of four, discuss in detail how you would incorporate an "applied research component" and a "pure research component" in your qualitative study and in your quantitative study. Present your results to the entire class.

LIBRARY EXERCISES

1. At your university library, locate a social work–related journal article that used a quantitative research approach. Using what you know about quantitative research, answer the following nine questions: (a) What was the problem area and research question? What were the study's concepts, independent variables, dependent variables, and operational definitions? (b) What were the hypotheses (if any)? (c) What were the extraneous variables (if any)? (d) Evaluate the study's research hypothesis in relation to the criteria as outlined in the chapter. (e) Was the hypothesis one- or two-tailed? (f) What were some rival hypotheses that the study could have contained? (g) How did the author overcome the four primary limitations of doing a quantitative study? (h) Did the author question any collective subjective beliefs? If so, what were they? (i) Did the quantitative study incorporate "human concern" for the client with effective social work practice? Explain, providing examples from the study.
2. At your university library, locate a social work–related journal article (four articles in total) where its main objective was to:
   - Describe variables and relationships
   - Predict and compare outcomes
   - Analyze components of interventions
   - Determine causal analyses

Knowing what you know about quantitative research at this point, comment on how each article met its objective.

3. Using one of the four journal articles above, comment on how well it strived toward:
   - Measurability
   - Objectivity
   - Reducing uncertainty
   - Duplication
   - Using standardized procedures
4. Using one of the four journal articles above, comment on how well its author(s):
   - Selected a problem area
   - Conceptualized variables
   - Operationalized variables
   - Identified constants and labeled variables
   - Formulated a research hypothesis
   - Developed a sampling plan
   - Selected a data collection method
   - Analyzed the data

NOTES ON CHAPTER 4

This chapter utilizes Studies J and K

Chapter 5

Qualitative Approaches to the Generation of Knowledge

CHAPTER OUTLINE

SELF-STUDY EXERCISES

1. In your opinion, was the qualitative research approach the appropriate one to use in Studies J and K? Why or why not?
2. What types of qualitative research questions are addressed in Studies J and K? Discuss in detail.
3. How are the steps of the qualitative research process as outlined in the chapter different from those as presented in Studies J and K? Discuss your answer in detail.
4. How, in your opinion, would the data collection methods used in Studies J and K change if a quantitative research approach had been used?
5. What type of interview(s) was used in Studies J and K? What type of interview would you have used? Why?
6. Do you believe that the use of focus groups would have been of benefit in Studies J and K? Justify your answer.
7. Do you believe that a quantitative research approach could have been used in Studies J and K? Justify your answer. How would the findings from a qualitative study differ from those of a quantitative study? Discuss in detail and relate your answer to Studies J and K.
8. What ethical considerations do you believe guided the author of Studies J and K? Discuss in detail.
9. In your own words, discuss what is meant by the qualitative research approach to knowledge generation. In your opinion, what might the implications have been for the results in Studies J and K if a qualitative research approach had *not* used?
10. Discuss the process of selecting problem areas and formulating research questions within qualitative research studies. Compare and contrast your response to quantitative research studies.
11. Discuss all of the steps in doing a qualitative research study. Use a social work example throughout your entire response.
12. What are the concepts and variables contained in Studies J and K? How would have they been conceptualized differently if a quantitative study had taken place?
13. In what other manner could the variables have been conceptualized and operationalized in Studies J and K? Discuss in detail.

14. Discuss the sequencing of steps in the qualitative research process. List, in your opinion, the sequence of steps that were utilized in Studies J and K. Do you believe that the flexibility of the steps played an important role in carrying out Studies J and K? Discuss in detail.
15. Discuss the ethical considerations associated with qualitative research studies such as Studies J and K. What were, in your opinion, the ethical limitations associated with the authors' choice of the qualitative research approach? Justify your answer.
16. Discuss the advantages and disadvantages of the qualitative research approach to knowledge generation. Use one common example throughout your discussion.
17. Describe in detail the five types of interviews that can be used when doing a qualitative research study. State how each type of interview could have been used to gather data for Studies J and K.

GROUP EXERCISES

1. Review Box 5.2. In groups of four, choose a social work–related research problem. Outline the process your group would follow to conduct a qualitative research study of the problem. How would the process differ if your group chose to conduct a quantitative study? Present your discussion to the entire class.
2. In groups of four, discuss what qualitative researchers do that quantitative researchers do not. What "research skills" do qualitative researchers have to have that quantitative researchers do not. Present your findings to the entire class.
3. In groups of four, construct a hypothetical codebook that could have been used in Study J. Repeat this exercise for Study K. Present your findings to the entire class.
4. *A Hard Question.* At this very beginning point in your social work research course, and after reading the Appendix, in groups of four, discuss the various cultural factors that you feel need to be taken into account when doing a qualitative social work research study. Do you feel any of these factors are different for doing an "applied" qualitative study verses a "pure" one? Discuss in detail and provide one common social work example in your discussion. Report back to the entire class what your group found.
5. *A Very Hard Question.* At this very beginning point in your social work course, and in groups of four, design a qualitative research study that proposes to answer a social work–related research question of your choice. Describe in detail how you could incorporate both an "applied" research component and a "pure" research component in the same qualitative study. Discuss the various cultural factors that you feel need to be taken into account when

including an "applied" component and a "pure" component in a qualitative study. Present your results to the entire class.

6. *A Very Very Hard Question.* At this very beginning point in your social work course, and in groups of four, design a qualitative research study that proposes to answer a social work–related research question of your choice. With the same research question, design a quantitative research study. Compare the advantages and disadvantages of using both research approaches in answering your research question, taking cultural factors into account (see Appendix). Describe in detail how you could incorporate both research approaches, qualitative and quantitative, in a single research study that answered the same research question. Present your results to the entire class. Do not read Chapter 6 to answer this question.

LIBRARY EXERCISES

1. At your university library, locate a social work–related journal article that used a qualitative research approach. Using what you know about qualitative research, answer the following five questions: (a) What was the problem area and research question? (b) What were the study's concepts, independent variables, dependent variables, and operational definitions? (c) How did the author overcome the limitations of doing a qualitative study? (d) Did the author question any collective subjective beliefs? If so, what were they? (e) Did the qualitative study incorporate "human concern" for the client with effective social work practice? Explain, providing examples from the study.
2. Using the above journal article, comment on how well its author(s):
   - Selected a problem area
   - Selected research participants
   - Selected a site or setting
   - Gained permission and access to the field
   - Entered the field and identified key informants
   - Selected a research design and data collection method
   - Recorded, logged, and analyzed the data

NOTES ON CHAPTER 5

This chapter utilizes Study A

Chapter 6

Using Both Research Approaches in a Single Study

CHAPTER OUTLINE

SELF-STUDY EXERCISES

1. Review Chapters 4 and 5. Discuss how both research approaches could have been used in Study A. Discuss how Study A could have been improved if both research approaches had been used.
2. Discuss in detail the advantages and disadvantages of using both research approaches within a single study. Provide specific examples within your discussion.
3. Discuss in detail the three models of combining both research approaches within a single study. Provide a social work example of each model.
4. Discuss the differences between simultaneous triangulation and sequential triangulation. Provide a social work example of each.
5. Reread Box 6.1 and take the social problem of violent crime. Discuss in detail how both research approaches could be used in a single research study in relation to the six criteria presented in Box 6.1.

GROUP EXERCISES

1. In groups of four, design a combined qualitative and quantitative study that employs two phases. Discuss why the phases are ordered in the sequence proposed.
2. In groups of four, design a combined qualitative and quantitative study that uses a dominant qualitative component and a less-dominant quantitative component. Discuss the approach to be taken in writing the introduction, the purpose statement, the research questions, and the methods.
3. In groups of four, design a combined qualitative and quantitative study that employs a mixed-methodological approach. Present this design as a visual diagram (or concept map) and identify the qualitative and quantitative components in the design.
4. *A Hard Question.* After reading the first six chapters in this book, and in the same groups of four that answered Group Exercise 6 from Chapter 5, reanswer this exercise—only now taking into account the contents of this chapter. Present your results to the entire class.

LIBRARY EXERCISE

1. At your university library, locate a social work–related journal article that used both research approaches within a single study. Knowing what you know about quantitative and qualitative research at this point, comment on how the article met its objective.

This chapter utilizes Study A

Chapter 7

Measuring Variables

CHAPTER OUTLINE

SELF-STUDY EXERCISES

1. Discuss why measurement is fundamental to social work research. Discuss the common components of the definitions of measurement as outlined in the chapter. Discuss how the measurement process is different from, and similar to, the quantitative and qualitative research approaches.
2. List and discuss the functions of measurement in the social work research process as outlined in the chapter. Discuss how measurement functions are different from, and similar to, the quantitative and qualitative research approaches.
3. Discuss what is meant by measurement validity. Provide an example of measurement validity via a social work example. Discuss how measurement validity is different from, and similar to, the quantitative and qualitative research approaches.
4. Discuss what is meant by measurement reliability. Provide an example of measurement reliability via a social work example. Discuss how measurement reliability is different from, and similar to, the quantitative and qualitative research approaches.
5. Discuss the relationship between measurement validity and measurement reliability as presented in this chapter. Provide a quantitative and qualitative social work example throughout your discussion.
6. Use Figure 7.1 to explain if the measuring instruments in Study A are both valid and reliable.
7. List and discuss the potential sources of measurement error as outlined in the chapter. Discuss how these errors are different from, and similar to, the quantitative and qualitative research approaches.
8. Discuss how a measuring instrument is assessed for its content validity. How can you tell if an instrument is content valid? Discuss how content validity is different from, and similar to, the quantitative and qualitative research approaches.
9. What is face validity? What is the difference between content validity and face validity? Provide a social work example throughout your discussion.
10. What is the difference between concurrent validity and predictive validity? Describe a situation in which you would use an instrument that has concurrent validity. Describe a situation in which you would use an instrument that has predictive validity. Discuss how concurrent validity and predictive validity are different from, and similar to, the quantitative and qualitative research approaches.
11. What does the test-retest method of reliability determine? Provide a social

work example of how it could be used.

12. What is the alternate-forms method of reliability? Discuss how it could be determined in a social work situation.
13. What is the split-half method of reliability? Discuss how it could be determined in a social work situation.
14. Discuss the various cultural factors that you feel need to be taken into account (see Appendix) when it comes to the measurement process in social work research.

GROUP EXERCISES

1. In groups of four, construct a 10-item self-administered questionnaire that measures a variable of your choice. What difficulties, if any, did you have with the construction of the questionnaire? As a class, discuss each questionnaire and the problems associated with its construction.
2. Choose one of the questionnaires developed in the above exercise and have the entire class fill it out. What were some of the problems encountered? Was the questionnaire understandable and answerable? Using Figure 7.1, explain if the questionnaire was both valid and reliable. What methods would you use to improve the validity and the reliability of this self-administered questionnaire?
3. In groups of four, discuss how the process of measurement is different in a quantitative study when compared to a qualitative one. Present your results to the entire class.
4. *A Very Very Hard Question.* After reading the first seven chapters and appendix in this book, in groups of four, discuss the various cultural factors that you feel need to be taken into account when delineating and measuring variables in a *qualitative* social work research study. Do you feel any of these factors are different for doing an "applied" *qualitative* study verses a "pure" one? Discuss in detail. Report back to the entire class what your group found.
5. *A Very Very Hard Question.* After reading the first seven chapters and appendix in this book, in groups of four, discuss the various cultural factors that you feel need to be taken into account when delineating and measuring variables in a *quantitative* social work research study. Do you feel any of these factors are different for doing an "applied" *quantitative* study verses a "pure" one? Discuss in detail. Report back to the entire class what your group found.

LIBRARY EXERCISE

1. At your university library, locate a social work–related article that makes use of a measuring instrument. If the measuring instrument is not included in the

article, find a copy of the instrument. Using what you know about measuring instruments answer the following two questions: (a) How were the validity and reliability of the instrument demonstrated? (b) Were any measurement errors mentioned? How were these errors compensated for or corrected?

NOTES ON CHAPTER 7

Chapter 8

Measuring Instruments

CHAPTER OUTLINE

SELF-STUDY EXERCISES

1. Discuss the role that standardized measuring instruments plays in the social work research process. Provide a social work example throughout your discussion.
2. List and discuss in detail the six questions that must be asked when selecting a standardized measuring instrument. Provide a simple social work example throughout your discussion.
3. List and discuss in detail the advantages of using standardized measuring instruments. Provide a social work example throughout your discussion.
4. List and describe the various formats that standardized measuring instruments can take. Provide a social work example of each format.
5. What are the differences between rating scales and questionnaire-type scales? Discuss the advantages and disadvantages of each. Provide a social work example throughout your discussion.
6. List and discuss the four different kinds of rating scales. Discuss the advantages and disadvantages of each. Provide a social work example throughout your discussion.
7. List and discuss the two different kinds of modified scales. Discuss the advantages and disadvantages of each. Provide a social work example throughout your discussion.
8. What are nonstandardized measuring instruments? Compare these instruments with standardized ones. Provide a social work example throughout your discussion.
9. List and discuss in detail the advantages and disadvantages of using nonstandardized measuring instruments. Provide a social work example throughout your discussion.
10. Do you feel the *GAS* as presented in Figure 8.1 has all the criteria to be classified as a standardized measuring instrument? Explain your answer in detail.
11. Discuss the two methods of maximizing the content validity of measuring instruments.
12. Using the points in the chapter, discuss how the response categories, continuum of ratings, and length of a measuring instrument can be determined.

13. Discuss the concepts of external and internal validity as they relate to the construction of standardized measuring instruments. Discuss in detail.
14. Using the points as outlined in the chapter, compare and contrast rating scales with questionnaire-type scales.

GROUP EXERCISES

1. In groups of four, construct a brief 10-item questionnaire that measures a social work–related variable of your choice. What difficulties, if any, did you have with the selection of the response categories and the continuum of ratings? Discuss each questionnaire and the problems in its construction with the entire class.
2. Choose one of the questionnaires developed in the above exercise and have the entire class fill it out. What were some of the problems encountered? Was the questionnaire understandable and answerable? Explain if the questionnaire was both valid and reliable. What methods would you use to improve the validity and the reliability of this self-administered questionnaire?
3. In groups of four, compare and contrast the advantages and the disadvantages of rating scales versus questionnaire-type scales as used in social work research. Construct a 10-item questionnaire on a social work–related topic of your choice. In developing the questions, use each of the rating and questionnaire-type scales discussed in this chapter. Label each question with the type of scale used. Present your questionnaire to the class.
4. In groups of four, discuss how the process of measurement is different in a quantitative research study when compared to a qualitative research study. Present your results to the entire class.

LIBRARY EXERCISE

1. At your university library, locate a standardized measurement instrument related to social work. Answer the following four questions: (a) How do you believe the measurement need was determined? Discuss in detail. (b) What type(s) of scale(s) is(are) utilized in the instrument? (c) How does the author demonstrate the instrument's internal and external validity? (d) Evaluate the instrument. What are its advantages and disadvantages?

NOTES ON CHAPTER 8

____

____

____

This chapter utilizes Study F

Chapter 9

Designing Measuring Instruments

CHAPTER OUTLINE

SELF-STUDY EXERCISES

1. Using the points as outlined in the chapter, list and briefly discuss the six functions of measuring instruments.
2. Explain the functions of the measuring instrument contained in Figure F-1. Support your answer by applying each of the six functions to the instrument.
3. Do you believe Figure F-1 is externally valid? Why or why not? Using the points as outlined in the chapter, explain what steps were (or should have been) taken to ensure the instrument's external validity.
4. Do you believe Figure F-1 is internally valid? Why or why not? Using the instrument design procedures as outlined in the chapter, discuss the aspects which contributed to and/or diminished the instrument's internal validity.
5. Using the points as outlined in the chapter, compare and contrast open-ended and closed-ended questions. What are the advantages and the disadvantages of using such questions? Discuss in detail.
6. Using Figure F-1 as an example, discuss the eight factors to consider when designing a measuring instrument. Do you believe the authors of the measuring instrument contained in Figure F-1 considered any of the above factors when constructing it? Why or why not? Which factors do you believe were most important to consider? Why?
7. What is the purpose of pretesting a measuring instrument? Why do you believe it was necessary to pretest standardized measuring instruments?

GROUP EXERCISES

1. In groups of four, construct a 10-item questionnaire. Did the group agree on the wording of the questions? Their meaning? How would you go about ensuring external and internal validity of the questions? How would you pretest your questionnaire? Present your questionnaire for discussion to the class.
2. In the same groups as for the above exercise, exchange your group's questionnaire with that of another group. Independently complete the questionnaire. Did all of the members in your group interpret the questions in the same manner? What questions were the focus of disagreement? What problems can your group predict in using the questionnaire to gather data? What are some possible solutions to these problems? Formulate a short list of do's and don't's for questionnaire construction. Discuss your list with the class.

LIBRARY EXERCISES

1. At your university library, locate a social work–related research article that describes the development of a standardized measurement instrument. Using the points as outlined in the chapter, answer the following five questions: (a) What function(s) does the instrument serve? (b) What steps were taken to ensure the instrument's external validity? Would you use the same steps? Why or why not? (c) What steps were taken to ensure the instrument's internal validity? Would you use the same steps? Why or why not? (d) Are the questions in the instrument open-ended, closed-ended, or a combination of the two types? What do you believe was the purpose of choosing the particular type(s) or question(s) used? Explain in detail. (e) Do you believe that the author pretested the questionnaire? Why or why not? How would you have gone about pretesting the questionnaire?
2. At your university library, locate two articles that discuss the construction of social work–related measuring instruments. How do the points as outlined in the chapter differ from those in the two articles? Do you believe any other guidelines may be necessary in instrument construction? If so, what are they?

NOTES ON CHAPTER 9

This chapter utilizes Study F

Chapter 10

Sampling

CHAPTER OUTLINE

SELF-STUDY EXERCISES

1. Discuss how sampling theory assists in the process of social work research. Why, in your opinion, were the sampling methods used in Study F? Explain in detail.
2. Discuss the purpose and the use of sampling frames in social work research. Describe the sampling frame in Study F. Was the sampling frame in Study F identical to the study's population? Why or why not?
3. Discuss the issue of generalizability in social work research. Do you believe the sample used in Study F was representative of the population from which it was drawn? Why or why not?
4. Discuss the differences between probability and nonprobability sampling. What are their comparative advantages and disadvantages? Justify your answer by using the points as outlined in the chapter.
5. List and discuss the different types of probability sampling procedures. Do you believe any probability sampling procedures were used in Study F? Why or why not? In your explanation discuss the sampling techniques used in Study F as outlined in the chapter.
6. Discuss the procedure of generating a random sample. Explain how the author of Study F might have used Table 10.1 to generate a random sample. Discuss the process in detail.
7. List and briefly discuss the different types of nonprobability sampling procedures.
8. Discuss how sampling errors vary with the size of the sample.
9. What, in your opinion, was the potential for sampling error in Study F? Discuss in detail.
10. List and discuss the various forms of nonsampling errors. What, in your opinion, may have been some of the nonsampling errors that may have occurred in Study F?
11. What suggestions could you provide to minimize nonsampling errors?

GROUP EXERCISES

1. Suppose you wanted the students in your class to participate in a research study. In groups of four, discuss what random sampling procedures could be used. Using Table 10.1, decide on a procedure, discuss how you would collect the data, and explain your decisions to the class. How does your study compare with those of the other groups? Discuss the problems associated with random sampling and possible solutions to the problems.
2. Suppose you design a research project that concerns all of the students of your university. In groups of four, decide on a sample size and discuss how you could use the four nonprobability sampling methods. Discuss the potential problems and possible solutions to the problems.

LIBRARY EXERCISES

1. At your university library, locate a social work–related research study that used a *probability* sampling procedure. Answer the following five questions: (a) What sampling procedure was used? (b) From what general population was the sample drawn? (c) Do you believe that the sample was representative of the population from which it was drawn? Why or why not? (d) What other sampling procedure could have been used? What would be the implications if this sampling method were used? (e) What changes could you suggest that would make the study more rigorous in terms of sampling procedures and/or controlling for nonsampling errors? Discuss in detail.
2. At your university library, locate a social work–related research study that used a *nonprobability* sampling procedure. Answer the following three questions: (a) What sampling procedure was used? (b) Could the author have used a different nonprobability sampling procedure? If so, which one? (c) In your opinion, does probability sampling or do nonprobability sampling procedures produce a more rigorous study? Justify your answer.

NOTES ON CHAPTER 10

Chapter 11

Group Designs

CHAPTER OUTLINE

SELF-STUDY EXERCISES

1. Discuss why very few social work research studies ever come close to "ideal" experiments. What are some of the reasons why it would be unethical to do "ideal" experiments with clients?
2. Discuss in detail each one of the six characteristics that are necessary to approach an "ideal" experiment in social work research. Provide a social work example in your discussion.
3. Design an "ideal" experiment with the general problem area of child sexual abuse.
4. Construct an "ideal" explanatory-level experiment with the research problem of suicide. What ethical problems did you run into?
5. Construct an "ideal" explanatory-level experiment with the research problem of abortion. What ethical problems did you run into?
6. In your own words, discuss why it is important for you to know the six characteristics of an "ideal" experiment when you design any given research study.
7. Why is it necessary to use at least one control group (or comparison group) when trying to design an "ideal" experiment?
8. Write an explanatory-level research hypothesis in which Variable A (some variable of your choice) is the independent variable and Variable B (some variable of your choice) is the dependent variable. Now rewrite the same hypothesis with the two variables reversed. Which hypothesis do you think is correct? Why? How would you go about testing the two hypotheses? Include in your discussion how you would address all six of the characteristics of an "ideal" experiment.
9. Discuss in detail the similarities and differences between the concepts of internal and external validity. Provide a social work example throughout your discussion.
10. List and discuss the threats to internal validity by using a common social work example of your choice.
11. List and discuss the threats to external validity by using a common social work example of your choice.
12. Design an "ideal" social work experiment that controls for all the threats to internal and external validity. You may select any topic that you desire.
13. List other factors that you feel could be added as additional threats to *internal validity* besides the ones presented in this chapter. Provide a rationale for your response.
14. List other factors that you feel could be added as additional threats to *external validity* besides the ones presented in this chapter. Provide a rationale for your response.
15. Discuss the differences among trend studies, cohort studies, and panel studies. Use a social work example throughout your discussion.
16. List all the group research designs and indicate the threats to internal and external validity that each design controls for. Provide a rationale for each

one of your responses. Provide a social work example to illustrate each one of your points.

17. Design a perfect group research study, at the explanatory level, that takes into account all the threats to internal and external validity. What ethical issues do you see if your study were in fact implemented?
18. Out of all the group research designs presented in this chapter, which one do you think is used most often in social work research? Why? Justify your answer. Which one do you think is least utilized? Why? Justify your answer.

GROUP EXERCISES

1. In groups of four, decide on a social work–related problem area. Design three hypothetical studies using one design from each of the three knowledge levels. For each study determine what data need to be gathered. Provide the graphic representation of the study detailing the *R*s, *O*s, and *X*s. Present the three designs to the entire class with a detailed explanation of the population and the sampling procedures.
2. In groups of four, discuss each of the threats to external validity and the threats to internal validity in the context of controlling for them. What problems do you foresee in attempting to control for all of the threats to internal and external validity? Present your discussion to the entire class.

LIBRARY EXERCISES

1. At your university library, identify a research article that comes closest to an "ideal" experiment. What were the characteristics that were missing in the study that prevented it from becoming an "ideal" experiment?
2. With the article you selected for Question 1, hypothetically redesign the study using the six characteristics for an "ideal" experiment.
3. At your university library, identify two social work research articles that focused on the same topic area. Which study do you feel had the most *internal validity*. Why? Justify your response. Provide a rationale as to why it is necessary to have higher degrees of internal validity for research studies at descriptive or explanatory levels than at the exploratory level.
4. At your university library, choose two social work research articles that focused on the same topic area. Which study do you feel had the most *external validity*? Why? Justify your response. Provide a rationale as to why it is necessary to have higher degrees of external validity for research studies at the descriptive or explanatory levels than at the exploratory level.
5. At your university library, find a published social work research article that controlled for as many threats to internal and external validity as possible. Go through the article and determine which internal and external validity factors the study controlled for, and which factors it did not control for.

Hypothetically redesign the study in such a way where you could control for the factors that the original study did not. After doing this, would your hypothetical redesigned study have been feasible? Discuss in detail.

6. At your university library, find a social work article that reports on a research study that used an *exploratory* research design. How could have this study been done using a "higher level" group research design?
7. At your university library, find a social work article that reports on a research study that used a *descriptive* research design. How could have this study been done using a "higher level" group research design?

NOTES ON CHAPTER 11

Chapter 12

Case Designs

CHAPTER OUTLINE

SELF-STUDY EXERCISES

1. Discuss in detail how a case design "significantly" differs from a group design (Chapter 11).
2. Discuss the purpose of a "case"as used in a case study.
3. Discuss the issue of generalizability in case study research.
4. Discuss how similar and different sampling procedures can be used in reference to group designs and case study designs.
5. Discuss in detail how a case study design can be used in *client assessment.* Compare and contrast the advantages and disadvantages of using some group designs and case study designs to help social workers assess client situations.
6. Discuss in detail how a case study design can be used in *interventions.* Compare and contrast the advantages and disadvantages of using some group designs and case study designs to help social workers in the *interventive* process.
7. Discuss in detail how a case study design can be used in assessing *client outcomes.* Compare and contrast the advantages and disadvantages of using some group designs and case study designs to help social workers assess client outcomes.
8. Discuss the necessary criteria that need to be met to evaluate outcome-oriented case studies. Provide a social work example in your discussion.
9. How does a "case" represent itself? Discuss in detail.
10. Discuss the three skills that are needed when a social worker generalizes from one case to another.
11. Discuss the necessary criteria that need to be met for evaluating the conceptual framework for a case study.
12. Discuss the differences between deterministic and probabilistic causation. Provide a social work example of each in your discussion.
13. What are intervening and extraneous variables? Discuss how they are similar in case study research and in group research. Provide a social work example of each in your discussion.
14. Compare and contrast the necessary criteria that need to be met to evaluate the clarity and accuracy of findings generated from a case study research design and from a group research design.

GROUP EXERCISE

1. Have the entire class select one common social work–related problem area. In groups of four, discuss how the problem could be researched with a group research design (Chapter 11) *and* with a case study research design. What

types of data would each design provide? What are the advantages of using a group design over a case study design, and vise versa? Discuss the generalizability of your hypothetical findings derived from your group design over your case study design. Have all groups report back to the entire class. What were the similarities and differences among the groups? Discuss the implications.

LIBRARY EXERCISES

1. At your university library, locate a social work–related research study (article) that used a group research design and another study (article) that used a case study design. Both studies must have addressed the same general problem area. What data did the study that used a group research design provide over the study that used a case study design, and vice versa? Discuss the advantages and disadvantages of using a case design over a group design with this problem area. Discuss how both types of designs, case and group, can be used to complement one another.
2. At your university library, locate an article that used a case study research design. Evaluate the article with the criteria presented in the chapter. How would you do the case study differently? Why? Discuss in detail using the contents of this chapter as a guide.

NOTES ON CHAPTER 12

This chapter utilizes Study B

Chapter 13

Structured Observation

CHAPTER OUTLINE

SELF-STUDY EXERCISES

1. Discuss what is meant by interval recording. Which one(s) of the four studies described in Study B used interval recording?
2. Discuss what is meant by frequency recording. Which one(s) of the four studies described in Study B used frequency recording?
3. Discuss what is meant by duration recording. Which one(s) of the four studies described in Study B used duration recording?
4. Discuss what is meant by magnitude recording. Which one(s) of the four studies described in Study B used magnitude recording?
5. Discuss what is meant by spot-check recording. Which one(s) of the four studies described in Study B used spot-check recording?
6. Discuss what is meant by permanent-product recording. How does it differ from the other methods of recording as outlined in the chapter? Which one(s) of the four studies described in Study B used permanent-product recording?
7. Discuss what is meant by observer reliability in social work research. Using the points as outlined in Chapters 7 and 13, discuss how you could establish observer and measurement reliability in Study 2 contained in Study B.
8. Using the points as outlined in the chapter, discuss what is meant by outside, indigenous, and self-observers. What category of observer was used in Study 1 described in Study B? In your opinion, was the choice of observer appropriate? Why or why not? Discuss in detail.
9. Discuss in detail how structured observation can be used as a data collection method in quantitative research studies (Chapter 4) and in qualitative research studies (Chapter 5). Provide one common social work example in your discussion.
10. Discuss in detail how structured observation can be used as a data collection method in group research studies (Chapter 11) and in case research studies (Chapter 12). Provide one common social work example in your discussion.

GROUP EXERCISES

1. In groups of four, decide on a positive behavior or mannerism of your social work research instructor. Assign a different type of data recording method to each group member. Individually record the target behavior. Compare your results. Use Figure 13.1 to discuss if the data collection methods were appropriate for the type of behavior, the information needs, and the relative expense. Were the methods reliable? Why or why not? Present your findings to the class.
2. In groups of four, refer to the class discussion generated in the above exercise. Define the categories of observers used by the groups. Which categories of observers would be most beneficial to this particular situation? Why? Present your discussion to the entire class.

LIBRARY EXERCISES

1. At your university library, locate a social work–related research article that uses any one of the six data recording methods for structured observation. Using Figure 13.1, discuss the method by answering the following three questions: (a) Which data recording method(s) was used? (b) Was the method(s) appropriate for the study's purpose? Why or why not? (c) What other method would have been appropriate to use in the study? Explain.
2. Using the same article as in the above exercise, discuss what type(s) of observers were used in the study. Was the choice of observer(s) appropriate for the study's purpose and methodology? Would other types of observers have been effective? Why or why not?

NOTES ON CHAPTER 13

This chapter utilizes Study D

Chapter 14

Survey Research

CHAPTER OUTLINE

SELF-STUDY EXERCISES

1. Using the points as outlined in the chapter, discuss the steps in the survey research process. Discuss how the above steps are interrelated with one another. Discuss how the author of Study D would have had to follow the steps as outlined in Figure 14.1. Explain.
2. Discuss the use of survey research in exploratory, descriptive, and explanatory studies. In your opinion, at what level on the knowledge continuum is Study D? Justify your answer.
3. Compare and contrast the cross-sectional and longitudinal approaches to survey research. What approach(es) did the author of Study D use? Justify your answer with information highlighting the points as presented in the chapter.
4. Discuss the advantages and the disadvantages of face-to-face interviewing. Could the researcher in Study D have chosen the face-to-face interview as a method of data collection? Why or why not? What would be the advantages and disadvantages of using the face-to-face interview data collection method in Study D?
5. Discuss the differences between group-administered questionnaires and mail surveys. Explain in what situation each method would be most appropriate.
6. What does the acronym CATI stand for? Discuss the advantages and the disadvantages of CATI in relation to other forms of data collection. In your opinion, would CATI have been appropriate to use in Study D? Explain.
7. Discuss in detail how surveys can be used as a data collection method in quantitative research studies (Chapter 4) and in qualitative research studies (Chapter 5). Provide one common social work example in your discussion.
8. Discuss in detail how surveys can be used as a data collection method in group research studies (Chapter 11) and in case research studies (Chapter 12). Provide one common social work example in your discussion.
9. Describe in your own words the purpose of survey research. Why are surveys useful? Describe the steps that a survey research study would take in reference to finding out how satisfied social workers are with their social work education.
10. Describe in detail the two main data collection methods that can be used in survey research. Provide a social work example of each, using one common research problem. In other words, how could your survey be conducted using questionnaires or interviews? How could it have been conducted using both? Discuss the advantages and disadvantages of using the two primary data collection methods.

11. Discuss in detail the two types of questionnaires that can be used in survey research. In which situations is one better than the other? Provide a rationale for your response. Use a social work example to illustrate your points.
12. What are the two types of questions that can be included in a questionnaire or interview schedule? Provide a social work example of each.
13. When is an open-ended item better to use than a closed-ended item? Provide a rationale for your response.
14. Discuss the commonalities and differences between personal interviews and telephone interviews used in survey research. In which situation is one better than the other?

GROUP EXERCISES

1. In groups of six, develop a 10-item questionnaire to survey your classmates' opinions on an issue relevant to social work. Group-administer the questionnaire to your class. Collect the completed questionnaires and return to the same group of six. What problems occurred in using the group-administered questionnaire as a data collection method? What are some potential solutions to these problems? Formulate a list of do's and don't's for group-administered questionnaires. Present your list to the class.
2. In the same group of six, designate three people as interviewers and three people as interviewees. Conduct face-to-face interviews in pairs of two using the questionnaire developed in the exercise above. Return to your group and discuss the following four questions. (a) What problems occurred in using the interview to gather data? (b) How did your experiences compare with the problems discussed in the chapter? (c) Which form of survey research would be best to use with your questionnaire? Why? (d) Would you revise your questionnaire? If so, how? Present your findings to the entire class.

LIBRARY EXERCISES

1. At your university library, locate a social work–related research article that used the survey as the data collection method. What type of survey research was used? What potential problems did you feel the researcher(s) encountered in using this type of data collection methodology? Discuss your answers in detail.
2. At your university library, locate a social work–related research article that used the mail survey method as the data collection method. What problems were encountered in collecting the data through the mail survey research method? What were the advantages of the data collection methodology used? Design a short hypothetical cover letter for the survey described in the article.

3. At your university library, locate a social work research article that used a mailed survey questionnaire to gather the data for the study. How could the study have used personal interviews rather than survey questionnaires to provide data to answer the research question? Provide a rationale for your response. What type of data would the interviews provide that the mailed questionnaire did not? Justify your answer.
4. For the study in Question 3, provide an in-depth critique using the contents of this chapter as a guide. Also, discuss areas of sampling, research design, operationalization of variables, generalizability, limitation, usefulness of findings, etc.
5. How would you have done the study in Question 3 differently, via a different survey method, given the same research question? Discuss in detail and be very specific. Keep in mind the context of the study (Chapter 2).

NOTES ON CHAPTER 14

Chapter 15

Participant Observation

CHAPTER OUTLINE

SELF-STUDY EXERCISES

1. What is participant observation? List and discuss how it can be used in social work research studies. What are its advantages? What are its disadvantages? Provide a social work research situation where you would use this type of nonsurvey data collection method. What are the main differences between structured observation (Chapter 13), surveys (Chapter 14), and participant observation? Provide one common social work example in your discussion.
2. Using the points as outlined in the chapter, discuss the steps in using participant observation as a data collection method.
3. Discuss in detail how participant observation can be used as a data collection method in quantitative research studies (Chapter 4) and in qualitative research studies (Chapter 5). Provide one common social work example in your discussion.
4. Discuss in detail how participant observation can be used as a data collection method in group research studies (Chapter 11) and in case research studies (Chapter 12). Provide one common social work example in your discussion.
5. Using your own words, define participant observation. Discuss how can it be used as a "research method" and as a "data collection method." Provide a social work example in your discussion.
6. Discuss the distinguishing features of participant observation as outlined in the chapter. Provide a social work example in your discussion.
7. Discuss when it is appropriate to use participant observation as a data collection method. Provide a social work example in your discussion.
8. Discuss the minimal conditions that must be met to use participant observation as a data collection method. Provide a social work example in your discussion.
9. Discuss the continuum of participant observation roles. When should we use one over the other? Explain in detail. Provide a social work example in your discussion.
10. Discuss the four ways to gather data by the participant observation method of data collection. Provide a social work example in your discussion.
11. Discuss how survey research interviews (Chapter 14) are different from participant observation interviews. Provide a social work example in your discussion.
12. Discuss the three ways to record data when using participant observation as a data collection method. Provide a social work example in your discussion.
13. Discuss the four types of field notes. When do you use one over the other? Provide a social work example in your discussion.

14. Discuss the three approaches to recording data gathered in qualitative research interviews. Provide a social work example in your discussion.
15. Discuss the ethical issues involved in using participant observation as a data collection method. How are these ethical issues different than using structured observation or surveys as data collection methods? Discuss in detail.

GROUP EXERCISES

1. In groups of four, select one common social work–relevant topic area. State a single research question and design three different research studies to answer your research question: one using structured observation as a data collection method, one using a survey as a data collection method, and the final one using participant observation as a data collection method. What types of data would be generated from each of the three data collection methods? Could you use all three data collection methods in a single study to answer the research question? Why, or why not? Explain in detail.
2. In groups of four, select one common social work–relevant topic area. State a single research question that needs to be researched. To answer your research question, construct one single research study that would use a group research design (Chapter 11) and a case research design (Chapter 12). In the same study, include a quantitative component (Chapter 4) and a qualitative component (Chapter 5). Collect data via structured observations (Chapter 13), surveys (Chapter 14), and participant observation. Do not collect irrelevant data. All data collected must directly be related to your research question.

LIBRARY EXERCISES

1. At your university library, locate a social work–related research article that used participant observation as the data collection method. What potential problems did you feel the researcher(s) encountered in using this type of data collection methodology? What were the advantages of the data collection methodology used? Discuss your answers in detail.
2. For the study in Question 1, provide an in-depth critique using the contents of this chapter as a guide. Also, discuss areas of sampling, research design, operationalization of variables, generalizability, limitation, usefulness of findings, etc.
3. How would you have done the study in Question 1 differently, via a different data collection method, given the same research question? Discuss in detail and be very specific. Keep in mind the context of the study (Chapter 2).

NOTES ON CHAPTER 15

This chapter utilizes Study C

Chapter 16

Secondary Analysis

CHAPTER OUTLINE

SELF-STUDY EXERCISES

1. Using the points as outlined in the chapter, define secondary analysis in your own terms. List some potential sources of data for a secondary analysis. Discuss in detail. What sources of data were used in Study C? Discuss in detail.
2. Compare and contrast the inductive and deductive processes in a secondary analysis. In your opinion, what process was used in Study C? Use the points as outlined in the chapter to support your answer.
3. Use the points as outlined in the chapter to discuss the use of secondary analysis in exploratory, descriptive, and explanatory research studies.
4. Discuss what is meant by reliability in a secondary analysis. Do you believe that the data used in Study C were reliable? Why or why not? Discuss in detail.
5. Discuss what is meant by validity in a secondary analysis. Do you believe that the data used in Study C were valid? Why or why not? Discuss in detail.
6. Using the points as outlined in the chapter, summarize the possible sources of error in a secondary analysis. Are any such errors present in Study C? Highlight each of the sources in your answer.
7. Discuss the problem of missing data in a secondary analysis. List the areas of missing data in Study C. Do you see any problems with data analyses when there are a lot of missing data? Explain. Do you believe that the missing data in Study C was influenced by any subjectivity or bias? Why or why not? Discuss in detail.
8. Discuss in detail the three types of data that are available for secondary analyses. Provide a social work example in your discussion.
9. Discuss in detail the specific steps of doing a secondary analysis using a social work problem area of your choice as an extended example.
10. List and discuss the four questions that need to be addressed when evaluating a data set. Provide a social work example in your discussion.
11. List and discuss in detail the advantages and disadvantages of doing a secondary analysis. As a data collection method, compare and contrast the advantages and disadvantages of secondary analyses with structured observations (Chapter 13), surveys (Chapter 14), and participant observation (Chapter 15).
12. Discuss in detail how secondary analyses can be used as a data collection method in quantitative research studies (Chapter 4) and in qualitative

research studies (Chapter 5). Provide one common social work example in your discussion.

13. Discuss in detail how secondary analyses can be used as a data collection method in group research studies (Chapter 11) and in case research studies (Chapter 12). Provide one common social work example in your discussion.

GROUP EXERCISES

1. In groups of four, decide on a social work–related problem area. Describe how you could carry out a secondary analysis of this problem. In your description, define the research hypothesis, sample, and the sources of data. What instruments would you use to collect the data? What research design would be most appropriate? Present your discussion to the entire class.
2. In groups of four, and using the hypothetical study you created in the above exercise, answer the following three questions: (a) Did you use an inductive or deductive process? (b) What were the potential sources of error in your study? (c) How could you determine the reliability and validity of your data? Present your answers to the entire class.

LIBRARY EXERCISES

1. At your university library, locate a social work–related research article that used a secondary analysis as a data collection method. What problems do you believe were encountered in using this method? Construct a short 10-item measuring instrument that could have been completed by the author to supplement the existing data. How do you believe your measuring instrument would have improved the author's study?
2. Using the research article that you located for the above exercise, answer the following five questions: (a) Was an inductive or deductive process used? Justify your answer. (b) Was the study's design exploratory, descriptive, or explanatory? Explain. (c) Do you believe the data were reliable and valid? Why or why not? (d) What were the sources of error in the study? (e) What suggestions could you make to improve the study?

NOTES ON CHAPTER 16

____

____

____

____

Chapter 17

Utilizing Existing Statistics

CHAPTER OUTLINE

SELF-STUDY EXERCISES

1. In your own words and using the points as outlined in the chapter, define how you could use existing statistics as a data collection method.
2. List some potential sources of data for a utilizing existing statistics as a data collection method. Discuss in detail.
3. Discuss what is meant by reliability when utilizing existing statistics as a data collection method. Discuss in detail.
4. Discuss what is meant by validity when utilizing existing statistics as a data collection method. Discuss in detail.
5. Discuss in detail the specific steps that you would take if you did a research study that utilized existing statistics as a data collection method using a social work problem area of your choice as an extended example.
6. List and discuss in detail the advantages and disadvantages of doing a research study that utilized existing statistics as a data collection method. As a data collection method, compare and contrast the advantages and disadvantages of utilizing existing statistics with structured observations (Chapter 13), surveys (Chapter 14), participant observation (Chapter 15), and secondary analyses (Chapter 16).
7. Discuss in detail how utilizing existing statistics can be used as a data collection method in quantitative research studies (Chapter 4) and in qualitative research studies (Chapter 5). Provide one common social work example in your discussion.
8. Discuss in detail how utilizing existing statistics can be used as a data collection method in group research studies (Chapter 11) and in case research studies (Chapter 12). Provide one common social work example in your discussion.

GROUP EXERCISES

1. In groups of four, decide on a social work–related problem area. Describe how you could carry out a research study that utilized existing statistics as a data collection method. In your description, define the research hypothesis, sample, and the sources of data. What instruments would you use to collect the data? What research design would be most appropriate? Present your discussion to the entire class.
2. In groups of four, and using the hypothetical study you created in the above exercise, answer the following three questions: (a) Did you use an inductive or deductive process? (b) What were the potential sources of error in your study? (c) How could you determine the reliability and validity of your data? Present your answers to the entire class.

LIBRARY EXERCISES

1. At your university library, locate a social work–related research article that utilized existing statistics as a data collection method. What problems do you believe were encountered in using this method? Construct a short 10-item measuring instrument that could have been completed by the author to supplement the existing data. How do you believe your measuring instrument would have improved the author's study?
2. Using the research article that you located for the above exercise, answer the following five questions: (a) Was an inductive or deductive process used? Justify your answer. (b) Was the study's design exploratory, descriptive, or explanatory? Explain. (c) Do you believe the data were reliable and valid? Why or why not? (d) What were the sources of error in the study? (e) What suggestions could you make to improve the study?

NOTES ON CHAPTER 17

This chapter utilizes Study E

Chapter 18

Content Analysis

CHAPTER OUTLINE

SELF-STUDY EXERCISES

1. Define content analysis. Discuss the similarities and differences between a secondary analysis and a content analysis.
2. Discuss the three characteristics of a content analysis as outlined in the chapter. How does each characteristic contribute to the validity and reliability in the research process? Does Study E demonstrate each of the three characteristics? Why or why not?
3. Discuss the four broad areas of classification in a content analysis as outlined in the chapter. How would you classify Study E? Justify your answer.
4. Discuss the process of developing the research question in studies that use content analysis as the method of data collection. In your opinion, what was the research question in Study E? Would you have formulated the same question? Why or why not?
5. Discuss the process of choosing the sample in studies that use content analysis as the method of data collection. Discuss the sampling methodology used in Study E. Would you have used the same sampling strategy? Why or why not?
6. Discuss the process of selecting the unit of analysis in studies that use content analysis as the method of data collection. What was the unit of analysis in Study E? What other unit of analysis could the authors of Study E have chosen?
7. Discuss the process of coding and analyzing data in studies that use content analyses as methods of data collection. Outline the procedure that was used in Study E for coding and analyzing the data. Would you have operationally defined the categories in the same way as the authors of Study E? Discuss in detail.
8. List and discuss in detail the advantages and disadvantages of doing a research study that utilized a content analysis as a data collection method. As a data collection method, compare and contrast the advantages and disadvantages of utilizing a content analysis with structured observations (Chapter 13), surveys (Chapter 14), participant observation (Chapter 15), secondary analyses (Chapter 16), and utilizing existing statistics (Chapter 17).
9. Discuss in detail how a content analysis can be used as a data collection method in quantitative research studies (Chapter 4) and in qualitative research studies (Chapter 5). Provide one common social work example in your discussion.
10. Discuss in detail how utilizing a content analysis can be used as a data collection method in group research studies (Chapter 11) and in case research studies (Chapter 12). Provide one common social work example in your discussion.

GROUP EXERCISES

1. In groups of four, decide on a social work–related problem area. Describe how you could carry out a research study that utilized a content analysis as a data collection method. In your description, define the research hypothesis, sample, and the sources of data. What instruments would you use to collect the data? What research design would be most appropriate? Present your discussion to the entire class.
2. In groups of four, and using the hypothetical study you created in the above exercise, answer the following three questions: (a) Did you use an inductive or deductive process? (b) What were the potential sources of error in your study? (c) How could you determine the reliability and validity of your data? Present your answers to the entire class.

LIBRARY EXERCISES

1. At your university library, locate a social work–related research article that utilized a content analysis as a data collection method. What problems do you believe were encountered in using this method? Construct a short 10-item measuring instrument that could have been completed by the author to supplement the existing data. How do you believe your measuring instrument would have improved the author's study?
2. Using the research article that you located for the above exercise, answer the following five questions: (a) Was an inductive or deductive process used? Justify your answer. (b) Was the study's design exploratory, descriptive, or explanatory? Explain. (c) Do you believe the data were reliable and valid? Why or why not? (d) What were the sources of error in the study? (e) What suggestions could you make to improve the study?

NOTES ON CHAPTER 18

Chapter 19

Historical Research

CHAPTER OUTLINE

SELF-STUDY EXERCISES

1. In your own words, define historical research.

2. What is the purpose of history?
3. Discuss the differences between presentism and antiquarianism. Provide a social work example in your discussion.
4. Discuss the process of developing the research question in studies that use historical research as the method of data collection.
5. What is fragmentary evidence? Explain in detail.
6. List and discuss in detail the advantages and disadvantages of doing a research study that utilized historical research as a data collection method. As a data collection method, compare and contrast the advantages and disadvantages of utilizing historical research with structured observations (Chapter 13), surveys (Chapter 14), participant observation (Chapter 15), secondary analyses (Chapter 16), utilizing existing statistics (Chapter 17), and content analyses (Chapter 18).
7. Discuss in detail how historical research can be used as a data collection method in quantitative research studies (Chapter 4) and in qualitative research studies (Chapter 5). Provide one common social work example in your discussion.
8. Discuss in detail how historical research can be used as a data collection method in group research studies (Chapter 11) and in case research studies (Chapter 12). Provide one common social work example in your discussion.
9. Discuss in detail how historical research, along with survey research, secondary analysis, content analysis, and utilizing existing statistics, can be viewed as research methods in their own right *and* as data collection methods.

GROUP EXERCISES

1. In groups of four, decide on a social work–related problem area. Derive a research question (or hypothesis) out of the problem area. Describe how you could carry out a historical research study that would answer your research question (or test your hypothesis). In your description, define the research question (or hypothesis), sample, and the sources of data. What instruments would you use to collect the data? What research design would be most appropriate? Present your discussion to the entire class.
2. In groups of four, and using the hypothetical study you created in the above exercise, answer the following three questions: (a) Did you use an inductive or deductive process? (b) What were the potential sources of error in your study? (c) How could you determine the reliability and validity of your data? Present your answers to the entire class.
3. In groups of four, design a quantitative research study that used historical research as a data collection method for answering a social work–related research question (or testing a hypothesis) of your choice. With the same research question (or hypothesis), design a qualitative research study. Compare the advantages and disadvantages of using both research ap-

proaches in answering the research question (or testing the hypothesis). Describe in detail how you could incorporate both research approaches, quantitative and qualitative, in a single research study that utilized historical research as a data collection method. Present your results to the entire class.

LIBRARY EXERCISES

1. At your university library, locate a social work–related research article that utilized historical research as a data collection method. What problems do you believe were encountered in using this method?
2. Using the research article that you located for the above exercise, answer the following five questions: (a) Was an inductive or deductive process used? Justify your answer. (b) Was the study's design exploratory, descriptive, or explanatory? Explain. (c) Do you believe the data were reliable and valid? Why or why not? (d) What were the sources of error in the study? (e) What suggestions could you make to improve the study?

NOTES ON CHAPTER 19

This chapter utilizes Studies E and F

Chapter 20

Selecting a Data Collection Method and Data Source

CHAPTER OUTLINE

SELF-STUDY EXERCISES

1. Discuss in detail what is meant by a data collection method. Provide a social work example in your discussion.
2. Discuss in detail what is meant by a data source. Provide a social work example in your discussion.
3. Discuss in detail how available data collection methods influence the selection of data sources, and vice versa. Provide a social work example in your discussion.
4. Discuss in detail how available data collection methods and data sources influence the selection of research problems and research questions, and vice versa. Provide a social work example in your discussion.
5. Discuss in detail how available data collection methods and data sources influence the selection of research designs, and vice versa. Provide a social work example in your discussion.
6. List and discuss in detail the criteria that can be used to select a data collection method. Provide a social work example in your discussion.
7. List and discuss in detail the criteria that can be used to select a data source. Provide a social work example in your discussion.
8. Describe in detail the main differences between obtrusive data collection methods (Chapters 13–15) and unobtrusive data collection methods (Chapters 16–19). When would you chose one over the other? Discuss in detail. Provide a social work example in your discussion.
9. Describe in detail how you could use an unobtrusive data collection method along with an obtrusive one in a single research study that focused on one specific research question (or hypothesis). Provide a social work example in your discussion.
10. Describe in detail how you could use two or more different data sources in a single research study that focused on one specific research question (or hypothesis). Provide a social work example in your discussion.
11. Describe how Study E could have used a different data collection method and data source to answer the same research question. What other data would this new data collection method and data source generate that the original one (content analysis) did not?
12. Describe how Study F could have used a different data collection method and data source to answer the same research question. What other data

would this new data collection method and data source generate that the original one (secondary analysis) did not?

GROUP EXERCISES

1. In groups of four, decide on a social work–related problem area. Derive a research question (or hypothesis) out of the problem area. Describe how you could carry out seven different hypothetical quantitative research studies that could answer your research question (or test your hypothesis) using each of the data collection methods listed on the top of Table 20.1. In your description, define all relevant variables (e.g., independent, dependent, extraneous, intervening), the research question (or hypothesis), potential rival hypotheses, the specific research design, the sample, the data collection method(s), and the data source(s) for each data collection method(s). Discuss the limitations of your hypothetical study. Present your discussion to the entire class.
2. Repeat Exercise 1 with seven different qualitative research studies.
3. Repeat Exercise 1 integrating a quantitative component and a qualitative component.

LIBRARY EXERCISES

1. At your university library, locate a social work–related research article that utilized any data collection method. What problems do you believe were encountered in using this method? What other method could the author have used to collect data? Why? Discuss in detail.
2. At your university library, locate a social work–related research article that utilized any data source. What problems do you believe were encountered in using this data source? What other data source could the author have used? Why? Discuss in detail.
3. Using the research article that you located for the above exercise, answer the following five questions: (a) Was an inductive or deductive process used? Justify your answer. (b) Was the study's design exploratory, descriptive, or explanatory? Explain. (c) Do you believe the data were reliable and valid? Why or why not? (d) What were the sources of error in the study? (e) What suggestions could you make to improve the study?

NOTES ON CHAPTER 20

This chapter utilizes Studies A–I

Chapter 21

Quantitative Data Analysis

CHAPTER OUTLINE

SELF-STUDY EXERCISES

1. Describe in detail each level of measurement. Use a social work example in your discussion. Discuss how the variable, educational level, could be classified at all four levels.
2. Describe the purpose of descriptive statistics. How can they be used in social work research situations? Provide a social work example in your discussion.
3. Describe the purpose of inferential statistics. How can they be used in social work research situations? Provide a social work example in your discussion.
4. Discuss how computers can help aid in the data analysis phase of the research process.
5. What are the benefits to the reader when statistics are reported in a journal article? Be specific and concrete in your response.
6. List and fully describe the three measures of central tendency and the two measures of variability. Provide a social work example throughout your discussion.
7. List and fully describe the two statistics that can help us to determine if there is an association between two variables. When is one used over the other? Why?
8. List and fully describe the three statistics that can help us to determine if there are any statistically significant differences between the means of two or more groups. Use a social work example throughout your discussion.
9. Describe the main differences between *t*-tests and ANOVA. When is one used over the other?
10. Read Study A. What statistics did the authors use? Did they use the statistics correctly? Why, or why not? Do you think that the use of statistics in the sample study increased your understanding of the study's findings? Why, or why not? What statistics, if any, do you think the authors should have used, but did not? Why?
11. Read Study B. What statistics did the authors use? Did they use the statistics correctly? Why, or why not? Do you think that the use of statistics in the sample study increased your understanding of the study's findings? Why, or why not? What statistics, if any, do you think the authors should have used, but did not? Why?
12. Read Study C. What statistics did the authors use? Did they use the statistics correctly? Why, or why not? Do you think that the use of statistics in the sample study increased your understanding of the study's findings? Why, or why not? What statistics, if any, do you think the authors should have used, but did not? Why?
13. Read Study D. What statistics did the author use? Did he use the statistics correctly? Why, or why not? Do you think that the use of statistics in the sample study increased your understanding of the study's findings? Why, or why not? What statistics, if any, do you think the author should have used, but did not? Why?
14. Read Study E. What statistics did the authors use? Did they use the statistics

correctly? Why, or why not? Do you think that the use of statistics in the sample study increased your understanding of the study's findings? Why, or why not? What statistics, if any, do you think the authors should have used, but did not? Why?

15. Read Study F. What statistics did the authors use? Did they use the statistics correctly? Why, or why not? Do you think that the use of statistics in the sample study increased your understanding of the study's findings? Why, or why not? What statistics, if any, do you think the authors should have used, but did not? Why?
16. Read Study G. What statistics did the author use? Did she use the statistics correctly? Why, or why not? Do you think that the use of statistics in the sample study increased your understanding of the study's findings? Why, or why not? What statistics, if any, do you think the author should have used, but did not? Why?
17. Read Study H. What statistics did the authors use? Did they use the statistics correctly? Why, or why not? Do you think that the use of statistics in the sample study increased your understanding of the study's findings? Why, or why not? What statistics, if any, do you think the authors should have used, but did not? Why?
18. Read Study I. What statistics did the authors use? Did they use the statistics correctly? Why, or why not? Do you think that the use of statistics in the sample study increased your understanding of the study's findings? Why, or why not? What statistics, if any, do you think the authors should have used, but did not? Why?

GROUP EXERCISES

1. In groups of four, decide on a social work–related problem area. Derive a research question (or hypothesis) out of the problem area. Describe how you could carry out a quantitative research study that would use statistics that could answer your research question (or test your hypothesis). In your description, define all relevant variables (e.g., independent, dependent, extraneous, intervening), the research question (or hypothesis), potential rival hypotheses, the specific research design, the sample, the data collection method(s), the data source(s) for each data collection method(s), and the specific statistics that you would use. Discuss the limitations of your hypothetical study. Present your discussion to the entire class.
2. With the same research question (or hypothesis) used in Exercise 1, design a qualitative study and answer the same questions contained at the end of Exercise 1.

LIBRARY EXERCISE

1. At your university library, locate as many articles as needed to demonstrate the four levels of measurement. If the measuring instruments are not included in the article(s), find copies of the instruments. Discuss how the authors used measurement by answering the following four questions: (a) Which variable(s) was(were) measured at the *nominal* level? (b) Which variable(s) was(were) measured at the *ordinal* level? (c) Which variable(s) was(were) measured at the *interval* level? (d) Which variable(s) was(were) measured at the *ratio* level?

NOTES ON CHAPTER 21

This chapter utilizes Studies J and K

Chapter 22

Qualitative Data Analysis

CHAPTER OUTLINE

SELF-STUDY EXERCISES

1. In your own words, describe the major differences between a qualitative data analysis and a quantitative data analysis. Provide a social work example in your discussion.
2. Discuss how you could answer a single research question through qualitative and quantitative data. Provide a social work example in your discussion.
3. What is the major purpose of a qualitative data analysis? What is the major purpose of a quantitative data analysis? Compare and contrast the two purposes in relation to the role that research plays in generating social work knowledge. Provide one common social work example in your discussion.
4. List and discuss all the assumptions that underlie the qualitative research approach that are directly relevant to the data analysis phase of a qualitative research study. Provide one common social work example in your discussion.
5. Discuss how you would go about preparing qualitative data in transcript form using the five substeps as outlined in the chapter. Provide one common social work example in your discussion.
6. Discuss how you would go about establishing a plan for qualitative data analysis using the two substeps as outlined in the chapter. Provide one common social work example in your discussion.
7. Describe in detail the purpose of first-level coding. Discuss how you would do first-level coding using the eight substeps as outlined in the chapter. Provide one common social work example in your discussion.
8. Describe in detail the purpose of second-level coding. Discuss how you would do first-level coding using the two substeps as outlined in the chapter. Provide one common social work example in your discussion.
9. Discuss in detail the purpose of interpreting qualitative data and building theory from the data. Discuss how you would interpret data using the two substeps as outlined in the chapter. Provide one common social work example in your discussion.
10. Discuss in detail the purpose of assessing the trustworthiness of a qualitative study's findings. Discuss how you would establish the a study's trustworthiness using the three substeps as outlined in the chapter. Provide one common social work example in your discussion.
11. Read Study J. Discuss how the authors must have used all of the steps and substeps as outlined in this chapter when they did their study. Provide specific examples in the study that directly relate to the steps and substeps as outlined in this chapter. How could the same research question be answered through a quantitative research approach? Discuss in detail. What different types of data would a quantitative study offer that a qualitative study does not, and vise versa? Explain in detail. After reading Study J, do you feel the authors did a credible qualitative research study? Why, or why not? What would you have done differently? Why?
12. Read Study K. Discuss how the author must have used all of the steps and

substeps as outlined in this chapter when he did his study. Provide specific examples in the study that directly relate to the steps and substeps as outlined in this chapter. How could the same research question be answered through a quantitative research approach? Discuss in detail. What different types of data would a quantitative study offer that a qualitative study does not, and vice versa? Explain in detail. After reading Study K, do you feel the author did a credible qualitative research study? Why, or why not? What would you have done differently? Why?

GROUP EXERCISES

1. In groups of four, decide on a social work–related problem area. Derive a research question (or hypothesis) out of the problem area that you wish to answer. Describe how you could carry out a qualitative research study that would answer your research question (or test your hypothesis). In your description, define all relevant variables (e.g., independent, dependent, extraneous, intervening), the research question (or hypothesis), potential rival hypotheses, the specific research design, the sample (research participants), the data collection method(s), and the data source(s) for each data collection method(s). Discuss in detail how you would go about analyzing data generated from your study using all the steps and substeps as outlined in the chapter. Discuss the limitations of your hypothetical study. Present your discussion to the entire class.
2. With the same research question (or hypothesis) used in the above exercise, design a quantitative study and answer the same questions contained at the end of the exercise using statistics as outlined in the previous chapter.
3. In groups of four, design a quantitative research study that used interviewing as a data collection method for a answering a social work–related research question (or testing a hypothesis) of your choice. With the same research question (or hypothesis), design a qualitative research study. Compare the advantages and disadvantages of using both research approaches in answering the research question (or testing the hypothesis). Describe in detail how you could incorporate both research approaches, quantitative and qualitative, in a single research study that utilized interviewing as a data collection method. Present your results to the entire class.

LIBRARY EXERCISE

1. At your university library, locate a social work–relevant article that used a qualitative research approach to answer a research question (or test a hypothesis). Evaluate the article's data analysis phase using the points as outlined in this chapter.

NOTES ON CHAPTER 22

Chapter 23

Case-Level Evaluation

CHAPTER OUTLINE

SELF-STUDY EXERCISES

1. Discuss in your own words the purpose of case-level evaluation designs. Use a social work example throughout your discussion.
2. List and discuss in detail the three requirements that case-level evaluation designs must have in order for them to be useful to social work practitioners and researchers. Use a social work example throughout your discussion.
3. List and discuss in detail the three *exploratory* case-level evaluation designs. Provide a social work example of each.
4. List and discuss in detail the two *descriptive* case-level evaluation designs. Provide a social work example of each.
5. List and discuss in detail the three *explanatory* case-level evaluation designs. Provide a social work example of each.
6. What do descriptive case-level evaluation designs have that exploratory ones do not? Provide a social work example in your discussion.
7. What do explanatory case-level evaluation designs have that descriptive ones do not? Provide a social work example in your discussion.
8. What is the major purpose of multiple-baseline case-level evaluation designs? Discuss in detail. Provide a social work example of all three types.
9. List and discuss in detail the advantages and disadvantages of case-level evaluation designs. Provide a social work example throughout your discussion.
10. When is it inappropriate to implement an *A*-phase when trying to achieve a case-level research design? Provide a social work example throughout your discussion.
11. In your own words, discuss the similarities and differences between case-level evaluation designs and group research designs as presented in Chapter 11. Use a social work example throughout your discussion.
12. In your own words, discuss the similarities and differences between *exploratory* case-level evaluation designs and *exploratory* group research designs as presented in Chapter 11. Use a social work example throughout your discussion.
13. In your own words, discuss the similarities and differences between *descriptive* case-level evaluation designs and *descriptive* group research designs as presented in Chapter 11. Use a social work example throughout your discussion.
14. In your own words, discuss the similarities and differences between *explanatory* case-level evaluation designs and *explanatory* group research designs

as presented in Chapter 11. Use a social work example throughout your discussion.

15. Design a perfect explanatory case-level evaluation study that takes into account all the threats to internal and external validity mentioned in Chapter 11. What ethical issues do you see if your study was in fact implemented?
16. Out of all the case-level evaluation designs presented in this chapter, which one do you think is used most often in social work research? Why? Justify your answer. Which one do you think is least utilized? Why? Justify your answer. Use a social work example throughout your discussion.
17. Discuss why case-level evaluation designs are nothing more than interrupted time series group designs as presented in Chapter 11. Justify your answer. Use a social work example throughout your discussion.

GROUP EXERCISES

1. In groups of four, decide on a social work–related problem area. Derive an *exploratory* research question out of the problem area. Describe how you could carry out all three *exploratory-level* quantitative case-level evaluations (i.e., *B, BC, BCD*) that could answer your research question using any one of the seven data collection methods discussed in Chapters 13–19 (i.e., Table 20.1). In your description, define and operationalize all relevant variables (e.g., independent, dependent, extraneous, intervening), the research question, potential rival hypotheses, the specific case-level evaluation design, the sample (research participants), the data collection method(s), and the data source(s) for each data collection method(s). Discuss the limitations of your hypothetical studies. Present your discussion to the entire class.
2. In groups of four, repeat Exercise 1 using the two *descriptive* case-level evaluation designs (i.e., *AB, ABC*). Use a different data collection method and data source.
3. In groups of four, repeat Exercise 1 using the three *explanatory* case-level evaluation designs (i.e., *ABAB, BAB, BCBC*). Use a different data collection method and data source.

LIBRARY EXERCISES

1. At your university library, find a social work article that reports on a research study that used an *exploratory* case-level evaluation design. What do you feel the article contributed to the knowledge base of social work? Why? Justify your response. How could have this study been done using a "higher level" design?
2. Repeat Exercise 1 with a *descriptive* case-level evaluation design.

NOTES ON CHAPTER 23

Chapter 24

Program-Level Evaluation

CHAPTER OUTLINE

SELF-STUDY EXERCISES

1. Why do you believe that program-level evaluation is important to the social work profession? Explain in detail using the points as outlined in the chapter.
2. Discuss how program-level evaluations complement case-level evaluations (Chapter 23). Provide a social work example in your discussion.
3. After reading Chapters 2, and 24, discuss the various political factors that are associated with doing a program-level evaluation. Provide a social work example in your discussion.
4. After reading Chapters 1, 2, and 24, discuss how a program-level evaluation can be an "applied" research study along with a "pure" research study. Provide a social work example in your discussion.
5. Discuss the various ways that a final report generated from a program-level evaluation can be useful to various stakeholder groups. Provide a social work example in your discussion.
6. Discuss some of the logistical problems that can occur when doing a program-level evaluation. Compare these problems with case-level evaluations. Provide a social work example in your discussion.
7. Discuss the various steps that you could use when anticipating logistical problems in a program-level evaluation. Compare these steps with the ones that you would use when doing a case-level evaluation. Provide a social work example in your discussion.
8. Discuss the differences between a formative program-level evaluation and a summative program-level evaluation. Compare and contrast these differences with "formative" case-level evaluations and "summative" case-level evaluations.
9. Discuss in detail how you would go about conducting a program-level evaluation that focuses on "*outcome.*" Be specific in your discussion and utilize as many of the concepts as you can from the preceding chapters in this book. Some of these concepts would be: problem area, research question, conceptualization of problem area and research question, operationalization of the variables, sampling strategy, research design, data collection methods, data sources, generalization of findings, etc.
10. Answer the above question focusing on a program's "*efficiency.*"
11. Answer Question 9 focusing only on a program's "*implementation.*"
12. How would you go about doing a needs assessment?
13. What are the main differences between normative needs and demand needs? Provide a social work example of each.
14. List and describe in detail the three different types of program evaluation

models. Provide a social work example of each. Discuss how each model complements one another.

15. Discuss how a program-level evaluation is really an application (or applied research) of all the principles as contained in this book. Do the same for a case-level evaluation. Provide a social work example in your discussion.
16. Discuss how a program-level evaluation can use each one of the seven different data collection methods contained in Parts V and VI in this book (e.g., Table 20.1). Provide a social work example in your discussion.
17. Discuss how a program-level evaluation could use each one of the eight case-level evaluation designs as outlined in the previous chapter. Provide a social work example in your discussion.

GROUP EXERCISES

1. In groups of four, decide on a program-level evaluation question that deals with a program's effectiveness (research question or hypothesis). Describe how you could carry out a *quantitative* program-level evaluation that would answer your research question or hypothesis. In your description, define all relevant variables (e.g., independent, dependent, extraneous, intervening), the research question (or hypothesis), potential rival hypotheses, the specific research design, the sample (research participants), the data collection method(s), and the data source(s) for each data collection method(s). Discuss in detail how you would go about analyzing data generated from your study. Discuss the limitations of your hypothetical program-level evaluation. Present your discussion to the entire class.
2. With the same research question (or hypothesis) used in the above exercise, design a qualitative study and answer the same questions contained at the end of the exercise.
3. In groups of four, describe in detail how you would evaluate the effectiveness and efficiency of your social work program.
4. After reading the appendix, and in groups of four, discuss the various cultural factors that need to be taken into account when doing a program-level evaluation. How are these factors different from the ones that need to be taken into account when doing a case-level evaluation? Discuss in detail and provide a social work example in your response. Report back to the entire class of what your group found.

LIBRARY EXERCISE

1. At your university library, locate a social work-relevant article that presents the results of a program evaluation. Evaluate the article using the contents of this entire book as a guide. How would you have done the study differently? Why? Be specific in your response.

NOTES ON CHAPTER 24

Chapter 25

Implementing Evaluations

CHAPTER OUTLINE

SELF-STUDY EXERCISES

1. Discuss the various principles that underlie the design of case-level evaluations and program-level evaluations. Provide a social work example in your discussion.
2. List and discuss all of the stakeholders who may benefit from a case-level evaluation and a program-level evaluation. Provide a social work example in your discussion.
3. List and discuss all of the stakeholders who may benefit from an "effectiveness" program-level evaluation of your social work program. Be specific in your discussion.
4. What is case-level decision making? What is program-level decision making? How do the two levels of decision making complement one another? Provide one common social work example in your discussion.
5. What is the monitoring approach to evaluation? Provide a social work example in your discussion.
6. List and discuss some of the ethical considerations when doing case- and program-level evaluations. Provide one common social work example in your discussion.
7. Describe in detail the main differences between planned interventions and crisis interventions. Provide one common social work example in your discussion.
8. Discuss how you select research designs for case-level evaluations and form program-level evaluations. Provide one common social work example in your discussion.

GROUP EXERCISES

1. In groups of four, decide on a program-level evaluation question that deals with a program's effectiveness (research question or hypothesis). Describe how you could combine a *quantitative* case- **and** a *quantitative* program-level evaluation at the same time that would answer your research question or hypothesis. In your description, define all relevant variables (e.g., independent, dependent, extraneous, intervening), the research question (or hypothesis), potential rival hypotheses, the specific research design, the sample (research participants), the data collection method(s), and the data source(s) for each data collection method(s). Discuss in detail how you would go about analyzing data generated from your study. Discuss the limitations of your hypothetical program-level evaluation. Present your

discussion to the entire class.

2. With the same research question (or hypothesis) used in the above exercise, design a qualitative case-study evaluation and a quantitative program-level evaluation and answer the same questions contained at the end of the exercise. Repeat the exercise with a quantitative case-level evaluation and a qualitative program-level evaluation.
3. In groups of four, describe in detail how you would evaluate the effectiveness and efficiency of your social work program by combining case-level evaluations to form a program-level evaluation.
4. After reading the appendix, and in groups of four, discuss the various cultural factors that need to be taken into account when doing a program-level evaluation. How are these factors different from the ones that need to be taken into account when doing a case-level evaluation? Discuss in detail and provide a social work example in your response. Report back to the entire class what your group found.

LIBRARY EXERCISE

1. At your university library, locate a social work–relevant article that presents the combined results of a case-level and program-level evaluation. Evaluate the article using the contents of this entire book as a guide. How would you have done the study differently? Why? Be specific in your response.

NOTES ON CHAPTER 25

PART II

Sample Research Studies

Bruce Bidgood
Leslie M. Tutty
Michael A. Rothery

Study 

An Evaluation of a Group Program for Men Who Batter Their Partners

THIS SAMPLE STUDY DESCRIBES a program evaluation of a community treatment program for assaultive men. The material presented here is a subset of a larger, complex study of groups serving women victims as well as male perpetrators (Bidgood, Tutty, & Rothery, 1991). In the interests of brevity, we have restricted our discussion to a few of many variables that were measured, and we shall focus on men alone.

GROUP TREATMENT OF MALE PERPETRATORS

Many authors argue that group treatment offers the widest range of benefits for most—though not all (Saunders, 1984)—men who batter. Currie (1984) and Saunders (1984) both suggest that group programs are less threatening than individual or couple therapy, reduce social isolation, and offer peer support. Groups also offer participants a variety of models and sources of feedback, increased possibilities for peer interaction, and a greater variety of activities (Edleson, 1984). Saunders (1984) argues that group programs can be extremely helpful in teaching men that they are not alone and that there are others who share the same problem.

As group treatment has become the main treatment for assaultive men, numerous variations in focus and style of intervention have emerged. For example, there are anger management groups, self-help groups, psycho-educational groups (Edleson & Syers, 1990), and coordinated community intervention programs (which refers to a model wherein groups are run as part of a larger community effort to reduce family violence). The program evaluated in the present study was of the last type.

Outcome Research on Groups for Perpetrators

Relatively few evaluations of men's group treatment programs have been reported in the literature. Of these, the most important criterion has been whether physical violence had ceased during and after the group. The limited available data suggest that men's groups can have several positive impacts:

1. Cessation of violence by a number of men (Edleson, Miller, Stone, & Chapman, 1985; Shupe, Stacey, & Hazlewood, 1984), that can be maintained, at least for up to six months after treatment (Edleson & Gruszynski, 1986 as reported in Gondolf, 1987; Shupe, Stacey, & Hazlewood, 1984; Gondolf, 1984 as reported in Gondolf, 1987).
2. Recidivism (Chen, Bersani, Myers, & Denton 1989) as measured by police rearrests may decrease, though this outcome obviously risks overestimating the cessation of violence, as many incidents do not result in charges being laid.
3. Related factors other than just cessation of abuse may also improve, such as the adoption of less traditional views of women and increased affective communication (Lund cited by Saunders & Harusa, 1986), and decreased anger, threat from female competence, depression, and jealousy (Saunders & Harusa, 1986).

It has been increasingly emphasized in the literature that physical and verbal/emotional abuse are to a degree independent issues. Physically abusive men are normally also guilty of high levels of emotional abuse, even terrorism—threats, extraordinary and hostile invasions of privacy, coerciveness, blackmail, and consistent assaults on confidence and self-esteem. It is especially important to note research indicating that treatment may lead to a cessation of physical violence while emotional attacks continue (Edleson & Grusznski, 1986 as reported in Gondolf, 1987).

The Current Study

The coordinated community group program evaluated in the present study is a feminist-informed program (Pressman, 1989), recognizing the impact of sociopolitical and economic factors, as well as attitudes and gender roles on establishing conditions that lead to men abusing their partners. Groups run from 10–12 weeks, with each session lasting from 2 to 3 hours. The leaders were social workers, with most groups led by a female-male co-therapy team.

The basic purpose of the men's groups is to help participants take responsibility for their violent behavior and learn more appropriate ways of expressing their feelings.

The group leaders identified several general goals for the men in their program. Of these, two will be focused on in this report:

1. To end physical violence, as well as psychological and emotional abuse.
2. To bring about changes in member's sex role attitudes.

METHODOLOGY

Research Design and Sample

The evaluation design used was a one-group pretest-posttest design. The participants in the study constitute a nonprobability availability sample. Every person referred to the program during the time the research took place was invited to participate. Fifteen groups and 104 men were studied. Of these, 71 men (68%) completed the program and were therefore available at the posttest.

Operational Definitions

Measures were chosen to fit with the stated objectives of the group. All were self-administered paper and pencil questionnaires, and, to the extent possible, only standardized instruments with proven reliability and validity were used.

The Index of Spouse Abuse

This index (Hudson & McIntosh, 1981) was utilized to assess the extent of physical and nonphysical abuse occurring between spouses. This 30-item instrument contains eleven statements on physical abuse and nineteen items on nonphysical abuse. Subjects respond to items using a 5-point response scale, and higher scores indicate greater severity of abuse globally and for each type (physical or nonphysical).

The index items, which were originally written to be answered by women with respect to their partners, were rewritten so that the measure could be administered to men as well.

The Conflict Tactics Scale

This scale is best known as one of the primary instruments used by Straus and his colleagues during landmark studies in the 1970s that documented the prevalence of domestic assaults against women in the United states. It measures partners' utilization of three distinct conflict resolution "strategies": reasoning, verbal abuse, and physical violence. Scores on the CTS are expressed as a percentage, with higher scores indicating a greater reliance on the specific strategy in question. The CTS was developed as an interview schedule; some modifications were necessary to incorporate it into a paper-and-pencil assessment package, and to compensate for other minor problems with the scale in its original form.

The Attitude Toward Marriage and the Family Scale

This scale was designed to measure traditional sex role attitudes in three areas of marital/family life: domestic, social, and sexual. With reasonably well-established reliability and validity, this measure consists of 29 items—respondents indicate their level of agreement with each on a 4-point scale. Scores range from 0 to 87, with higher scores indicating a more traditional sex role orientation.

Limitations

In research with perpetrators there is always concern about the extent to which their responses to self-report instruments may be distorted by a tendency to overestimate positive change and underestimate abuse in their relationships. Different strategies are employed by researchers to deal with this problem, which often entail gathering information against which the men's claims can be corroborated. In this study we could not, for ethical reasons, obtain corroboration from the men's partners; we did cross-check the men's self-described changes with ratings provided by group leaders. As a second check, the Marlowe-Crowne Social Desirability Scale (which measures a respondent's tendency to distort information in an effort to "look good") was used to compensate statistically for any client tendencies to give socially desirable answers (Crowne & Marlowe, 1960).

Fortunately, the men in the sample did not score significantly highly on this scale relative to established population norms, there was no significant change in their social desirability scores over the course of treatment, and an analysis of findings using Marlowe-Crowne scores as a control variable did not affect the findings as reported in Table A-1.

Despite the existence of a waiting list of previously assessed clients for each treatment group, it proved unfeasible to use these to form a suitable comparison group. The lack of a meaningful control or comparison group poses significant potential problems with internal validity.

The loss of subjects experienced in this research is not unusual in research with this population. As an interesting tangential note, information beyond the measures reported here was gathered, in order to study questions other than those reported in this chapter.

When dropouts and completers were compared using some of these other measures, it appeared that the dropouts had significantly lower self-esteem and were significantly more socially isolated. Such findings suggest (a good topic for future research) that there may be a subpopulation of assaultive men who are depressed and isolated, and who may need extensive pregroup individual help or extra support and encouragement if they are going to connect with group treatment successfully.

Finally, in an ideal world, random selection of participants would support safer generalization of our results to other assaultive men, and an opportunity to follow up with the subjects would allow us to estimate how successfully gains were maintained.

FINDINGS

As Table A-1 indicates, client participation in the program was associated with positive change respecting critical outcome criteria. The significance of these changes was assessed using a correlated t-test for each of the variables.

Attitudes toward marriage and the family shifted in the direction of less traditional attitudes regarding gender roles, and there was a decline in nonphysical as well as physical abuse. While there was a slight increase in the respondents' reported use of reasoning as a strategy for resolving conflict, this change was not statistically significant.

DISCUSSION

As noted earlier, it was not possible to incorporate a control or comparison group into the design for this study. Had we been able to do so, this would have provided us with additional confidence in our findings; the possibility that the changes observed in Table A-1 are due to factors other than the treatment program cannot confidently be ruled out without having a no-treatment group available for comparison. It is also regrettable that without follow-up, we cannot know if changes made in the course of group treatment were maintained after treatment is terminated.

TABLE A-1 MEAN SCORE AT PRETEST AND POSTTEST ($N = 71$)

Variable	Pretest	Posttest	Difference	t-Value
Attitudes toward marriage and family	30.6	26.9	-3.7	2.7^a
Spouse abuse (global)	19.7	11.1	-8.6	3.7^a
• physical	18.8	10.6	-8.2	3.9^a
• nonphysical	21.5	11.5	-10.0	3.9^a
Conflict tactics:				
• reasoning	28.6	31.3	2.7	0.5
• verbal abuse	16.8	10.0	-6.8	2.3^b
• violence	4.1	1.0	-3.1	3.0^a

$^a = p \le .05$; $^b = p \le .01$

Nevertheless, it is encouraging to see significant change in directions that are consistent with goals suggested in the literature and endorsed by the group leaders. In the case of physical and nonphysical abuse, two separate instruments were sensitive to these changes, and this adds credibility to the findings.

Future research can focus on many interesting questions about which little is yet known regarding a population that is rightly considered difficult to help. As examples, studies of drop-outs could be very useful, and continued attention to the stability of gains during follow-up periods of two years or more will also be welcome. In the meantime, findings such as those presented provide encouraging tentative evidence for the efficacy of methods that clinicians have evolved for helping to alleviate the threat of continuing violence against women.

REFERENCES

BIDGOOD, B., TUTTY, L.M., & ROTHERY, M.A. (1991). *An evaluation of the coordinated family violence treatment program in the Waterloo area.* Waterloo, Ontario: Wilfrid Laurier University Centre for Social Welfare Studies.

CHEN, H., BERSANI, C., MYERS, S., & DENTON, R. (1989). Evaluating the effectiveness of a court sponsored abuser treatment program. *Journal of Family Violence, 4*, 309-322.

CROWNE, D.P., & MARLOWE, D. (1960). A new scale of social desirability independent of psychopathology. *Journal of Consulting Psychology, 24*, 349-354.

CURRIE, D. (1984). A Toronto model. *Social Work with Groups, 7*, 179-189.

EDLESON, J. (1984). Working with men who batter. *Social Work, 29*, 237-241.

EDLESON, J., MILLER, D., STONE, G., & CHAPMAN, D. (1985). Group treatment for men who batter: A multiple base-line evaluation. *Social Work Research and Abstracts, 21*, 18-21.

EDLESON, J., & SYERS, M. (1990). Relative effectiveness of group treatments for men who batter. *Social Work Research & Abstracts, 26*, 10-17.

GONDOLF, E. (1987). Evaluating programs for men who batter: Problems and prospects. *Journal of Family Violence, 2*, 95-108.

HOTALING, G., & SUGARMAN, D. (1986). An analysis of risk markers in husband to wife violence: The current state of knowledge. *Violence and Victims, 1*, 101-124.

HUDSON, W., & MCINTOSH, S. (1981). The assessment of spouse abuse: Two quantifiable dimensions. *Journal of Marriage and the Family, 42*, 873-885.

PRESSMAN, B. (1989). Treatment of wife-abuse: The case for feminist therapy. In B. Pressman, G. Cameron, & M. Rothery (Eds.), *Intervening with assaulted women: Current theory, research and practice*. Hillsdale, NJ: Lawrence Erlbaum.

SAUNDERS, D. (1984). Helping husbands who batter. *Social Casework, 65*, 347-353.

SAUNDERS, D., & HARUSA, D. (1986). Cognitive-behavioral treatment of men who batter: The short-term effects of group therapy. *Journal of Family Violence, 1*, 357-372.

SHUPE, A., STACEY, W., & HAZLEWOOD, L. (1984). *Violent men, violent couples*. Toronto, ON: D.C. Heath.

John V. Flowers
Curtis D. Booarem

Study **B**

Four Studies Toward an Empirical Foundation for Group Therapy

THE DIFFICULTY OF OUTCOME EVALUATION in group therapy reflects a more complex version of the problem of psychotherapy evaluation in general. Since it has been demonstrated that using specific, operational outcome measures is more promising than global or personality assessment for measuring a single client's progress in therapy (Ciminero, Calhoun, & Adams, 1977; Mischel, 1977), it follows that situationally specific assessment is easier to accomplish when the group focuses on a single type of problem for all members. This is probably why the greatest proportion of research in "behavioral" group therapy has been with groups of clients with homogeneous problems (Upper & Ross, 1979, 1980, 1981).

Within groups of clients with heterogeneous problems, the most common assessment methods have been of a global or personality type (Strupp & Hadley, 1977, Bergin & Lambert, 1978). When more specific measures have been employed, the most common methods use the client or the therapist(s) to rate improvement on the problem(s) being addressed. Unfortunately, this form of assessment is unsound, since reliability is unknown and validity is unassessed and compromised by response bias.

Flowers and his associates (1981, 1980a, 1980b) have employed a modified (7 instead of 5 anchored points) version of Goal Attainment Scaling (GAS) to address situationally specific client goals without relying on client or therapist ratings (Kiresuk & Sherman, 1968). In this method of assessment, prior to the group session, clients write down problem disclosures that could be made in group and the name of one rater per problem outside the therapy group who could judge the client's progress on the goal of resolving this problem. In the next session the client can write down different potential problem disclosures, the same problem disclosures, or a mix. If the instructions were to write two problem disclosures prior to each group session, in sixteen weeks' duration, a client could write from two to 32 potential problem disclosures. Every problem actually disclosed in the therapy group becomes a client-selected goal for therapy, and never-disclosed problems become control goals. Both types of goals are rated by external raters unaware of goal type.

In this research, it has been shown that clients improve more on disclosed than never-disclosed problems, improve more on problem disclosures rated as higher than lower in intensity, and improve more on problem disclosures discussed in higher than lower cohesion sessions. While the GAS methodology employed in these studies potentially eliminates many of the problems that plague research on heterogeneous therapy groups, the goals (problem disclosures) were still client selected, and clients might have selected disclosures (therefore goals) that were going to improve because of factors other than group therapy.

The present paper reports the results of four studies. Study 1 addresses the methodological issue mentioned above to determine if client selection of disclosures biases the Goal Attainment Scaling methodology. In Study 1, instead of being client selected, the disclosures (and therefore the goals) were randomly selected for group disclosure and discussion. While this addresses the issue of selection bias, it still leaves the issues of actual group work unresolved. Even with randomly selected disclosures, any differential goal improvement could be because of the single act of disclosure rather than because of the subsequent group work done on the disclosure.

Study 2 addresses the issue of whether the amount of time spent working on a client's problem, or the frequency of positive and negative statements from other group members in such a discussion, affects client improvement. While these results partially answer the question of the effect of group work on client improvement, the variable of the client's emotional response and its change because of what other group members say is also an important factor in therapeutic change.

Study 3 addresses this question by inspecting what pattern of client emotional induction and reduction in group therapy maximizes client outcome.

While the first 3 studies help verify the GAS methodology and show its utility as a group outcome assessment method, the question of whether specific goal attainment relates to overall improvement remains open. The common method of employing specific measures along with some more standard personality measure to determine if there has also been "real," "general," or "more profound" changes as well (Bergin & Lambert, 1978) was not employed in these studies because it creates a theoretical polyglot and encourages the worst form of eclecticism. If the overall importance of the specific client change is to be assessed, it must be measured by devices or methods that are theoretically consistent with the nature of the group process and the specific measures employed. The final study here reports the results of an attempt to devise a general assessment device based on the DSM III to assess overall change without theoretical bias. Such a general assessment device, if verified, would augment the more specific assessment techniques generally employed in behavioral group therapy.

STUDY 1

Method

Subjects on a waiting list for group therapy at a community clinic were contacted and asked if they would be willing to participate in a group with the following specific rules:

1. The group would meet for 1.5 hours weekly for 16 weeks.
2. Clients would come to each group session group with two potential problem disclosures (numbered 1 and 2) written down with the name and address of a person outside the group who could rate the client's progress in resolving that problem.
3. The client agreed not to talk to any indicated rater about anything that happened in the group.
4. If the client was willing to talk during a session, one of the leaders would specify which problem to disclose (randomly chosen, 1 or 2), with the clear understanding that the other problem was not to be disclosed in that or subsequent sessions.
5. In subsequent sessions after a disclosure, the client could talk about the problem disclosed in a previous session or ask to talk about something new, which again required that two problem disclosures be written down, and that the problem discussed be chosen randomly.

Subjects

The subjects (3 males, 5 females) ranged in age from 23 to 41 (mean = 27.7). The first eight people contacted from the list all agreed to participate in the group and abide by the rules of disclosure. All subjects were guaranteed participation in another therapy group without the above restrictions if they finished the experimental group. All subjects finished the treatment attending an average of 14.5 sessions each.

Therapists

The therapists were a male and female co-therapy team trained to conduct behavioral group therapy (Flowers & Schwartz, 1985).

Outcome Measures

Fifty different disclosures were made in the 16 group sessions. Two of these were on the not-to-disclose list, which eliminated both those disclosures and the previously paired disclosures from research consideration; therefore, 46 random disclosures and paired 46 never-disclosed problems with identified raters were employed in the outcome research. The external raters who had been identified were contacted within one week of the group's termination and were asked to rate the client's progress on the goal of resolving each disclosed and never-disclosed problem on a Likert type seven-point scale in the general form:

In terms of resolving the __________ problem, in the last 4 months (Client Name) is:

1. Much worse
2. Worse
3. Somewhat worse
4. Unchanged
5. Somewhat improved
6. Improved
7. Greatly improved

Ninety of the 92 goal assessments were returned.

Results

The 45 goals that had been randomly picked to be discussed in the therapy group were rated 5.34 compared to 4.48 for goals randomly selected never to be discussed (t (43) = 4.33, $p < .001$), indicating a significant client improvement even when the goal had been randomly selected to be discussed.

While Likert scales are commonly analyzed parametrically, the scale is not ratio; hence the same data were analyzed employing the Wilcoxon test to assure that the interval nature of the scale was not creating the significant difference (sum of positive pairs = 499, sum of negative pairs = 96, $p < .001$).

STUDY 2

Introduction

These results demonstrate that the differential improvement shown on the GAS between disclosed and never-disclosed problems (goals) occurs even when the disclosures are randomly elicited. This verifies that both previous and future differential results in more normally conducted groups, wherein the client can chose what to disclose, are not merely due to the client's choice of problem disclosures and goals. What this study does not resolve is whether it is merely disclosure, or the subsequent group work, that contributes to client improvement, which is the focus of Study 2.

Method

Subjects in three successive therapy groups at a community clinic volunteered and were studied for 10 one and one-half hour sessions. All subjects wrote two possible problem disclosures prior to each session, with the name of an outside rater who could assess the subject's progress on the goal of resolving the disclosed problem. A subject could disclose no problem, either problem, both problems, or a problem not written prior to the group in the session. If the disclosure was a problem not written prior to the group, it was written by the client after the session.

Subjects

Twenty-three subjects (10 male, 13 female) ranging in age from 19 to 44 years (mean = 27.2) completed the experimental group sessions.

Therapists

The therapists were three male and female co-therapy teams trained to conduct behavioral group therapy (Flowers & Schwartz, 1985).

Outcome Measures

The first two sessions in each group were used to train the judges (graduate students in a practicum class who were not yet qualified to see clients) who collected data for the next eight sessions. Three judges independently assessed (and signaled with an arrow that could point to "on goal" or "off goal" and another arrow that pointed to a client name) whether the group was discussing a client goal (i.e., talking about a disclosure the client had made). A fourth judge recorded the time the group spent discussing the problem when two of the three judges agreed that the group was discussing a specific client's goal. A fifth and sixth judge recorded the frequency of positive and negative statements made by all group members except the client while the timer was on (Flowers, Booarem, Brown, & Harris, 1974). All judges observed the group through a one-way mirror. At the end of the ten sessions, a goal list of discussed and never-discussed problems was made for each client along with the outside raters the clients had indicated could rate any improvement on the goal. These external raters were then contacted to rate the clients' progress on the goals.

Results

Of 2160 scheduled minutes, 2040 actually occurred. In the 2040 potential minutes, at least two judges agreed that 1666 were spent discussing a specific client's goals that were eventually rated by the external raters. Of the 74 goals that were discussed in the 24 sessions (3 groups times 8 sessions each), 72 had external raters specified and 68 ratings were returned by external raters (mean = 5.48). The improvement on the 68 client goals correlated significantly ($r = .32$, $p < .001$) with the time spent discussing each goal.

In a separate analysis, the improvement on the 68 discussed and rated goals correlated significantly ($r = .68$, $p < .001$) with the frequency of positive plus negative statements per minute as rated by the fifth and sixth judges. The frequency of positive and negative statements per minute per goal was calculated and varied from .20 to 2.91. The 34 goals with the lowest positive plus negative rating per minute (intensity) were rated at an improvement rate of 4.76 compared to 6.18 for the 34 goals with the highest intensity (t (66) = 5.39, $p < .001$). An ANOVA of goal improvement by group was not significant (F (2,65) = 18) demonstrating that the 3 groups were equivalent in terms of this measure of client improvement.

STUDY 3

Introduction

This study demonstrates that client improvement is not merely due to the client disclosing the problem (and the therapeutic goal) but is positively influenced by the amount of time spent in group work, and is more influenced by what might be called the "intensity" of the discussion. While the frequency of emotional statements made by other group members during a discussion correlates with the client change on what was discussed, this does not assess any differential response of the client during the group work. Instead of the "intensity" of the discussion, Study 3 assesses the effect of the client's emotionality during the discussion on outcome.

Method

In Part 1 of this study, clients in three separate therapy groups at a community clinic completed 16 one and one-half hour sessions. After the session, each member wrote down a brief version of what he or she had disclosed in the session and indicated a rater as in the previous studies. All the group members and therapists rated each disclosed problem on a seven-point Likert-type scale:

1. No emotion evidenced
2. Very little emotion evidenced
3. Little emotion evidenced
4. Some emotion evidenced
5. Moderate emotion evidenced
6. Considerable emotion evidenced
7. A great deal of emotion evidenced

Each problem was rated for the highest emotion level reached by the discloser during the problem discussion and the subsequent lowest level the discloser reached prior to the end of that group session. The reason that reduction can be rated after the problem discussion is completed is that groups often return to disclosing members late in the group to assess how they are feeling. Every disclosed problem was given an emotional induction-reduction score based on the mean difference over all ratings (other clients and therapists) between the highest and lowest level of emotion rated during the problem discussion. After the termination of therapy, the outside raters were contacted for ratings in the previous study.

In Part 2, clients in a therapy group completed 16 sessions of 1.5 hour duration. Prior to the group session the therapists were given a random number list that instructed them to attempt to either induce or abort emotional induction of each problem as it was disclosed. In all cases where emotionality was induced, whether by therapist design or not, maximum reduction was always attempted during the session. Thus, the therapists attempted to randomly generate a set of discussed problem disclosures which had either (1) a maximum difference between the highest and subsequent lowest level of emotionality (obtained by inducing maximum emotion and subsequently reducing it to minimum levels), or (2) a minimum of such difference (obtained by inducing minimum emotion). The same data as above were collected. The group members were unaware of the independent variable.

Subjects

In Part 1, 23 subjects (14 female and 9 male) of ages ranging from 21 to 56 years (mean = 32.4) completed the 16 group sessions.

In Part 2, 8 subjects (4 male and 4 female) of ages ranging from 23 to 35 (mean = 25.6) completed the 16 group sessions.

Therapists

The therapists were four male and female co-therapy teams trained to conduct behavioral group therapy (Flowers & Schwartz, 1985).

Outcome Measures

In Part 1 of this study, of the 93 problem disclosures that had potential external raters, 86 ratings of goal improvement were returned by mail. These goals were given an emotional difference rating based on the mean difference between high and low emotionality ratings by the group members and leaders during that goals discussion.

In Part 2, 50 separable problem disclosures were actually made to the group, of which the therapists were successful in keeping the problem disclosure in the correct predetermined category of emotional induction (mean rating of 4 or below for low induction, 5 or above for high induction) in 43 cases. Seven problem disclosures were made that could not be induced (4) or could not be held to low emotional induction (3).

Results

In Part 1, the 43 goals with the highest emotional induction-reduction difference were rated at 5.59 compared to 4.63 for the low emotional induction-reduction goals ($t\ (84) = 3.86$, $p < .001$).

In Part 2, of 43 disclosed goals, 31 had external raters and 27 ratings were returned. One goal was discarded randomly to achieve the even number of goals necessary for a split half procedure, and the 13 with the highest emotional induction were given external ratings of 5.67 compared to 4.85 for the 13 with the lowest emotional induction ($t\ (24) = 2.98$, $p < .01$).

STUDY 4

Introduction

While the previous three studies demonstrate the efficacy of the GAS methodology for assessing specific outcome in heterogeneous client groups, they do not demonstrate that improvement on specific therapeutic goals is related to overall client improvement. As previously stated, this is not an easily resolved assessment question. Most measures of overall improvement are both theory specific and inconsistent with the specific problem approach of behavioral group therapy. Study 4 is devoted to testing the reliability and concurrent validity of a general measure of client improvement based on the DSM III as well as testing if specific outcome results are paralleled by more generalized results. Specifically, clients in three therapy groups were assessed both on the GAS methodology and on a more general measure derived from the DSM III.

Method

Persons in three successive therapy groups at a community clinic were subjects for this study. Each subject understood that he or she would undergo four hours of individual counseling to prepare for group therapy, 24 one and one-half hour sessions of group therapy, and 4 hours of individual counseling at the end of the group to determine if more group therapy was appropriate. All subjects wrote two potential problem disclosures on a card prior to each group therapy meeting as in the previous studies. At the end of the 24 sessions a goal list of discussed and never-discussed problems was made for each client along with the raters the clients had indicated as potential judges who were contacted for their ratings after the termination of the therapy groups.

Subjects

Of the 27 subjects initially assigned to the three groups, 24 (9 male, 15 female) of ages ranging from 17 to 49 years (mean = 29.4) completed the group and individual sessions.

Outcome Measures

Thirteen therapists (none of whom conducted the group sessions) conducted the initial four individual therapy sessions and were in fact determining the client's appropriateness for group. These therapists filled out an 80-item DSM III questionnaire on each client designed by the first author on the basis of research by McDowell (1982) and Nicolette (1982).

Fifteen therapists (none of whom had conducted the group sessions) conducted the four postgroup individual sessions after group and were in fact determining the clients' continued need for group therapy. All therapists filled the same 80-item DSM III questionnaire used by the pregroup therapists and were led to believe the research was a diagnostic reliability study, which was in fact going on at the clinic concurrently with the present research.

At the end of group therapy, one of the group therapists was randomly selected to fill out the same DSM III diagnostic questionnaire on each client. The other therapist in each group filled out the DSM III questionnaire twice, with the instruction to generate both the most optimistic and most pessimistic reasonable assessment of the client. Both therapists knew these data were to be used to evaluate the group's effectiveness.

The numerical answer (1 to 5) to each of the 80 questions on each client was entered into a computer program designed by the first author. This program yields a list of all DSM III diagnoses that might describe this client's problems and indicates if there is substantial or merely provisional evidence for each possible diagnosis. Thus, each of the 24 subjects received a full, computer-run DSM III diagnosis before group therapy and received four such diagnoses after the group terminated.

Client goals discussed and never discussed were sent to the indicated external raters as in the previous studies.

Results

Concurrent Validity

Prior to group therapy the 24 subjects (24 computer runs) had a total of 35 DSM III diagnoses rated as substantial, or 1.46 each. After group therapy, the 24 subjects' computer-run tests yielded 20 DSM III diagnoses rated as substantial, or .83 each ($t\ (23) = 4.73$, $p < .001$). Thus, the individual independent therapists rated the subject as significantly less pathological after group therapy than before.

Since some of the diagnoses for which there was substantial evidence prior to group therapy became diagnoses for which there was provisional evidence after therapy, a second analysis was conducted in which each subject was given two pathology points for any substantial diagnosis and one point for any diagnosis for which there was some evidence. Prior to group therapy the 24 subjects had an average of 4.04 pathology points each, compared to 2.71 after group therapy ($t\ (23) = 7.52$, $p < .001$). Since these data are clearly not interval in nature, the same data were analyzed by a Wilcoxon test to determine if the results were created by a violation of the parametric assumptions. The results (sum of positive ranks = 268.5, sum of negative ranks = 7.5, $p > .001$) clearly indicated that the significant differences in pathology before and after the therapy group were not a result of a violation of parametric assumptions.

Of 127 disclosures made in group, 123 had external raters and of 106 never made, 101 had raters indicated. These were sent to the raters with a return rate of 115 disclosures made and 91 never made. Problems discussed in the group were rated with greater improvement (mean = 5.57) than the goals never discussed (mean = 4.65, $t\,(204) = 5.82$, $p < .001$). To be certain the results were not due to the noninterval aspect of the Likert scale, the same data were analyzed with a Mann-Whitney. These results were a $U1 = 2910.5$ and $U2 = 7554.5$, $z = 4.56$, $p < .001$, indicating that the results were not due to the nonparametric nature of the Likert type scale rating used.

Reliability

The 24 subjects were evaluated as having .46 substantial diagnoses each by the group therapists who filled out a single assessment, making the most accurate diagnosis they could. This was significantly different ($t\,(23) = 3.19$, $p < .001$) from the evaluation given by the subsequent individual therapists (.83). These results indicate that the group therapists who had worked with the clients perceived them as significantly less pathological than the subsequent individual therapists.

The same 24 subjects were rated at means of .71 substantial diagnoses when this rating was derived from the average of the most optimistic and pessimistic evaluation from the other three group therapists. These results are not significantly different from the subsequent evaluations of the individual therapists (0–83). Thus, when the group leader is asked to give a range of pathology rather than give a single point estimate, the middle of this range is closer to another independent therapist's judgment of the client's present functioning than is the group leader's best estimate.

DISCUSSION

The use of client disclosures in the therapy group as goals in a Goal Attainment Scaling (GAS) assessment procedure makes the GAS method extremely easy to use in group therapy research. The use of client-specified raters, unaware of what goals have and have not been therapeutically addressed, eliminates the potential biasing effect of a rater wishing the intervention to be shown effective or ineffective. The present study strongly suggests that client selection of the goal to be assessed does not affect the outcome and suggests that this method of assessment of client outcome measures primarily the effect of the therapy group on client change. While there can still be response bias, it biases both experimental and control goals, thus should not yield false positive results.

This methodology provides an alternative to random assignment and control groups in the design of clinical research when the more traditional experimental control is difficult or impossible. The use of control goals rather than control groups means that every subject, in a sense, is part of a simplified multiple baseline design that is not limited to clearly observable units of behavior. This is not to say that every problem of assessment has been or even can be resolved by this method. Not all goals can have raters, raters are not equally reliable, and the reliability is presently unknown.

Studies 2 and 3 use this methodology to inspect other aspects of group therapy. Study 2 demonstrates that both the time spent discussing the disclosure and intensity (number of positive and negative statements by other members) during the group work significantly affect the outcome. The fact that intensity is a more powerful agent than time spent is both seductive and dangerous.

Simply increasing intensity could lead to group casualties just as easily as it could increase positive outcome (Lieberman, Yalom & Miles, 1973; Flowers, Booarem, & Seacat, 1974). Positive change is not induced by merely increasing group session intensity, but by increasing intensity within a safe context, Specifically, intensity as measured here is made up of both positive and negative statements, not merely negative ("encounter") statements that are too prevalent in some group work.

Study 3 begins the process of investigating the variables involved in making the intensity factor work safely. Both positive and negative statements induce emotion and while emotional induction motivates change, the present study demonstrates it is the difference between emotional induction and emotional reduction that leads to positive outcome in group therapy. Clients who leave the group in a state of emotional induction without subsequent reduction may be prime candidates for change in a negative direction, i.e., casualty status. The work of Lieberman, Yalom and Miles (1973) suggests, that such unsafe induction may be because of an overabundance or overintensity of negative messages in the group session. This area should be addressed in future research to clearly determine what is safe and unsafe group practice.

The results of the final study replicate the results of previous work, i.e., behavioral group therapy works on the specific goals addressed in the therapy. However, this study also indicates that these results are also paralleled by the more general result of less overall pathology, strengthening the case for the significance, as well as the validity, of the results. This DSM III method of assessment is based on the assumption that pathology is reflected in diagnosis and that client improvement is indicated when a diagnosis that was a possibility is removed in the course of therapy. This assumption and therefore the assessment methodology will be weakened when the pathology is not reflected in diagnosis as in cases of family system pathology, or not necessarily reflected in individual disorders such as in low social skills. It would also be weakened in cases of confused rather than generally severe disorders; however most highly confusing disorders (e.g., Bipolar, Borderline) are also severe, nevertheless, this methodology would have to be independently verified as a general measure of improvement in such cases.

The evaluations of the group therapists under two different sets of instructions (optimistic and pessimistic) indicate that an even easier method than that employed in this study may be possible in future research. The group therapists (one per group) instructed to fill out the 80-item questionnaire to make the most accurate diagnosis, knowing that the rating was to be used to assess the group's effectiveness, evaluated the clients as less pathological than the subsequent therapists, who thought the evaluation was part of a diagnostic reliability study. This seems to be yet another example of therapist bias in the direction of self-interest in outcome evaluation.

On the other hand, when the other therapist in each group was asked to fill out two questionnaires on each client—one indicating the most optimistic and one indicating the most pessimistic pathological possibilities—the average of the number of DSM III diagnoses produced by these two ratings was almost identical to the subsequent evaluations of the presumably less biased individual therapists. Thus, the evaluation of global improvement may be able to be done by the therapist, provided he or she is asking the right questions—i.e., the range of pathology possible rather than the best assessment of the client's present status.

The use of the DSM III as the global measure of client improvement in group therapy (or any therapy for that matter) has a number of advantages. First, unlike other global measures, the DSM III method is not linked to a single theory of therapy. This method addresses pathology rather than personality and can be used with any other method of specific assessment. Additionally, the method employs a universal language that is understandable by therapists of any persuasion. Finally, the present method of assessment is sensitive enough to reflect changes brought about by group therapeutic intervention. At present, the DSM III outcome assessment method suffers from some of the same limitations that the DSM III itself suffers; it is limited in showing systems changes (i.e., marital or family) that are not also indicated by changes in individual pathology, and it may give falsely high pathology scores in diagnostically confusing cases.

REFERENCES

BERGIN, A.E., & LAMBERT, M.J. (1978). The evaluation of therapeutic outcomes. In S.L. Garfield & A.E. Bergin (Eds.), *Handbook of psychotherapy and behavior change: An empirical analysis*. New York: Wiley.

CIMINERO, A.R., CALHOUN, K.S., & ADAMS, H.E. (1977). *Handbook of behavioral assessment*. New York: Wiley.

FLOWERS, J.V., BOOAREM, C.D., BROWN, T.R., & HARRIS, D. (1974). An investigation of a technique for facilitating patient to patient therapeutic interactions in group therapy. *Journal of Community Psychology, 2,* 39-42.

FLOWERS, J.V., BOOAREM, C.D., & HARTMAN, K.A. (1981). Client improvement on higher and lower intensity problems as a function of group cohesiveness. *Psychotherapy: Theory, Research, and Practice, 18,* 246-251.

FLOWERS, J.V., BOOAREM, C.D., & SEACAT, G. (1974). The effect of positive and negative feedback on members' sensitivity to other members in group therapy. *Psychotherapy: Theory, Research, and Practice, 11,* 346-350.

FLOWERS, J.V., HARTMAN, K.A., MANN, R.J., KIDDER, S., & BOOAREM, C.D. (1980). The effects of group cohesion and client flexibility on therapy outcome. In D. Upper & S.M. Ross, (Eds.). *Behavioral group therapy, 1980*. Champaign, IL: Research Press.

FLOWERS, J.V., & SCHWARTZ, B. (1985). Behavioral group therapy with clients with homogeneous problems. In S.M. Ross & D. Upper (Eds.), *Handbook of behavioral group therapy*. New York: Plenum Press.

FLOWERS, J.V., TAPPER, B., KIDDER, S., WEIN, G., & BOOAREM, C.D. (1980). Generalization and maintenance of client outcome in group therapy. In D. Upper & S.M. Ross (Eds.), *Behavioral group therapy, 1980*. Champaign, IL: Research Press.

KIRESUK, T.J., & SHERMAN, R.E. (1968). Goal attainment scaling: A general method for evaluating comprehensive community mental health programs. *Community Mental Health Journal, 17,* 443-453.

LIEBERMAN, M.A., YALOM, I.D., & MILES, M.B. (1973). *Encounter group: First facts*. New York: Basic Books.

MCDOWELL, D.J. (1982). *Psychiatric diagnosis: Rater reliability and prediction using "psychological rating scale for diagnostic classification."* Unpublished Doctoral Dissertation. Denton, TX: North Texas State University.

MISCHEL, W. (1977). On the future of personality research. *American Psychologist, 32,* 246-254.

NICOLETTE, M. (1982). *Interrater reliability of the psychological scale for diagnostic classification*. Unpublished Masters Thesis. Denton, TX: North Texas State University.

STRUPP, H.H. (1978). Psychotherapy research and practice: An overview. In S.L. Garfield & A.E. Bergin (Eds.), *Handbook of psychotherapy and behavior change: An empirical analysis*. New York: Wiley.

STRUPP, H.H., & HADLEY, S.W. (1977). A tripartite model of mental health and therapeutic outcomes. *American Psychologist, 32,* 187-196.

UPPER, D., & ROSS, S.M. (1979). *Behavioral group therapy, 1979*. Champaign, IL: Research Press.

UPPER, D., & ROSS, S.M. (1980). *Behavioral group therapy, 1980*. Campaign, IL: Research Press.

UPPER, D., & ROSS, S.M. (1981). *Behavioral group therapy, 1981*. Champaign, IL: Research Press.

Michael W. Stephens
Richard M. Grinnell, Jr.
Judy L. Krysik

Study C

Victims of Child Sexual Abuse: A Research Note

CHILD SEXUAL ABUSE is not a recent phenomenon and has received considerable attention over the years (e.g., Howes, 1986; Sgroi, 1982). Indeed, child sexual abuse has been occurring for quite some time (e.g., Finkelhor & Hotaling, 1984; Howes, 1986; Russell, 1983). The most recent data of the American Humane Association (Russell & Trainor, 1984) report an increase in the number of reported cases across the United States. In a six-year period from 1976 to 1982 there was an increase in the number of reported cases from 1,975 to 22,918. At the present time similar national data are not available for Canada.

One of the reasons for an increase in reporting may be a loosening of the operational definition of child sexual abuse. Historically, the meaning attached to child sexual abuse was only incest that involved sexual intercourse. In fact, the terms "child sexual abuse" and "incest" were often used interchangeably (Faria & Belohlavek, 1984).

Over the years, various authors have defined child sexual abuse along a range from a narrow extreme to a more open, less restrictive definition (e.g., Butler, 1978; Giaretto, 1982; Justice & Justice, 1979; Sgroi, 1982; Wyatt & Peters, 1986).

PURPOSE OF STUDY

The rising incidence of child sexual abuse poses many social work practice and research questions. One of the greatest concerns of child care workers today is that of the victim. The focus of this study was on the variables related to the victim in an attempt to present Canadian-based data about the victims of child sexual abuse.

METHODOLOGY

The Setting

In Canada, child welfare is a provincially legislated responsibility. In Alberta, the Province of Alberta Child Welfare Act was passed by the Alberta Legislature on May 31, 1984, and proclaimed on July 1, 1985. This act forms the basis for child welfare intervention in Alberta. The Ministry that administers the child welfare legislation for the province is Alberta Social Services. Any allegation of child sexual abuse must be referred to Alberta Social Services for investigation purposes.

The delivery of child welfare services in Alberta occurs through a decentralized system located in six geographic regions. This study was carried out in one of Alberta's largest regions, which includes a large metropolitan city and the surrounding rural territory. Five geographic offices offer an investigation/intake program within the region.

Operational Definition

To be consistent with the study's setting, we adopted the operational definition of child sexual abuse as legislated by the Province of Alberta Child Welfare Act:

> A child is sexually abused if the child is inappropriately exposed or subjected to sexual contact, activity, or behavior.
>
> Section 1 (3) (c) p. 6.

Criteria for Sample Inclusion

Three criteria had to be satisfied in order for a child sexual abuse case to be included in the study. First, cases alleging child sexual abuse had to be referred to Alberta Social Services during the 1985 calendar year. The abuse itself did not have to occur in 1985, but must have been referred for investigation between January 1, 1985 and December 31, 1985.

The location to which the child sexual abuse was reported was the focus of the second criterion. To be included in this study the referral had to be made to the specified region mentioned above. The second criterion was met if the referral was actually investigated by a child welfare worker within the region under study.

The third criterion to be considered was assessment. To be included in the study, the investigating social worker was required to have assessed that child sexual abuse had indeed occurred.

The sample was therefore defined as all cases of alleged child sexual abuse referred to Alberta Social Services in 1985; investigated by a child welfare worker within the identified region; and in which the alleged sexual abuse was assessed as actually having occurred.

Sample

Having defined the sample via the above three criteria, the next step was to gather an inventory of all child welfare files. The study initially identified a preliminary group of 539 alleged victims who met the first two criteria. These 539 files were then reviewed to screen out those that did not meet the third criterion. This process rendered 191 cases in which the investigating social workers concluded that child sexual abuse had occurred. It is these 191 victims that form the final sample for this study.

Validity and Reliability

A data-gathering instrument was designed based upon a review of professional literature on child sexual abuse. Three employees of Alberta Social Services tested the instrument to affirm its content validity. Upon completion of this process additions, modifications, and deletions were made in format and operational definitions of the instrument to increase validity.

A test for interrater reliability rendered an error rate of less than one percent. Twenty percent of all files (109) included in this study were randomly checked for reliability of data collection. Seven errors were present in a total of 9,146 responses. Where there was error (disagreement between the principal data gatherer and the person checking reliability) the files were rechecked and corrections were made.

FINDINGS AND DISCUSSION

Four separate variables are highlighted in this article: victim, victim's family, perpetrator, and occurrence. Each variable will be delineated into related subvariables for presentation purposes.

Victim

Perhaps the largest body of literature concerning child sexual abuse is that which exists about the victim (e.g., Helfer, 1982). This study reports on five victim-related subvariables: gender, age, relationship to the perpetrator, number of perpetrators, and previous history as a victim. These five subvariables were chosen because of their prevalence in the literature.

The first of five subvariables concerning the victim was the child's gender. Mrazek, Lynch, and Bentovim (1983) have stated that there are significantly larger numbers of reported female child sexual abuse victims than male victims. Other authors indicate similar findings (Erickson, Walbek, & Seely, 1988; Pierce & Pierce, 1985b). Generally, the literature indicates that between 80 to 90 percent of all reported victims are female (e.g., Pierce & Pierce, 1985b). Our analysis of Canadian data is in agreement with the findings presented below. As can been seen from Table C-1, 84 percent of all reported victims of child sexual abuse were female.

Age of the victim at the onset of abuse was the second subvariable examined. Meddin (1985) reported that the younger child is viewed as being at greater risk of sexual abuse than the older child. An interesting relationship between gender and age of the child sexual abuse victim is indicated by many studies. For example, the age of a male victim at the time of reporting was significantly lower than for female victims (Russell, 1983). This study found that the mean age at onset of abuse for males and females was 8.3 years. Furthermore, this study's findings were congruent with the literature in which the mean age for males at the onset of abuse was 8 years compared to 8.4 years for females.

The third subvariable studied was the relationship of the victim to the perpetrator. Relationship to the perpetrator can be further broken down into two categories: intrafamilial or extrafamilial. For the purposes of this study, intrafamilial child sexual abuse occurred when there was a blood or legal familial relationship between the victim and the perpetrator. Extrafamilial child sexual abuse occurred when there was no blood or legal familial relationship between the victim and the perpetrator.

Summit (1980) reported that the vast majority of perpetrators came from the victim's family. This study also identified intrafamilial child sexual abuse as predominant. In 54 percent of all reported cases the perpetrator was the individual in the father role. In addition, once all intrafamilial relationships were accounted for, 79 percent of child sexual abuse victims were related either by blood or legal ties to the perpetrator. The remaining 21 percent of perpetrators

TABLE C-1 VICTIMS OF CHILD SEXUAL ABUSE

Variables		Number	Percent
Gender:	Males	30	16%
	Females	161	84%
Mean Age of Child at Onset of Abuse (in years):	Males	8.0	
	Females	8.4	
	Combined	8.3	
Relationship to the Perpetrator:			
Father Role (Biological)		49	27%
Father Role (Nonbiological)		49	27%
Mother Role (Biological)		3	2%
Female Sibling		2	1%
Male Sibling		17	9%
Uncle		12	6%
Male Cousin		7	4%
Grandfather		7	4%
Significant Other (Nonrelated)		38	21%
Missing Data		7	
Previous History as a Victim:			
Yes		38	26%
No		109	74%
Missing Data		44	
Number of Different Perpetrators:			
Single Perpetrator		179	94%
Multiple Perpetrators		11	6%
Missing Data		1	

were not related to the victims.

The child's previous history as a victim (i.e., physical abuse, sexual and emotional abuse, neglect) was the fourth subvariable examined. Pierce and Pierce (1985a) reported that over one-third of all substantiated cases of child sexual abuse had been previously reported as allegations of abuse other than sexual. Canadian data yield similar results (e.g., Corsini-Munt, 1982). In this study, a previous history of child abuse had been recorded for 26 percent of the 191 child sexual abuse victims.

The final subvariable examined was the number of different perpetrators involved with the victim. Evidence indicates that victims with multiple perpetrators have greater difficulty in treatment after the occurrences than do those with a single perpetrator (e.g., Greenburg, 1983). This study reports that 94 percent of

TABLE C-2 VICTIMS OF SEXUAL ABUSE AND THEIR FAMILIES

Variables	Number	Percent
Parental Structure:		
Two Parent	115	61%
Single Parent	71	38%
Extended Family	2	1%
Missing Data	3	
Other Known Family Victims:		
None	107	60%
One	44	25%
Two	26	14%
Three	2	1%
Missing Data	12	
Known Prior Sexual Abuse of Parents:		
Mother	29	58%
None	17	34%
Father	3	6%
Both	1	2%
Missing Data	141	

the victims had a single perpetrator, while six percent experienced multiple perpetrators. Data from the U.S. are similar in that only one perpetrator was involved in 90 percent of 304 child sexual abuse cases (Pierce & Pierce, 1985a).

Victim's Family

Many variables have been associated with the family of the child sexual abuse victim. This section examines three: parental structure, other known family victims, and known prior sexual abuse of parents (see Table C-2).

Parental structure was the first of three subvariables concerning the victim's family. Family constellation is important to every child, especially in terms of risk to the child's safety and development. There is a large body of literature concerning family structure in relation to child sexual abuse (Dietz & Craft, 1980). This study defined parental structure as the adult(s) responsible for the child victim. Possibilities of family structure include: one natural parent, both natural parents, one natural parent and another parent, or an extended family living arrangement.

Upon reviewing the literature, Mannarino and Cohen (1986) found that the majority of child sexual abuse victims were living with both parents at the time

TABLE C-3 PERPETRATOR CHARACTERISTICS

Variables		Number	Percent
Gender:	Male	186	98%
	Female	4	2%
	Missing Data	1	
Mean Age of Perpetrator at Onset (in years):	Male	27.5	
	Female	22.5	
	Combined	27.0	
Previous History of Abuse as a Victim:			
Yes		16	67%
No		8	33%
Missing Data		167	
Previous History of Abuse as a Perpetrator:			
Yes		91	100%
No		0	0%
Missing Data		100	
Relationship to the Victim:			
Father Role (Biological)		49	27%
Father Role (Nonbiological)		49	27%
Significant Other (Nonrelated)		38	21%
Male Sibling		17	9%
Uncle		12	5%
Male Cousin		7	4%
Grandfather		7	4%
Mother Role (Biological)		3	2%
Female Sibling		2	1%
Missing Data		7	

of the abuse. This study's findings were consistent with those of Mannarino and Cohen. Sixty-one percent of the victims of child sexual abuse were living in two-parent families at the time of abuse. In comparison, Pierce and Pierce (1985a) found that 25 percent of victims were living in homes headed by a single parent. Once again, this study was similar in its findings in that 38 percent of the victims were living in single-parent homes at the onset of abuse.

The Perpetrator

There are many issues to be considered when examining the perpetrator in child sexual abuse. This section considers five subvariables: the perpetrator's

TABLE C-4 VICTIMS AND SITUATIONAL VARIABLES

Variables		Number	Percent
Primary Sexual Act:			
Fondling of Genitalia		79	46%
Vaginal Penetration		40	24%
Attempted Vaginal Penetration		12	7%
Exposure		9	5%
Anal Penetration		8	5%
Fellatio		5	3%
Cunnilingus		3	2%
Kissing		2	1%
Not Classified		8	5%
Missing Data		21	
Mean Duration of Abuse (in months):	Male	15.0	
	Female	21.7	
	Combined	21.1	
Frequency:			
Multiple Occurrences		126	79%
Single Occurrence		34	21%
Missing Data		31	

gender, mean age of the perpetrator at the onset of abusive behavior, previous history of abuse as a victim, previous history of abuse as a perpetrator, and relationship to the victim (see Table C-3).

The first subvariable concerning the perpetrator was gender. There is an abundance of literature indicating that males predominate in the commission of child sexual abuse (Finkelhor & Hotaling, 1984). This study's findings are clearly consistent with the literature in that 98 percent of the perpetrators were male.

The literature suggests (e.g., Pierce & Pierce, 1985a), that the mean age of the perpetrator was 34 years. This study's findings indicate that the mean age of the perpetrator (male and female combined) at the onset of abuse to be 27.0 years—seven years younger than the U.S. data.

One of the prime issues regarding sexual offenders is their relationship to the victim. Many studies in the literature point out that the vast majority of perpetrators are from within the child's family (Summit, 1980). This study found that 79 percent of all perpetrators were in fact from within the child's family. More specifically, these perpetrators were usually men in the father role. Only 21 percent of the perpetrators were individuals outside of the family, or in other words, of no relation to the victim.

The Occurrence

The fourth variable that plays an important role in the study of child sexual abuse is the occurrence itself. Three subvariables related to the occurrence were considered: the primary sexual act, duration of the abuse, and the frequency of occurrence (see Table C-4).

The first subvariable regarding the occurrence is the primary sexual act. Attitudes toward child sexual abuse are documented to be influenced by the abusive activities that occur (Wilk & McCarthy, 1986). For example, as people in authority, social workers tend to be more tolerant of one incident of fondling than they are of multiple events of sexual intercourse (Finkelhor, 1983). Also related to the type of activity is the question of upon whom the sexual act was performed. The victim may be coerced into performing a sexual act on the perpetrator just as frequently as the perpetrator victimizes the child.

Berliner and Conte (1981) reported that 64 percent of the time the primary abusive act was fondling of genitalia. This study also reports that fondling was the sexual act that occurred most frequently. Furthermore, Baumann, Kasper and Alford (1984) found that penetration occurred in less than one-third of child sexual abuse cases. This analysis found that vaginal penetration took place in 23 percent of the child sexual abuse cases—approximately 10 percentage points less than the U.S. data.

The second subvariable to be considered in regard to occurrence is the duration of abuse. Studies indicate that large numbers of child sexual abuse situations continue for years prior to the victim's disclosure to a person in authority. Again this study was congruent with the literature. The mean duration of abuse for males and females combined was 21.1 months.

Frequency of occurrence in child sexual abuse has been given due attention in the literature (Finkelhor, 1983). The difference between a single occurrence and multiple occurrences is an important consideration in victim treatment and perpetrator disposition. Berliner and Conte (1981) have reported that the majority of cases (66%) include multiple occurrences. In contrast, they found that only 17 percent of the cases consisted of a single incident of abuse. This study was consistent with the above data. Multiple occurrences were present in 79 percent of the cases, as opposed to 21 percent reporting single occurrences.

IMPLICATIONS

Monitoring the profiles of the victim, the family, and the perpetrator have great implications for human service professionals concerned with child sexual abuse. Community education can be focused to the population with the greatest need. Armed with characteristic data, child care workers may be able to identify the victim, thereby preventing further abuse.

In constructing the four tables presented in this study, the authors found a great deal of missing data. Missing information for any one variable ranged as high as 87 percent. This has implications for the development of a standardized data collection format to be used in child sexual abuse investigations.

The similarity of Canadian data to that from the United States has implications for further service development. The United States has a proliferation of information concerning child sexual abuse. Treatment programs, policymakers, and child care workers could benefit greatly from the experience and expertise developed in the southern half of this continent. However, further study is necessary to validate and track the apparent current similarities.

SUMMARY

In summary, this research note has presented Canadian-based data on the victims of child sexual abuse. The information was compiled from the files of one Alberta Social Service region. Specific variables described were: characteristics of the victim, the victim's family structure, a profile of the perpetrator, as well as details pertaining to the sexually abusive occurrence.

At the risk of overgeneralizing, this study found that a majority of the victims of child sexual abuse were females whose average age was 8.4 years, with single perpetrators who were their fathers. In addition, a majority of the victims did not have previous histories of sexual abuse. They came from two-parent families and there were no other known family victims. The perpetrators were males whose average age was 27.5 years old. The primary sexual act included multiple occurrences of the fondling of genitalia.

REFERENCES

ALBERTA SOCIAL SERVICES. (1984). *Province of Alberta Child Welfare Act.* Edmonton, AB: Author.

BAUMANN, R.C., KASPER, J.C., & ALFORD, J.M. (1984). The child sex abusers. *Corrective and Social Psychiatry, 29-30,* 76-81.

BERLINER, L., & CONTE, J.R. (1981). Sexual abuse of children: Implications for practice. *Social Casework, 62,* 601-606.

BUTLER, S. (1978). *Conspiracy of silence.* San Francisco, CA: New Glide Publications.

CORSINI-MUNT, L.A. (1982). A Canadian study: Sexual abuse of children and adolescents. In B. Schlesinger (Ed.), *Sexual abuse of children: A resource guide and annotated bibliography.* Toronto, ON: University of Toronto Press.

DIETZ, C.A., & CRAFT, J.L. (1980). Family dynamics of incest: A new perspective. *Social Casework, 61,* 602-609.

ERICKSON, W.D., WALBEK, N.H., & SEELY, R.K. (1988). Behavior patterns of child molesters. *Archives of Sexual Behavior, 7,* 77-86.

FARIA, G., & BELOHLAVEK, N. (1984). Treating female adult survivors of childhood incest. *Social Casework, 65,* 465-477.

FINKELHOR, D. (1983). Removing the child—prosecuting the offender in cases of sexual abuse: Evidence from the National Reporting System for Child Abuse and Neglect. *Child Abuse and Neglect, 7,* 195-205.

FINKELHOR, D., & HOTALING, G.T. (1984). Sexual abuse in the national incidence study of child abuse and neglect: An appraisal. *Child Abuse and Neglect, 8,* 23-33.

GIARETTO, H. (1976). Humanistic treatment of father daughter incest. In R.E. Helfer & C.H. Kempe (Eds.), *Child abuse and neglect: The family and the community* (pp. 120-144). Cambridge, MA: Ballinger.

GIARETTO, H. (1982). *Integrated treatment of child sexual abuse: A treatment manual.* Berkeley, CA: Science and Behavior Books.

GREENBURG, N. (1983). Remarks to the national medical center's conference on sexual abuse. In D. Finkelhor, Removing the child—prosecuting the offender in cases of sexual abuse: Evidence from the national reporting system for child abuse and neglect. *Child Abuse and Neglect, 7,* 195-205.

HELFER, R.E. (1982). A review of the literature on the prevention of child abuse and neglect. *Child Abuse and Neglect, 6,* 251-266.

HOWES, C. (May 25, 1986). Incest: Dark secrets confronted. *Calgary Herald,* 1.

JUSTICE, B., & JUSTICE, R. (1979). *The broken taboo: Sex in the family.* New York: Human Sciences Press.

MANNARINO, A.P., & COHEN, J.A. (1986). A clinical-demographic study of sexually abused children. *Child Abuse and Neglect, 10,* 17-23.

MEDDIN, B.J. (1985). The assessment risk in child abuse and neglect case investigations. *Child Abuse and Neglect, 9,* 57-62.

MRAZEK, P.J., LYNCH, M.A., & BENTOVIM, A. (1983). Sexual abuse of children in the United Kingdom. *Child Abuse and Neglect, 7,* 147-153.

PIERCE, R.L., & PIERCE, L.H. (1985a). Analysis of sexual abuse hotline reports. *Child Abuse and Neglect, 9,* 37-45.

PIERCE, R.L., & PIERCE, L.H. (1985b). The sexually abused child: A comparison of male and female victims. *Child Abuse and Neglect, 9,* 191-199.

RUSSELL, A.B., & TRAINOR, C.M. (1984). *Trends in child abuse and neglect: A national perspective.* Denver, CO: American Humane Association.

RUSSELL, D.E. (1983). The incidence and prevalence of intrafamilial and extrafamilial sexual abuse of female children. *Child Abuse and Neglect, 7,* 133-146.

SGROI, S.M. (Ed.). (1982). *Handbook of clinical intervention in child sexual abuse.* Toronto, ON: Lexington Books.

SUMMIT, R. (1980). *Typical characteristics of father-daughter incest: A guide for investigation.* Unpublished paper. Los Angeles, CA: Harbor UCLA Medical Center.

WILK, R.J., & MCCARTHY C.R. (1986). Intervention in child sexual abuse: A survey of attitudes. *Social Casework, 67,* 20-26.

WYATT, G.E., & PETERS, S.D. (1986). Issues in the definition of child sexual abuse in prevalence research. *Child Abuse and Neglect, 10,* 231-240.

James R. Moran

Study D

Social Work Education and Students' Humanistic Attitudes

SOCIAL WORK IS BASED on humanitarian ideals. The social work code of ethics calls for belief in the dignity of human beings, respect for individual differences, and a commitment to improving the general welfare (Lemmon, 1983). Professional social work education must be concerned with both the knowledge and the value base of social work (Koerin, 1977). Consequently, social work educators seek to shape students' attitudes so as to develop a commitment to strive for individual and institutional arrangements that will have a humanistic impact on clients (Howard & Flaitz, 1982). Concern with values and attitudes may be even more important in the future, as social workers are forced to deal with cutbacks in social programs and a public that is less than enthusiastic about raising taxes to support the needy. It thus is important that social work educators evaluate their impact on values and attitudes. The study reported in this paper examined the relationship between undergraduate social work education and the humanistic attitudes of social work students.

Previous research into the relationship between social work education and values/attitudes has produced contradictory results. A comparison of beginning and graduating MSW students' attitudes toward equal rights and commitment to service found no significant differences in attitude between those who had finished their studies and those who had not (Varley, 1963). Cyrns (1977) found that social work graduate students actually had more negative attitudes toward human nature and the causes of poverty than did social work undergraduate students. Two longitudinal studies reported positive, but statistically non-significant, changes in attitudes toward equal rights when comparing MSW students at the beginning and end of their education (Varley, 1963; Judah, 1979). However, Sharwell (1974) found a significant positive change in graduate social work students' attitudes on such issues as the extensiveness of public assistance programs and the effect of programs on recipients' motivation to work. Finally, a study of undergraduate social work education showed a significant positive relationship between the number of social work courses completed and attitudes toward persons on public assistance (Merdinger, 1982).

The study reported here differs from most of the previous research: It focuses entirely on undergraduate social work students. It also attempts to control for several factors likely to be related to the students' attitudes. The study is based on the premise that students who have completed more social work courses will have more humanistic attitudes than will students who have completed fewer courses.

METHODOLOGY

A cross-sectional sample was used for this research. The setting was an accredited baccalaureate program located within a southeastern state university of approximately 14,000 students. The sampling frame consisted of all 275 students enrolled in social work courses during Spring semester 1985. A random sample of 150 was drawn from this universe. In order to ensure adequate variability in the number of social work courses completed, the sample was stratified on the basis of enrollment in lower or upper division courses; one half of the sample was selected from each level.

Subjects were requested to complete a questionnaire that collected demographic data and specific details about the social work courses they had completed. The instrument also measured the students' humanistic attitudes. The questionnaire was distributed by faculty during class periods with the request that it be completed outside of class and be returned at the next class meeting. In addition to the questionnaire, the respondents were provided with an informed consent statement that explained the general purpose of the study and guaranteed confidentiality.

Of the 150 students in the sample, 112 returned completed questionnaires. Of those who did not take part, seven stated that they did not want to participate; the other 31 simply did not return the questionnaire or the consent form. To assess the degree that those who responded were representative of the total sample, the gender and race of the respondents and all majors in the Social Work department were compared. Respondents were 71.4 percent female and 26.8 percent nonwhite, while all majors were 65.5 percent female and 22.9 percent nonwhite. While this certainly does not eliminate the possibility of selection bias, it does indicate some degree of representativeness on the part of the sample.

Students' humanistic attitudes were assessed with the Social Humanistic Ideology Scale. This scale measures attitudes about human nature, social justice, human rights, and individual freedom. The authors of the scale report the alpha reliability coefficients for these subscales at .68, .76, .48, and .64, respectively. They also indicate the study's content validity (Howard & Flaitz, 1982).

Only the two subscales with the highest reliability coefficients were used for this study. The "human nature" section of the instrument examines perceptions of the needs and motivations of clients of social service programs. It also examines respondents' perceptions of the role that individual pathology plays in economic success or failure. The "social justice" subscale assesses attitudes about the fairness in the distribution of life-sustaining resources. Specific items deal with the use of social action to achieve a more just society, economic reform, and efforts to redress past injustices against members of minority groups. Both subscales consisted of ten statements to which students were asked to respond by checking one of five options. The choices varied from strongly agree to strongly disagree. Each item received a score from 1 to 5; higher scores indicated stronger identification with humanistic attitudes. Thus, the possible range of scores for each subscale was from a low of 10 to a high of 50.

Students were asked to list the number of social work courses they had completed to date. Since the data were collected at the end of the semester, courses in which students then were enrolled were considered completed courses. Additional data were collected on respondents' age, gender, and race.

Regression analysis examined the relationship between humanistic attitudes and social work education. Two separate dependent variables were utilized in the analysis. They were the scores from the human nature and social justice subscales.

The primary independent variable was the number of social work courses completed by the respondents. Age, gender, and race also were treated as independent variables in the regression models. Age was measured in years. Gender was represented by a dummy variable with a value of 1 for male and 0 for female. Race was represented by a dummy variable with a value of 1 for nonwhite and 0 for white. This approach allowed the influence of age, gender, and race to be controlled while examining the primary relationship of interest.

RESULTS

The scores on the human nature subscale varied from a low of 18 to a high of 45 with a mean score of 32. The social justice scores varied from 22 to 45 with

TABLE D-1 CORRELATION COEFFICIENTS

Variables	Age	Male	Non-white	Social Justice	Human Nature
Number of Social Work Courses	.1530	-.0415	.0539	.0900	.3395*
Age		.0548	-.0706	-.1692	-.1522
Male			-.0638	-.1827	-.1950
Nonwhite				.2870	.0292
Social Justice					.3954*

* = Significant at $p < .05$

a mean score of 32.5. The number of social work courses completed by the respondents varied from 1 to 9 with a mean of 4.08. The age of the students varied from 18 to 59 with a mean of 22.2 years. There were 32 male respondents and 80 female respondents. The racial composition of the group was 82 whites and 30 nonwhites.

Table D-1 presents the zero-order correlation coefficients for the variables used in the regression models. These results show the relationship between social work education and students' humanistic attitudes. There was a statistically significant and positive relationship between the number of social work courses completed and attitudes concerning human nature. However, the correlation between the number of courses and attitudes concerning social justice was not statistically significant. Table D-1 also shows that there is no significant association between the four independent variables. This is important because regression analysis attempts to examine the relationship between the dependent variable and each of the independent variables, while controlling for the effects of the other variables in the model. For example, the relationship between humanistic attitudes and social work education can be looked at while holding the effects of age, gender and race constant. The lack of strong correlations between the independent variables indicates that regression analysis is an appropriate procedure by which to attempt to evaluate their independent effects.

Table D-2 and Table D-3 display the results for the two regression models. The explanatory power of the equations was poor, with only 17.7 percent of the variance in the human nature score explained and 15.7 percent of the variance explained for the social justice score. The adjusted R^2s for the human nature and social justice models were .142 and .123, respectively. This means that when adjusted for sample size and the number of independent variables, the models explain even less of the variance. However, an examination of the residuals plotted against the predicted values and each independent variable revealed no pattern of nonrandomness. In addition, histograms of the residuals were essentially normal. Thus, although the models explain little of the variance, there appears to be no violation of the basic assumptions of regression analysis.

TABLE D-2 REGRESSION RESULTS FOR HUMAN NATURE SUBSCALE ($N = 99$)

Variables	Coefficient	Standard Error	BETA	*t*-test	*p*
Number of Social Work Courses	.8098	.2159	.3569	3.75	.0003
Age	-.2325	.1163	-.1978	-1.99	.0485
Male	-2.1713	1.2469	-.1643	-1.74	.0849
Nonwhite	.0382	1.2000	.0030	.03	.9747
Constant	34.3161				
		$R^2 = .177$	$f = 5.039$		
		Adjusted $R^2 = .142$	$p = .0010$		

Statistical significance was obtained for two variables in the human nature equation, but for only one in the social justice model. The number of completed social work courses had a statistically significant ($p = .0003$) and positive relationship with the score on the subscale for human nature, but was not statistically significant in the social justice equation. Age had a significant ($p = .0485$) negative relationship with the human nature score and negative but nonsignificant relationship to the social justice score. As indicated by the male dummy variable results, gender had a nonsignificant relationship to both human nature and social justice. Race, as represented by the dummy variable for nonwhite, had a statistically significant ($p = .0013$) and positive relationship to the social justice score—it was not statistically significant in the human nature model.

TABLE D-3 REGRESSION RESULTS FOR SOCIAL JUSTICE SUBSCALE ($N = 103$)

Variables	Coefficient	Standard Error	BETA	*t*-test	*p*
Number of Social Work Courses	.2361	.1949	.1145	1.21	.2287
Age	-.1690	.1073	-.1486	-1.58	.1184
Male	-1.5087	1.1024	-.1274	-1.37	.1743
Nonwhite	3.5355	1.0665	.3091	3.32	.0013
Constant	34.8337				
		$R^2 = .157$	$f = 4.562$		
		Adjusted $R^2 = .123$	$p = .0020$		

The standardized coefficients (betas) show the relative importance of the independent variables in the models. The social work courses variable had the largest standardized coefficient in the human nature equation while the variable for nonwhite had the largest in the social justice model.

DISCUSSION

Although the coefficient for age was statistically significant only in the human nature equation, its negative direction in both of the models is important. It was noted earlier that several studies found a negative relationship between social work education and student attitudes. However, none of these studies attempted to control for the influence of age. If the negative relationship between age and attitudes also was present in past research, it would provide a partial explanation for some of the contradictions in the findings. This may be especially true in studies comparing undergraduate and graduate students. While not conclusive, it suggests that we may need to pay particular attention to older students when addressing issues related to social work values and attitudes.

Although the author had no *a priori* expectation about the role of race in the models, the results for the nonwhite variable require closer examination. This variable had the smallest beta coefficient and did not achieve statistical significance in the human nature equation. However, in the social justice model it had the largest beta coefficient and was the only statistically significant variable. In other words, nonwhites scored higher than whites on the social justice subscale, but essentially were no different on the human nature subscale. A partial explanation for this finding may exist in the specified items on the social justice subscale. Out of the ten items, two related directly to issues of redressing injustices to minority groups, while the other eight dealt primarily with issues related to reducing poverty. Because of the high rates of poverty and economic deprivation faced by nonwhites, it seems likely that nonwhite respondents would be more inclined to feel strongly about these particular items. In other words, the findings on race may be due to the construction of the particular subscale rather than offer any evidence that nonwhites are more concerned with social justice than whites are.

The most surprising finding was that the number of social work courses had a positive relationship with attitudes about human nature, but essentially no relationship to the students' attitudes toward social justice. Entering the variables singly into the models showed that the number of courses explained 10.7 percent of the variance in the score for human nature but only 1.4 percent of the variance in the score for social justice. Similarly, the standardized regression coefficient for this variable was almost twice as large as any of the others in the human nature equation, but was the smallest coefficient in the social justice model.

There are several possible explanations for this finding. First, the social work curriculum may stress issues of human nature more than issues of social justice. Second, students may start the program with more positive attitudes toward issues of social justice and hence change may be less likely. Third, it is possible that students' attitudes toward human nature are more easily influenced than their attitudes towards social justice are. There also may be an interaction between these three possibilities and other explanations not mentioned. The data permit tentative examination of the first two alternatives.

While a content analysis of each course would be necessary to thoroughly explore the issue of the curriculum's focus, an overall impression can be gained by examining the general content and titles of the nine social work courses. It appears that the programs' curriculum is balanced between courses that tend to emphasize individual issues and those that emphasize social issues. There does not seem to be a lack of courses that normally deal with issues of social justice. For example, three of the nine courses cover history and social policy issues, while a fourth course deals with the organization of social welfare systems. Clearly no firm conclusion can be drawn without a detailed analysis of each course's content. However, the general focus of the courses casts doubt on the argument that the curriculum favors material dealing with human nature over material reflecting issues of social justice.

The second alternative can be examined through a comparison of mean scores on the two subscales. Although the regression results show that the number of completed social work courses has a positive relationship to the human nature score and essentially no relationship to the social justice score, the overall means are roughly equal at 32.0 and 32.5, respectively. This suggests that the social justice score must be higher than the human nature score for students beginning the program. In this study, students who had completed only one social work course had mean scores of 29.9 for the human nature scale and 32.8 for the social justice scale. This indicates that the students had to make greater changes in their attitudes about human nature than in their attitudes about social justice and thus may have been more susceptible to the education process along this dimension. However, the low initial scores on human nature raise the alternative explanation that the change was simply regression to the mean rather than the result of the number of social work courses completed.

Although the findings of this study are important, there are several limitations. One of these is the cross-sectional approach used in this research. Comparing different students at various points in the educational process opens the possibility that any observed differences in their attitudes may be the result of differences between the students rather than the influence of the social work courses completed. The small sample size is another limitation and perhaps is related to the lack of variance explained by the regression models. Furthermore, only one undergraduate social work program was examined. This program may not be representative of social work programs in general. In addition, it is possible that the particular geographical location of the program biased the results in some manner. Thus, this study may be limited in its external validity.

CONCLUSION

This research study lends partial support to the hypothesis that the number of completed social work courses is positively related to students' humanistic attitudes. Furthermore, it appears that social work education has a stronger influence on attitudes about human nature than on those about social justice. This tentative finding may suggest that students start the program with more positive attitudes about social justice than about issues related to human nature, thus making change in the former set of attitudes less likely.

It is important to note that this research merely examined the situation as it is, rather than what may be possible. In other words, looking at the impact of the number of social work courses completed is only one way of examining the relationship between social work education and attitudes. Further research is needed on the manner in which social work educators attempt to influence values and attitudes. It is possible that particular methods may work better with some attitudes than with others. For example, it may be found that discussion may best influence attitudes about issues such as human nature whereas an action-oriented or experiential approach is needed to affect attitudes concerning social justice. There also is a need for research that examines the relationship between attitudes and actions. Changing attitudes is an important first step, however. Effective social work practice demands that humanistic attitudes become translated into action. The exploration of these issues is critical if social work education is to meet its mandate of producing practitioners committed to our code of ethics and who are willing to work for the improvement of the general welfare.

REFERENCES

CYRNS, A.G. (1977). Social work education and student ideology: A multivariate study of professional socialization. *Journal of Education for Social Work, 13*, 44-51.

HOWARD, T.U., & FLAITZ, J. (1982). A scale to measure humanistic attitudes of social work students. *Social Work Research and Abstracts, 18*, 11-18.

JUDAH, E.H. (1979). Values: The uncertain component in social work. *Journal of Education for Social Work, 15*, 79-86.

KOERIN, B. (1977). Values in social work education: Implications for baccalaureate degree programs. *Journal of Education for Social Work, 13*, 84-90.

LEMMON, J.A. (1983). Legal issues and ethical codes. In A. Rosenblatt & D. Waldfogel (Eds.), *Handbook of clinical work* (pp. 853-865). San Francisco, CA: Jossey-Bass.

MERDINGER, J.M. (1982). Socialization into a profession: The case of undergraduate social work students. *Journal of Education for Social Work, 18*, 12-19.

SHARWELL, G.R. (1974). Can values be taught? A study of two variables related to orientation of social work graduate students toward public dependency. *Journal of Education for Social Work, 10*, 99-105.

VARLEY, B.K. (1963). Socialization in social work education. *Social Work, 8*, 102-109.

Craig W. LeCroy
Cynthia C. Goodwin

Study E

New Directions in Teaching Social Work Methods: A Content Analysis of Course Outlines

SOCIAL WORK EDUCATION has undergone considerable change in the last two decades. As Constable (1984, p. 366) states "in the mid-1960s it became evident that developments in knowledge and in practice were outrunning the possibility of a single prescribed curriculum for the MSW degree." However, new curriculum issues surfaced with the greater acceptance of diversity within social work programs. Social work educators began to debate each other. One such dispute involved the generic versus specific focus of social work education (Leighninger, 1980). Another debate looked at the extent to which a common foundation of practice exists (Aigner, 1984; Hartman, 1983).

Several attempts have been made to interpret and understand the nature of curriculum changes in social work education. For example, several articles have analyzed the Curriculum Policy Statement, compared it with its predecessor, and put it into the context of present-day social work education (Constable, 1984; Aigner, 1984; Hokenstad, 1984). Some educators examined the issues arising from these changes from a historical perspective, by seeing how changes took place and interpreting their significance (Constable, 1984). One study designed a questionnaire to examine ways in which generic content was being taught in graduate social work curricula (Bakalinsky, 1982).

Although various methods have added to our understanding of social work education, there is very little current information on course content in graduate schools of social work. Guzzetta (1982) conducted a content analysis of MSW programs, and found little change in overall program design. Yet, no information is available on the topics covered or the focus of instruction in practice courses. No scholar has been able to interpret this information in light of new CSWE policy and the changes occurring in the profession. That void prompted the present research, which uses course outlines to examine the content of graduate-level direct practice courses.

METHODOLOGY

The sources of data used in the study were the outlines for foundation practice courses currently being used by faculty who teach social work methods. The 93 schools of social work represented in the CSWE list of accredited graduate programs were conducted by telephone. Of all the schools conducted, 80 (87%) agreed to participate. Of the 93 schools contacted, 65 percent are represented in the final sample (i.e., submitted course outlines). In terms of the geographical distribution of the sample, 21 percent of the schools are in the West, 25 percent are in the East, 27 percent are in the Midwest, and 27 percent are in the South.

Each school was asked to provide the names of faculty members teaching a first-year direct practice or methods course. The 354 faculty members were requested to send a copy of their current course outline. A follow-up letter was sent to nonrespondents eight weeks after the initial mailing. A total of 188 course outlines was received. About 10 percent of the outlines were not usable because the outline was for an elective course rather than a required direct practice course. Some of the same outlines were submitted by more than one instructor, hence the actual number of course outlines does not match the number of course instructors.

The final response rate, which was based on the number of faculty identified and the number of course outlines received, was 58 percent, typical for this type of study (See Bakalinsky, 1982; Lauderdale, Grinnell, & McMurtry, 1980). The complexity of the sampling method makes it difficult to validate the accuracy of the data. However, over half of the schools that have MSW programs are represented and the response rate of the instructors meets expectations.

RESULTS

The following data were taken from the course outlines: topics covered in the course units, required readings, course assignments, and course textbooks. All of the data were subjected to an interrater reliability evaluation. The entire sample of course outlines was used in the reliability analysis. Each variable was categorized by two research assistants. Definitions were used for each variable to train the raters and enhance consistency in ratings. The authors used Cohen's kappa to calculate interrater reliability. It is a more conservative and reliable estimate than percent agreement because it controls for chance agreement.

The results of the reliability analysis are presented in Table E-1. In general, all of the data, except treatment process under course units, show adequate reliability.

Course Units

Each course outline was examined to determine the content covered throughout the class. Courses would typically be divided into sections labeled "the client-worker relationship" or "data collection." These course units were grouped into 10 categories. The number of units used in each course outline is presented in Table E-2 (percentages are based on total number of course outlines in the sample, $N = 170$).

The most frequently covered unit was Treatment Process (72%). This is not surprising: Social work methods courses should cover basic treatment issues such as contracting and goal setting. In addition, most courses dealt with introductory materials, the social work relationship, and assessment. Few of the courses covered crisis intervention, and only 19 percent presented material on research and practice evaluation. The recent emphasis on practice evaluation by CSWE (1982) makes the latter finding particularly striking. The new Curriculum Policy Statement directs schools to prepare students to "evaluate their own practice and contribute to the generation on knowledge for practice" (Council on Social Work Education, 1982, p. 8). Perhaps social work programs currently use research courses to meet this objective. Nonetheless, the best forum still is undetermined. Without clear guidelines, practice evaluation may receive inadequate coverage. Worse yet, it may not be taught at all.

Very few courses read published research. A count of the authors determined the number of research articles listed as required reading. Required reading was defined as any material listed in the course outlines that the instructor clearly expected the students to read. These articles had to include the use of systematic observation and standardized procedures to be considered research. Our results revealed a mean of only .67—less than one article per course. Few courses used research articles in addition to the required textbooks. Although CSWE states that recent research be taught in practice courses (Council on Social Work Education, 1982, p. 8), evidence suggests that only small numbers of empirical studies are actually incorporated into syllabi.

The CSWE guidelines are quite clear: "Both the professional foundation and the advanced concentration curricula must give explicit attention to the patterns

TABLE E-1 INTERRATER RELIABILITY OF COURSE OUTLINE VARIABLES (COHEN'S KAPPA)

Course Units		Course Texts	
Introduction	.95	Compton & Galaway	.100
Social Work Relationship	.92	Hepworth & Larsen	.97
Ethnic-sensitive Practice	.87	Germain & Gitterman	.100
Data Collection	.72	Green	NA
Assessment	.75	Pincus & Minahan	NA
Crisis Intervention	NA	Garvin & Seabury	NA
Treatment Process	.52	Shulman	NA
Research/Evaluation	.79		
Termination	.83		
Secondary Texts		**Assignments**	
Hollis & Woods	.83	Assessment	.73
Ruperstein & Block	.85	Final exam	.96
Germain & Gitterman	.92	Midterm exam	.98
Pincus & Minahan	NA	Term Paper	.86
Egan	NA	Written Assignment	.63
Compton & Galaway	NA	Interview	.78
		Log	NA
		Experience	NA
Required Reading[a]			
Research articles	.76		
Minority articles	.82		

[a]Interrater reliability based on Pearson's Correlation Coefficient.
NA = not applicable, frequency of occurrence not large enough.

and consequences of discrimination and oppression, providing both theoretical and practice content about groups that continue to be subjected to oppression and those that are emerging into new social roles with greater freedom and visibility" (Council on Social Work Education, 1982, p. 6). Analyses of course outlines indicate that only 31 percent of practice courses devoted much attention to ethnic sensitivity issues. This appears to be a serious omission: Professional social work practice necessitates study of these issues.

Required Reading

We compiled a list of the textbooks and readings most frequently used in practice courses. It was an effort to better understand the nature of those courses;

TABLE E-2 COURSE UNITS USED IN THE DIRECT PRACTICE COURSES

Textbooks	Percent of Sample	Number of Occurrences
Introduction	70.6	120
Social Work Relationship	61.8	105
Ethnic-sensitive Practice	30.6	52
Data Collection	46.5	79
Assessment	68.2	116
Crisis Intervention	5.9	10
Treatment Process	71.8	122
Research/Practice Evaluation	17.6	30
Termination	54.1	92

Note: The textbooks listed in this table are cited as references.

textbook choice reveals much about the instructor's methods and assumptions.

Analysis of the list of required readings indicates that ethnicity issues (i.e., theoretical approaches to ethnicity, unrelated to particular ethnic groups) were completely absent from 42 percent of the course outlines. Another 22 percent of the course outlines included one or two articles on a minority group. Less than a quarter of the course outlines included a unit on minorities. These results suggest a need to reexamine the status of minority content in the curriculum.

Table E-3 lists the primary textbook for the class. Only one textbook was considered "primary"; if two or more textbooks were used, then the textbook with the larger amount of required reading was designated the primary textbook. Since many courses used more than one textbook Table E-4 lists other required

TABLE E-3 REQUIRED TEXTBOOKS USED IN COURSES

Textbooks	Percent of Sample	Number of Times Used
Compton & Galaway	17.1	29
Hepworth & Larsen	12.9	22
Germain & Gitterman	4.1	7
Green	2.9	5
Pincus & Minahan	3.5	6
Garvin & Seabury	3.5	6
Shulman	2.4	4

Note: The textbooks listed in this table are cited as references.

TABLE E-4 SECONDARY TEXTBOOKS USED IN COURSES

Textbooks	Percent of Sample	Number of Times Used
Hollis & Woods	8.2	14
Ruperstein & Block	4.7	8
Germain & Gitterman	4.7	8
Pincus & Minahan	3.5	6
Egan	2.9	5
Compton & Galaway	2.9	5

Note: The textbooks listed in this table are cited as references.

textbooks, designated "secondary textbooks." Both tables show the number of times each textbook was used, according to the course outlines.

Table E-3 shows that the two most frequently used textbooks are the Compton and Galaway and the Hepworth and Larsen. Both books cover many of the course units reviewed earlier, such as: knowledge and values in social work, the social worker/client relationship, and the treatment process. However, the two texts differ in the presentation of the material. The Hepworth and Larsen text is competency-based and skills-oriented; the Compton and Galaway book follows a generic format. For example, in Compton and Galaway, treatment process is presented in a problem-solving format: The authors offer a conceptual framework rather than a guide to action.

In contrast, Hepworth and Larsen describe treatment process in an action-oriented set of guidelines for practice. In the past, social work methods classes

TABLE E-5 MOST FREQUENTLY GIVEN ASSIGNMENTS

Assignments	Percent of Sample	Number of Times Assignment Appeared In Sample
Assessment Evaluation	22.4	38
Final Exam	21.2	36
Midterm Exam	20.0	34
Term Paper	15.9	27
Written Assignment	15.3	26
Analysis of an Interview	11.8	20
Log of a Placement	3.5	6
Personal Experience	2.9	5

frequently used the Pincus and Minahan textbook. Its popularity dropped sharply: At the time of this study, only 3.5 percent of practice courses used it as primary text. The text lacks clear practice guidelines; this may account for its recent disfavor. Compton and Galaway replaced Pincus and Minahan as the most popular textbook because the former is more easily translated into those guidelines. Thus, it appears that action-oriented and task-centered methods are increasingly being used to teach social work practice. The newer models of education probably are the result of increased emphasis on social work practice outcomes. However, these speculations clearly are open to many interpretations.

Assignments

We also derived data on the types of grading criteria from the course outlines. Table E-5 presents these results. The most frequent assignments were assessments and psychosocial evaluations. Most of the assignments represent typical course requirements: exams, finals, term papers, and written assignments. Two assignments were assigned infrequently: analysis of an interview (11.8% of courses) and journal of placement experiences (3.5% of courses). It is hard to determine if this differs from previous practices.

Skills Training

In order to assess the extent to which courses included skills instruction a short questionnaire was attached to the course outline request. Some instructors returned course outlines but failed to return the questionnaire; they received follow-up letters and phone calls. Almost all (92%) of the instructors included in the study completed the additional questionnaire. A majority of the courses (70%) included some type of skills instruction. A few (12%) had none. Along with more of a competency-based curriculum, it appears practice courses incorporate more skills content than ever before. Historically, it was assumed that students would learn the necessary skills in the field. Schools of social work now try to ensure that practice skills are learned in the classroom and refined in the field.

DISCUSSION

Various attempts have been made to understand current directions in social work. Those attempts never examined the way social work practice is taught in schools of social work across the country.

This analysis suggests some interesting patterns in the teaching of social work and raises some important questions. For example, how consistent are MSW courses in schools of social work across the country? This study found reasonable consistency in basic educational content. In particular, most courses included units on the social worker/client relationship, assessment, treatment process, and termination. Many courses used similar reading for these units. Classic articles such as Seabury's (1976) article, "The Contract: Uses, Abuses and Limitations" Kadushin's (1963) article "Diagnosis and Evaluation for Almost all Occasions," and Germain and Gitterman's (1976) "Social Work Practice: A Life Model" were used in most of course readings. A large number of the required readings come from professional journals.

In a review of CSWE policy changes, Constable (1984, p. 367) notes that programmatic "differences, together with more obvious differences in the way programs identify themselves and conceive of their purpose, suggest that MSW programs are becoming less comparable over time." However, the data from this study suggest that the basic methods of social work education are comparable, at least in the first year. The advanced curriculum may be less comparable, but the initial year of direct practice appears to be fairly uniform. This leads to a further question. How comparable should we expect social work courses to be? This question (like many others) about social work education needs further study.

While there may be some common features across curricula there are clearly omissions in curriculum content. The most glaring omission is that only 30.6 percent of the course outlines included a unit on ethnic practice. In addition, the analysis of required readings found that general minority content was absent in 42 percent of the course outlines. These two findings suggest that many courses do not include anything directly relevant to ethnic practice. Ethnic content perhaps is covered in discussion and lecture. Alternatively, this "missing" content may be included in other courses. In addition, the CSWE call for increased emphasis on minority content may have resulted in the assimilation of these issues into every course unit. Nonetheless, 42 percent of courses had no readings on ethnic-sensitive practice. Students should read about minority issues relevant to the practice of social work. The CSWE requirement for increased minority content may ultimately contribute to a lack of minority content. Further research should examine this issue.

This omission calls into question the willingness of schools to conform to CSWE curriculum policy. The low percentages of research and practice evaluations also form such doubts.

Although there is a degree of uniformity in the social work curriculum, the profession lacks standardized course content. If, as Constable and others argue, social workers are becoming less comparable with each other, then perhaps CSWE should support efforts toward producing greater conformity in the foundation year.

The authors propose that the course units identified in Table E-6 be included in all foundation year practice courses. This table represents the curriculum units frequently used in social work classes for direct practice. If the profession wants to increase uniformity across social work schools, a more standard curriculum is needed to enhance this consistency. Table E-6 serves as a preliminary

TABLE E-6 SUGGESTED CURRICULUM FOR SOCIAL WORK PRACTICE

1. Purpose and Objectives of Social Work Practice
2. Conceptual Frameworks for Social Work Practice
3. Knowledge and Values for Social Work Practice
4. The Social Work Relationship
5. Data Collection and Initial Contacts
6. Social Work Interviewing
7. Social Work with Special Populations
8. Assessment and Diagnosis
9. Contracting and Goal Setting
10. Treatment Strategies
11. Practice Evaluation
12. Termination

guide. A more detailed set of recommendations could be provided to schools of social work. These recommendations might describe common objectives for suggested course units. However, increased consistency of educational objectives through uniform procedures is likely to be controversial.

There are several limitations to this study. The sampling frame consisted of only 58 percent of the population. The reliability of the sample is open to question; the sample itself must be interpreted in a circumspect fashion. It should also be noted that the meaning of the data is based on the authors' interpretation. For example, the idea that action-oriented task centered approaches are replacing the conceptual approaches is based solely on analysis of required textbooks for the courses. Furthermore, changes of this nature cannot be established in cross-sectional research study.

This study rests on the assumption that course syllabi reflect what is actually taught. Course outlines give one type of picture. In many ways it is an incomplete picture of what actually happens in a course. A course outline does not record the lectures, exercises and class discussions. In addition, the authors' categorizations may not accurately reflect content. For example, practice evaluation appeared to be omitted from most of the courses. However, practice evaluation may be covered under different course units, such as intervention procedures or termination. Nevertheless, course outlines are highly revealing documents. They are important symbols of educational values of social work. They also carry suggestions for the improvement of social work education.

REFERENCES

AIGNER, S.M. (1984). The curriculum policy: Implications of an emergent consensus. *Journal of Education for Social Work, 20*, 5-14.

BAKALINSKY, R. (1982). Generic practice in graduate social work curricula: A study of educators' experience and attitudes. *Journal of Education for Social Work, 18*, 46-54.

COMPTON, B., & GALAWAY, B. (1984). *Social work process* (3rd ed.). Homewood, IL: Dorsey.

CONSTABLE, R.T. (1984). Social work education: Current issues and future promise. *Social Work, 29*, 366-376.

COUNCIL ON SOCIAL WORK EDUCATION. (1982). *Curriculum Policy for the Master's Degree and Baccalaureate Degree Programs in Social Work Education*, document No 82-310-0GR. New York: Council on Social Work Education.

EGAN, G. (1975). *The skilled helper: A model for systematic helping and interpersonal relating*. Monterey, CA: Brooks-Cole.

GARVIN, C.D., & SEABURY, B.A. (1984). *Interpersonal practice in social work: Process and procedures*. Englewood Cliffs, NJ: Prentice-Hall.

GERMAIN, C., & GITTERMAN, A. (1980). *The life model of social work practice*. New York: Columbia University Press.

GREEN, J. (1982). *Cultural awareness in the human services*. Englewood Cliffs, NJ: Prentice-Hall.

GUZZETTA, C. (1982). MSW education: The present state. Unpublished paper, Hunter College. Cited in Hokenstad, M.C., Jr. (1984). Curriculum directions for the 1980s: Implications of the new curriculum policy statement. *Journal of Education for Social Work, 20*, 15-22.

HARTMAN, A. (1983). Concentrations, specializations and curriculum design in MSW and BSW programs. *Journal of Education for Social Work, 19*, 79-85.

HEPWORTH, D.H., & LARSEN, J. (1982). *Direct social work practice: Theory and skills*. Homewood, IL: Dorsey.

HOKENSTAD, M.C. (1984). Curriculum directions for the 1980s: Implications of the new curriculum policy statement. *Journal of Education for Social Work, 20*, 15-22.

HOLLIS, F.E., & WOODS, M.E. (1981). *Casework: A psychosocial theory* (3rd ed.). New York: Random House.

LAUDERDALE, M.L., GRINNELL, R.M., JR., & MCMURTRY, S.L. (1980). Child welfare curricula in schools of social work; A national study, *Child Welfare, 59*, 531-541.

LEIGHNINGER, L. (1980). The generalist-specialist debate in social work. *Social Service Review, 54*, 1-12.

PINCUS, A., & MINAHAN, A. (1973). *Social work practice: Model and method*. Itasca, IL: Peacock.

RUPERSTEIN, H., & BLOCK, M.H. (1982). *Things that matter: Influences on helping relationships*. New York: Macmillan.

SHULMAN, L. (1984). *The skills of helping* (2nd ed.). Itasca, IL: Peacock.

Barbara Thomlison
Irene Hoffart

Study 

An Evaluation of the Social Support Component of a Perinatal Program for Adolescents

ADOLESCENT PREGNANCY is associated with a large number of negative consequences to both the young mother and her child. Research findings have indicated that pregnant and parenting adolescents face educational, economic, and social-emotional difficulties (Sherman & Donovan, 1991). Some authors suggest that social support is effective in minimizing these risks (Rothery & Cameron, 1985; Tracy, 1988). Improving social support in the provision of services is considered to be an important program component to avert poor outcomes for pregnant and parenting adolescents (Sherman & Donovan, 1991).

SOCIAL SUPPORT

Crockenburg (1986) reports that teenage mothers overwhelmingly turned to their friends, mothers, siblings, and sometimes to boyfriends and professionals for social support. Unfortunately, pregnancy frequently disrupts these relationships and precipitates negative consequences.

Presence of social support can minimize physical and mental health risks to both the young mother and her infant. Social support facilitates higher educational and occupational achievement, reduces the strain of pregnancy and impact of related problems, and increases self-confidence (Unger & Wandersman, 1985).

Miller and Whittaker (1988) indicate that social support resources also increase mothers' social competency, thus promoting infant well-being and preventing family breakdown. The healthy development of the infant is positively associated with the number of close supportive family members identified by the mother (Crockenburg, 1986).

Perceived Social Support

Social support is most effective when there is a fit between the individual and the type of support offered. A good fit occurs when the adolescent mother perceives her social support as beneficial. Perceived social support is positively related to better adjustment in mothers, better health and development in their children, increased satisfaction with life, and decreased worries about parenting (Unger & Wandersman, 1985; Sherman & Donovan, 1991).

Most recent research findings also view social support as an important marker in minimizing risks to the young mother's and her infant's well-being (Turner, Grindstaff, & Phillips, 1990). Thus, it is essential that perinatal programs include activities designed to improve young women's perceptions of social support.

THE PROGRAM

The community-based perinatal program evaluated in the present study constitutes the primary source of social support and intervention for many pregnant adolescents in a large metropolitan area with a population of 670,000. Referrals to the program are received from health and social service professionals and clients themselves. Services are available to women between 12 to 19 years of age.

Clients can enter the program at any time during the perinatal period. The program is mandated to provide services for up to 30 days after the birth of the baby. At this time, services are terminated and clients in need of further services and assistance are referred to other community social service agencies.

Provision of program services is system-centered, in the sense that the availability of services defines treatment. If the needed services are not available the client is referred elsewhere.

The program's philosophy is based on research findings which suggest that poor pregnancy outcomes may be preventable (Unger & Wandersman, 1985). The application of the program philosophy is aimed at pregnant women known to be at risk for a poor outcome due to health, economic, or social conditions. Case management activities directed toward the fulfillment of the program goal include assessment, counseling, referral of clients at risk for health and social factors, and enhancement of social-educational opportunities for the young women and their families. Poor nutrition, self-care and exercise habits, substance use, excessive stress, lack of medical supervision, and inadequate social support resources are the primary foci of intervention by the professional staff.

As can be noted, social support is only one of the multitude of problem areas addressed by the program. To improve aspects associated with social support, professional, community-based nurses provide supportive counseling to the adolescent, her family, and significant others.

Purpose

The original purpose of the larger project was to report on the findings regarding all of the components of the program. These aspects included services to improve medical supervision and nutrition, to modify lifestyle habits such as substance use, to provide health promotion services such as self-care, and to promote effective parenting practice and infant-mother well-being.

The purpose of the present study is to report the findings of an evaluation of only one of the program's components: improvement of adolescents' perceived social support. In view of the literature outlined above it is possible to hypothesize that the program intervention will improve the pregnant adolescent's satisfaction with the perceived social support she receives.

METHODOLOGY

This section describes the study's population, design, and instrumentation.

Population

The study's population was admitted to the program in the years of 1987 to 1989 inclusive. All of the 581 females served by the program over the three-year study period entered the program voluntarily. The intake data indicate a consistent and increasing rate of program entry, with 31% in 1987, 34% in 1988, and 35% in 1989.

A variety of agencies and individuals served as clients' referral sources. Twenty-one percent were referred by several social and health agencies. Other referrals came from the clients' school (16%), themselves (14%), friends and relatives (13%), and their doctor (13%) in approximately the same proportion. For 23% of the population, the referral source was unknown.

At intake, the clients had an average age of 16.9. During case management, the clients were interviewed at the agency on average 3.5 times. Approximately 60% were separated from their families. Many lived with their mother (41%) or both parents (46%), while 56% maintained contact with the baby's father during their stay with the program. At the time of intake, the clients were, on average, 4.5 months pregnant. Nearly one quarter (22%) reported having had a previous pregnancy.

Design

The program's closed perinatal files ($N = 581$) constituted the study's unit of analysis. At the time of intake, each client's psychosocial history associated with familial, psychological, social, health, and lifestyle factors was assessed through an interview format and documented in the client's file. The closed case record review provided data on a variety of adolescent, infant, and service delivery variables. The perceived social support scores and the demographic variables reported in this study were a small part of the overall larger project.

The study used a one-group pretest-posttest design. Clients' perceptions of social support were measured at two different points of their contact with the program. Pretest scores were obtained at the initial interview, and posttest scores were obtained at the termination of the program. Some missing data for pretest or posttest measurements decreased the sample from 581 to 500 clients. The variables used to describe the population (i.e., client's age, year of admission, referral source, length of pregnancy, number of interviews, contact with baby's father, and previous pregnancy) were gathered at admission.

Measuring Instrument

A list of eight sources of perceived support were used to derive the final social support scores (Figure F-1). Each client rated, on a ten-point partition scale, her perception of support received from each of the eight people described in Figure F-1. The scale ranged from zero (no support) to nine (maximum support). The overall social support scores were computed by summing the scores and dividing by the number of individuals rated.

FINDINGS AND DISCUSSION

A paired *t*-test was used to determine if the perceived social support scores significantly changed from pretest to posttest. As can be seen from Table F-1 on page 160, the difference (i.e., .2) between pretest and posttest scores was statistically significant ($t = 2.7$, $p = .007$).

Though the difference was significant, it was very small and in the direction

This group of questions is about the client's perception of the social support she receives. Eight sources of support are listed below. Please ask the client to rate each source by circling the number which best describes her perception. Check off sources that are not applicable.

To derive the Social Support Score add all numbers circled and divide by the number of sources rated.

	Perceptions of Social Support										
Sources of Support	*None*								*Maximum*		*NA*
1. Baby's father	0	1	2	3	4	5	6	7	8	9	__
2. Brother	0	1	2	3	4	5	6	7	8	9	__
3. Sister	0	1	2	3	4	5	6	7	8	9	__
4. Grandfather	0	1	2	3	4	5	6	7	8	9	__
5. Grandmother	0	1	2	3	4	5	6	7	8	9	__
6. Boyfriend	0	1	2	3	4	5	6	7	8	9	__
7. Peer/Friend	0	1	2	3	4	5	6	7	8	9	__
8. Other	0	1	2	3	4	5	6	7	8	9	__

Total Score __
Average Social Support Score __

FIGURE F-1 PERCEPTIONS OF THE SOCIAL SUPPORT MEASURING INSTRUMENT

opposite to the one predicted. As can be seen from Table F-1, the average score at pretest (M = 5.6) was slightly higher than the average score at posttest (M = 5.4). The hypothesis that the perceived social support scores would increase from pretest to posttest is not supported.

The absence of improvement in social support scores encourages further examination of the program's social support component. The adolescent's infrequent interviews at the agency (on average 3.5 times) may have played a role in diminishing differences in scores. This interpretation is supported by Rothery & Cameron (1985), who report that the level of the pregnant adolescent's contact with a nurse can make a difference in program outcome.

Considering the problems and lifestyle practices of the young mothers, their scores are comparatively high both before and after the intervention (5.4 and 5.6 out of a possible 9). The clients in the present sample may be satisfied with their social support because many of them live with one or both of their parents.

This is in line with the argument that many pregnant and parenting adolescents experience social emotional difficulties because they do not live in family-supported settings (Thomlison & Krysik, 1991; Tracy, 1988).

TABLE F-1 MEANS AND STANDARD DEVIATIONS OF SOCIAL SUPPORT SCORES AT PRETEST AND POSTTEST ($N = 500$)

Pretest		Posttest		Difference			
Mean	SD	Mean	SD	Mean	SD	t	p
5.6	2.6	5.4	2.8	.2	-.2	2.7	.007

LIMITATIONS

Instrumentation, use of a single data source, history, and maturation constitute the primary limitations of the present study. The instrument used by the program was not inclusive of all types of social support and was not standardized. The scores varied from 0 to 9, providing a broader range than is usually recommended (Mueller, 1986). As a result, it is not entirely clear how the ratings of social support were carried out and if the raters were consistent in their assessments.

Rothery and Cameron (1985) indicate that the type and nature of actual provision of social support is critical to comprehensive assessment. Incomplete assessment may affect program case management and outcome.

Use of a single data source in measuring program effectiveness represents another limitation of the study because other potentially relevant areas were not explored. For instance, if the evaluation had focused on mothers' and infants' physical health rather than social well-being, it may have resulted in different findings.

Finally, the absence of control group may contribute to such internal validity threats as history and maturation. Transitional effects associated with the period of adolescence make the threat of maturation particularly relevant, because clients' rapid developmental changes may have prevented capture of the true results (Quinton & Rutter, 1988).

SUMMARY

Several suggestions associated with the present functioning of the program emerge from the study. It is possible that the failure of the social support to improve resulted from the use of nonstandardized assessment instruments, lack of differentiation between adolescents' developmental levels, lack of service follow-up, and system-focused rather than client-focused services.

First, the data collection forms used by programs must be consistent and clear. Inappropriate data collection instruments can prevent the program from demonstrating the full extent of its effectiveness. The quality of information is improved when multiple standardized instruments are used.

Second, one should not assume that all adolescents are at the same level of maturity, because the phase covers a long time span (Landy, Cleland, & Schubert, 1984). The social support is likely to differ among adolescents who are not equivalent in developmental stages and life events (Tracy, 1988). Services differentiated on the basis of developmental stages may improve outcome.

Third, research studies indicate that support provided to the adolescent mother declines by the end of the baby's first year (Mercer, Hackley, & Bostrom, 1984). The present perinatal program is mandated to terminate its services soon after the infant's birth. Absence of differences in scores may indicate that the program intervention is not long enough to produce real impact. The young mother and her child(ren) may need sustained program intervention or follow-up for at least a year after the baby's birth.

Finally, preliminary findings suggest that outcomes may differ in a client-focused rather than system-focused service provision (Ontario Ministry of Community and Social Services, 1991). The use of a "wrap-around service" concept by other programs resulted in cost-effective, integrated networking of services and may benefit the perinatal programs as well (Greenley, Littman, & Robitchek, 1990).

In conclusion, linkage of policy, research, and programming is essential in meeting the needs of young mothers and their infants. An integrated system of care can help minimize the risks associated with adolescent pregnancy.

REFERENCES

CROCKENBURG, S.B. (1986). Professional support for adolescent mothers: Who gives it, how adolescent mothers evaluate it, what they would prefer. *Infant Mental Health Journal, 7*, 48-58.

GREENLEY, J.R., LITTMAN, P.S., & ROBITCHEK, C.G. (1990). Two pilot programs of services to SED youngsters in Wisconsin. *Proceedings of the Third Annual Children's Mental Health Conference*, Tampa, Florida, February.

LANDY, S., CLELAND, J., & SCHUBERT, J. (1984). The individuality of teen-age mothers and it implication for intervention strategies. *Journal of Adolescence, 7*, 171-190.

MERCER, R.T., HACKLEY, K.C., & BOSTROM, A. (1984). Adolescent motherhood: Comparison of outcome with older mothers. *Proceedings of the Fifth Annual Meeting of the California Perinatal Association*, San Diego, California, September.

MILLER, J.L., & WHITTAKER, J.K. (1988). Social services and social support: Blended programs for families at risk of child maltreatment. *Child Welfare, 67*, 161-173.

MUELLER, D.J. (1986). *Measuring social attitudes: A handbook for researchers and practitioners.* New York: Teachers College.

ONTARIO MINISTRY OF COMMUNITY AND SOCIAL SERVICES (1991). *Nine Ontario communities become part of better beginnings, better futures.* Toronto, Ontario, Canada: The Ontario Prevention Clearinghouse Newsletter.

QUINTON, D., & RUTTER, M. (1988). *Parenting breakdown: The making and breaking of inter-generational links.* Aldershot, England: Avery.

ROTHERY, M., & CAMERON, G. (1985). Understanding family support in child welfare: A summary report. *Ontario Ministry of Community and Social Services*. Waterloo, Ontario, Canada; Wilfrid Laurier University.

SHERMAN, B.R., & DONOVAN, B.R. (1991). Relationship of perceived maternal acceptance-rejection in childhood and social support networks of pregnant adolescents. *American Journal of Orthopsychiatry, 61*, 103-113.

THOMLISON, B., & KRYSIK, J. (1991). Toward validating an instrument for rating restrictiveness: An expert panel approach. *Proceedings of the Fourth Annual Children's Mental Health Conference*, Tampa, Florida, February.

TRACY, E. (1988). Social support resources of at-risk families: *Implementation of social support assessments in an intensive family preservation*. Doctoral dissertation, University of Washington.

TURNER, R.J., GRINDSTAFF, C.F., & PHILLIPS, N. (1990). Social support and outcome in teenage pregnancy. *Journal of Health and Social Behavior, 31*, 43-57.

UNGER, D. G., & WANDERSMAN, L.P. (1985). Social support and adolescent mothers: Action research contributions to theory and application. *Journal of Social Issues, 41*, 29-45.

Leslie M. Tutty

Study G

An Evaluation of a Vocational Rehabilitation Program for Ex-Psychiatric Patients

THE NEEDS OF EX-PSYCHIATRIC PATIENTS living in the community are substantial. Most live on below-poverty-level government benefits—78 percent in a recent study in Hamilton, Ontario (Kearns, Taylor, & Dear, 1987). However, not being employed creates problems beyond economic considerations. If ex-psychiatric patients do not have the work skills and social skills necessary to keep a job, they are not only financially incapacitated, but are denied a potential source of self-worth and stable social integration. Walsh (1982) has suggested that perhaps the most important road out of the mental health system for ex-mental patients is employment or volunteer work.

LITERATURE REVIEW

It has not been clear whether available community mental health programs actually assist ex-psychiatric patients to reintegrate into the community or to find work. Re-hospitalization rates and employment are most often used as the measure of whether such programs are successful. However, Anthony, Cohen, and Vitalo (1978) concluded that the best demographic predictor of employment across a number of studies was previous employment history, a factor unrelated to program effectiveness. Employment rates after hospitalization have been consistently in the range of 20 to 30 percent employed at follow-up, regardless of the length of time after hospitalization (Anthony, Buell, Sharratt, & Althoff, 1972). A recent study estimated that 62 percent of patients discharged from hospitals were unemployed six months after discharge (Fischer, Goering, Lancee, & Wasylenki, 1981).

Studies of rehabilitation programs for the psychiatrically disabled indicate that positive changes in employment often decrease dramatically and re-hospitalization rates increase as the support of the program is withdrawn (Test, 1981). In the long run, few programs appear to have a positive impact on clients utilizing only employment and re-hospitalization as outcome measures. Other indicators of effectiveness such as client skill and activity levels have been suggested as additional outcome measures (Anthony et al., 1978). Willer and Biggin (1976) found that social factors such as interpersonal skills, personal relations, use of leisure time, control of aggression, and employment, in combination with personal factors such as general affect and physical health, are indeed related to success of community tenure. A wider assessment of the complexities of the lives of psychiatrically disabled clients is, therefore, suggested in evaluating whether vocational rehabilitation programs actually assist reintegration back into the community.

PROGRAM DESCRIPTION

The Redirection Through Education program (R.T.E.) at Seneca College of Applied Arts and Technology in North York, Ontario, was originally developed to address both the employment and the interpersonal needs of young psychiatrically disabled adults. Situated within a community college campus, the shift in identity from "patient" to "student" is seen as a crucial element of the program. Similar vocational rehabilitation programs in educational settings have been only recently described in the literature (Farkas & Anthony, 1989). In comparison, most vocational programs provide job-training in sheltered situations, while some offer opportunities for job placements in the community. Few include an educational component similar to the R.T.E. program—an essential element since many of these young adults have not completed high school and an increasing number of job training programs require high school graduation.

Interviews with R.T.E. staff and inspection of the written program objectives and student files suggested that the objectives of staff and students are similar. The staff reported such student aims as an increase in self-esteem, being better able to function socially, and an improvement in both physical and emotional well-being. In the staff's view, the program's focus is therapeutic, centering on intrapersonal and interpersonal functioning. The program's written materials stress educational and vocational objectives that are compatible with the community college setting. The staff mentioned that not all of the students necessarily obtain employment after the program. However, given the social isolation of many psychiatrically disabled individuals, the staff consider the social interaction component of the program as critical. The congruence in objectives of staff, students, and written materials suggests that the R.T.E. program is evaluatable.

RESEARCH DESIGN

Sample

Two groups were targeted as sources of information in evaluating the effectiveness of the R.T.E. program: former students, who had attended the program during the past three or four years and current students. Information from the current students ($N = 77$) was gathered as they proceeded through the program during Week 1, Week 11, and the last week, Week 20. However, only 26 students completed the entire R.T.E. program. Information from other students who had either left the program before completion or were unavailable for testing was utilized for comparison purposes.

The follow-up sample consisted of all former students who could be contacted by mail. Of 122 questionnaires that were mailed to former R.T.E. students, 46 (39%) were returned completed, 15 (12%) were returned with no forwarding address.

Sample Characteristics

Information from the student files on the current ($N = 77$), as well as former ($N = 122$) R.T.E. students, was used to obtain a description of student characteristics. Over half of the students were in the 18 to 29 age range, with another third aged 30 to 40 years. There was an equal gender split. Psychiatric diagnoses were primarily schizophrenia or schizo-affective disorders (over 40%). Another 20 percent were depressed, with the remaining diagnoses primarily consisting of anxiety and manic-depressive disorders. Almost 90 percent of the students took medication, with the largest proportion being prescribed major tranquilizers (over 50%). Approximately 40 percent of the students took further medication to counteract side-effects from the primary medication. Over 65 percent of the students had been previously hospitalized in a psychiatric facility once or twice, while another 30 percent had been hospitalized three or four times.

In regard to education level, 75 percent of R.T.E. students had not completed high school, of these 40 percent had only a Grade 11 education or less. Over 60 percent of the students had no previous work experience or had worked for a total of only one or two years. Of those who had jobs, 40 percent had worked in unskilled positions, with a further 33 percent having had experience in clerical work.

These demographics suggest that R.T.E. students are severely disabled with disorders that necessitate the long-term use of psychotropic medication. The majority of students had past educational difficulties, which would have further exacerbated their search for employment. Given the age of the students (on average in their late 20s and 30s), the shortness of the average duration of job experience suggests difficulty in maintaining employment once it was obtained.

Measurement of Objectives

A number of factors were considered in choosing measures to evaluate the objectives of the R.T.E. program. First, Schulberg and Bromet (1981) suggest that a comprehensive evaluation of community mental health programs should include measures of social adaptation, psychiatric status, quality of life, satisfaction with services, vocational performance, and environmental conditions.

Self-report, paper-and-pencil measures, which could be mailed to former students, were utilized rather than conducting in-depth face-to-face interviews. A broadly based sample of responses was thought to be more useful in addressing the questions raised by R.T.E. staff, such as how many graduates were employed. Although the response rates of mailed questionnaires are typically lower than that of other forms of follow-up evaluation, there are compensations. Warner, Berman, Weyant, and Ciarlo's (1983) study on follow-up methods found that, although response rates for the mailed questionnaires were only half as high as for face-to-face or telephone interviews, they were the least affected by socially desirable responses.

Finally, evaluation measures were chosen that would address the six objectives identified by both staff and students as being central to the R.T.E. program.

Objective 1

The first objective was to increase the self-esteem of R.T.E. students. This objective was measured by the adult version of the Coopersmith Self-Esteem Inventory (Coopersmith, 1988) which is a 25-item self-report measure. Test-retest reliability studies have reported correlations of .88 over five weeks, and .70 over three years. Research on the adult version (Ahmed, Valliant, & Swindle, 1985) has yielded an internal reliability score of .75 using Cronbach's alpha coefficient. Several convergent validity studies that compared the Coopersmith to other scales of self-esteem or self-acceptance have shown correlations in the .45 to .65 range (Coopersmith, 1988). The range of scores is from 0 to 100. Higher scores are indicative of greater self-esteem.

Objective 2

The second objective was to improve the social adjustment of R.T.E. students. This objective was measured by the Social Adjustment Scale (SAS-SR) (Weissman & Bothwell, 1976). This self-report scale was derived from a structured interview procedure measuring how well one is performing in, and how one feels, about seven key areas of social functioning: work, social activities, leisure activities, relationships with extended family, economic independence, marital roles, and parental roles. It has reasonably high test-retest stability (mean coefficient of .80 over two time periods) and high internal consistency (alpha = .74) (Edwards, Yarvis, Mueller, Zingale, & Wagman, 1978). Two questions from the marital subscale regarding the frequency of sexual intercourse were excluded since they seemed unnecessarily personal. The range of scores is from 1 to 5. Higher scores are indicative of greater difficulty in social adjustment.

Objective 3

The third objective was to increase the level of functioning of R.T.E. students. This objective was measured by the R.T.E. staff using the Level of Functioning Scale (Carter & Newman, 1976). This is a brief, global rating scale developed for use with the psychiatrically disabled population. The scale contains nine levels that describe a range of functioning from being considered normal to being totally dependent on others to meet one's needs. A test of the construct validity of the Level of Functioning Scale found a correlation of .58 with a measure of social functioning that focused on vocational, educational, and skill roles. Newman (1980) examined the psychometric properties of global rating scales and found high inter-rater reliability with experienced clinicians and researchers, from .70 to .90. In a comparison of six brief rating scales (Green & Gracely, 1987) this scale was preferred on the basis of reliability, sensitivity to change, construct validity, group relevance, and clinical utility. Its use in predicting re-hospitalization in outcome evaluations of mental health services has been suggested (Krowinski & Fitt, 1978). The range of scores is from 1 to 9. Higher scores indicate more independent functioning.

Objective 4

The fourth objective was to increase the life satisfaction of R.T.E. students. This objective was measured by the Client Satisfaction with Life Domains Scale (Andrews & Withey, 1976) which is a 15-item self-report questionnaire that provides a general gauge of satisfaction with place of residence, family relationships, friends, employment, leisure time, and finances. Internal consistency reliabilities estimates range from .67 to .87, and factor analysis has been used to describe evidence for the confirmed construct validity of the measure (Lehman,

1983). The range of scores is from 1 to 105. Higher scores indicate greater satisfaction.

Objective 5

The fifth objective was to establish employment/educational experiences for R.T.E. students. A follow-up questionnaire was constructed to document former R.T.E. students' experiences after the program in seven areas: current employment, employment since the R.T.E. program, current student status, educational programs attended, involvement in other mental health programs, involvement in other vocational training programs, and re-hospitalizations.

Objective 6

The last objective was to determine the R.T.E. students' satisfaction with the R.T.E. program. Three questions were added to the questionnaire that was developed to measure Objective 5. The three questions were designed to investigate students' satisfaction with the R.T.E. program. The questions were: (1) whether all or most of their needs had been met, (2) how satisfied were they with the program, and (3) whether they would recommend the program to a friend.

Limitations

The lack of availability of a larger sample of young adults with psychiatric disabilities from which to select a comparison group placed limitations on the choice of research design. A comparison group utilizing a community mental health program located in the community was a theoretically possible alternative, but a group with participants functioning at a similar level could not be found. A waiting list comparison group would have strengthened the design of the research, however, there was generally not a waiting list available. The lack of a comparison group in a quasi-experimental pretest-posttest design means that the results are primarily descriptive in nature and must be interpreted carefully (Grinnell & Stothers, 1988). For example, scores might improve because of an event occurring outside of the R.T.E. program that affected all participants. Without a comparison group the effects of the historical event would be interpreted as a treatment effect.

Testing in itself could influence scores such that students would improve because of a practice effect rather than the influence of the program. This is more likely to occur with tests of skill or knowledge than on measures of attitude or personal functioning such as those chosen for the present study. Most of the evaluation measures chosen have high test-retest reliability, so that practice effects are not likely.

Mortality, or loss of participants, is a further threat to the internal validity of an evaluation, however such attrition is common with psychiatrically disabled populations. Many programs report substantial rates of early dropouts from rehabilitation facilities (Beard, Malamud, & Rossman, 1978). Of the total 77 current R.T.E. students, 43 (58%) graduated from the program, three left to take employment, one left to go to another program, one student died, and 28 did not complete the program (37%). The students who did not complete were most likely to leave early in program cycle: 12 students dropped out in the first month; another 13 left before the end of ten weeks. Thus, those students who remained may have been different from those who dropped out.

To test for this possibility, independent *t*-tests were conducted on the scores of R.T.E. graduates as compared to nongraduates, tested during the first week in the program. These yielded no significant differences on any of the measures utilized, with the exception of one item from the Satisfaction With Life Domains Scale, which showed that graduates of R.T.E. were significantly more satisfied ($p < .05$) with their health than were students who ultimately left the program. This suggests that, since dropouts were indistinguishable from graduates on most measures, mortality should not be considered a significant threat to the internal validity of the evaluation.

Another threat to the internal validity of the study is that the follow-up group was self-selected, through their willingness to return the questionnaires. It was not possible to locate all past R.T.E. students for inclusion in the follow-up research, given the high mobility of the population (Sheets, Prevost, & Reihman, 1982). However, it is likely that the students who responded were functioning highly and may have felt more positively about the R.T.E. program. Student file information was utilized to examine the characteristics of the previous students who answered the follow-up questionnaire as compared to those who did not, in an attempt to test the magnitude of this bias. The 44 respondents were about twice as likely to have graduated from the R.T.E. program than those who did not return their questionnaire (59% versus 26%). It is logical that students who successfully completed the program would be more willing to make the effort to provide feedback.

Secondly, the respondents were more educated (75% had grade 12 or 13 education and above, versus 56 percent of nonresponders). More educated students were likely less uncomfortable responding to the long and somewhat complex set of mailed questionnaires. Finally, the respondents were more likely to have lived at home during the time that they attended the R.T.E. program. This factor may be solely as a result of the fact that parents could forward the questionnaire to their offspring if they were no longer living at home. There were no major differences in diagnosis, medication, or previous work experience.

This comparison suggests that there is a bias in favor of more highly functioning former students responding to the follow-up questionnaire. While the return rate of 39 percent attained from the follow-up population is quite respectable for mailed questionnaires, this sample is not representative of the entire population of R.T.E. students. Nevertheless, the follow-up component of this study is an important element given the previously mentioned research that has suggested that clients in mental health programs do well until the programs stop (Test, 1981).

FINDINGS AND DISCUSSION

The scores of the 26 current students, all of whom graduated from the program, were included in a repeated measures analysis of variance. In the repeated measures comparison of current R.T.E. students ($N = 26$), significant positive changes were found between Week 1 and Week 20 on three of the four objectives measured: self-esteem ($p < .01$), social adjustment ($p < .05$), and level of functioning (rated by the R.T.E. counselors) ($p < .01$). The change in the satisfaction with life domains was not significant (see Table G-1).

To compare the current R.T.E. students with the former students who answered the follow-up questionnaire, independent *t*-tests were performed on scores from all students at Week 1 of the R.T.E. program (62 of the total 77 students completed the measures in Week 1) with the 44 former students who responded to the follow-up questionnaire (see Table G-2). A *t*-test resulted in significant differences on all three objectives measured at follow-up: self-esteem ($p < .001$), social adjustment ($p < .01$), and satisfaction with life domains ($p < .05$).

Although the comparisons in these results cannot be interpreted with as much confidence as the repeated measures analysis of current students, since two different groups of students are involved, they support the idea that R.T.E. students make positive changes while in the program that are maintained after the program.

Self-Esteem (Objective 1)

The normative score of adults aged twenty to thirty-four on the Coopersmith Self-Esteem Index is 76, with a standard deviation of 18.8 (Coopersmith, 1988). At Week 1 of the R.T.E. program, the students had average scores of 45, clearly much lower than the normative group. Although these scores significantly increased by follow-up (mean = 60.5), they are still lower than the norm. R.T.E. students significantly increased their self-esteem as they progressed through the program ($p < .01$). In addition, the average self-esteem score for the follow-up students was significantly greater ($p < .001$) than for the current group of students at Week 1 of the R.T.E. program.

TABLE G-1 MEAN SCORE COMPARISON OF CURRENT R.T.E. STUDENTS FOR WEEK 1 AND WEEK 20 ($N = 26$)

Objective	Week 1	Week 20	*p*
1. Self-esteem (range 0 - 100)	45.0	56.3	.01
2. Social adjustment (range 1 - 5)	2.4	2.2	.05
3. Level of functioning (range 1 - 9)	6.0	6.8	.01
4. Life Satisfaction (range 1 - 105)	67.7	69.3	NS

Social Adjustment (Objective 2)

R.T.E. students made significant improvements in their social adjustment from the beginning to the end of the program. Since the majority of R.T.E. students were not married, and had no children, there were few responses to these two subscales. Current R.T.E. students were not working, with the exception of three who were in a job placement as part of R.T.E. program. The small number of respondents in these areas made the three subscale scores uninterpretable.

The two role areas that were characterized by the most difficulty, irrespective of the time of assessment, were the Social & Leisure and the Economic subscales. In responding to questions about social and leisure activities at the start of the

TABLE G-2 MEAN SCORE COMPARISONS OF CURRENT R.T.E. STUDENTS AT WEEK 1 AND FORMER R.T.E. STUDENTS AT FOLLOW-UP

Objective	Current ($N = 26$)	Former ($N = 44$)	Difference	*p*
1. Self-esteem (range 0 - 100)	45.0	60.5	15.5	.001
2. Social adjustment (range 1 - 5)	2.4	2.0	-.4	.01
3. Level of functioning (range 1 - 9)	5.6	NA	NA	-
4. Life satisfaction (range 1 - 105)	69.0	75.6	6.6	.05

NA = Staff unable to rate level of functioning for former R.T.E. students at follow-up

R.T.E. program, 16 percent of the 62 students ($N = 10$) indicated that they had no friends. Looking only at the students who were included in the repeated measures analysis, at the beginning of R.T.E. 38 percent said they had no friends or only one friend. By the end of the program, 71 percent (as compared to 8% in Week 1) of the same group, reported that they had nine or more friends; not one student reported having no friends or only one. This is a significant change in individuals for whom social interaction is typically very difficult.

Level of Functioning (Objective 3)

On the average, all students who began the R.T.E. program were functioning in mid-level 5 on the Level of Functioning Scale. Level 5 indicates that emotional stability and stress tolerance are sufficiently low that successful functioning in the social, vocational, and educational realms is marginal (Carter & Newman, 1976). Perhaps not surprisingly, when one looks at the scores of students who completed all three ongoing assessments in the study, the average level of functioning started at level 6. In level 6, the person's vocational and social areas of functioning are stabilized, but only because of direct therapeutic intervention. For students who completed the R.T.E. program the average level of functioning rose to 6.8 by the end of Week 20. Level 7 indicates that the person is functioning and coping well socially and vocationally; however, symptom reoccurrences are sufficiently frequent to necessitate some form of regular therapeutic intervention. The staff clearly perceived changes in students as they progressed through the program that paralleled the changes that the students themselves reported.

Life Satisfaction (Objective 4)

There are no established norms for the Satisfaction with Life Domain Scale. In comparison to Baker and Intagliata's (1982) community group of chronic mental health clients ($N = 118$), R.T.E. students were less satisfied on all items at the start of the program. The follow-up participants more closely approximated the levels of satisfaction obtained in Baker and Intagliata's study.

R.T.E. students ranked most areas on the Satisfaction with Life Domains Scale in the "mixed" to "mostly satisfied" range. The lowest area of satisfaction, irrespective of time tested, was feelings about one's economic situation, which were consistently in the "mostly dissatisfied" range. There were no significant improvements in satisfaction with life domains as students progressed through the R.T.E. program. However, twenty weeks is a relatively brief period of time in which to make changes that could result in significant changes to the general quality of life. R.T.E. participants are, after all, students, mostly financed through government assistance. Since many of the domains are influenced by income level (i.e., satisfaction with food, clothes, and housing), one might expect to find an improved quality of life after the program, when graduates are more likely to be working. Such an improvement was demonstrated in the comparison of follow-up students to students at the beginning of the R.T.E. program.

Employment and Education (Objective 5)

Of the former R.T.E. students who responded to the follow-up questionnaire, 35 percent were employed either full- or part-time at the time of the survey (of the 35% who were working, about half worked full-time). Over half (57%) of the R.T.E. students who responded to the survey had worked at some time since completing the R.T.E. program.

One method of interpreting the significance of these levels of employment is to compare them with the most commonly cited employment statistics (Anthony et al., 1978), based on American populations of psychiatric patients in the community. Compiled from a review of studies from 1960–1966, Anthony and colleagues calculated that employment rates after discharge from hospital appear to fall between 20 to 30 percent, regardless of the time period sampled. During a further review in 1978, Anthony and colleagues suggested that the previous rate of post-hospital employment was likely an overestimate and that a more accurate range would be 10–30 percent employed at follow-up.

The R.T.E. employment rate for previous students from six months to four years after attending the program was 35 percent, which is slightly better than Anthony's "best case scenario." However, in the two decades since Anthony's 1972 article was published, significant changes such as massive deinstitutionalization of psychiatric patients have occurred. Another crucial change is the identification of the young adult chronic patient. As compared to older chronic psychiatric clients, these younger individuals consistently display greater difficulty in the domains of psychiatric symptoms, daily living skills, behavior problems, social isolation, and alcohol and drug abuse problems (Sheets et al., 1982). These changes suggest that Anthony's statistics may, in fact, overestimate how many of the current community sample should be expected to be working, since many will be functioning with more difficulty in the community than the past population.

Another appropriate comparison is based on employment statistics from recent Canadian studies. In a Montreal study, for example, only 5–6 percent of the participants were working (O'Loughlin, Laurendeau, & Gagnon, 1989). In a study in Hamilton, Ontario (Kearns et al., 1987), only 21 percent of 66 clients were working in any regular fashion, but half of these were employed in sheltered workshops. In comparison to these more regionally appropriate employment statistics, the 35 percent employed rate of former R.T.E. students is impressive, even considering the probable bias in that those who returned the evaluation forms were likely among the most highly functioning students.

Perhaps the most striking change for R.T.E. students was in their sources of

TABLE G-3 PERCENTAGE INCOME SOURCES OF FORMER STUDENTS BEFORE AND AFTER THE R.T.E. PROGRAM ($N = 44$)

Income Sources	Before	After	Difference
Employment	0.0	35.6	35.6
Welfare	47.8	13.3	34.5
Family Benefits	10.9	28.9	18.0
Family Support	19.6	4.4	15.2
Disability Pension	6.5	6.7	0.2
Unemployment Insurance	6.5	8.9	2.4
Training Allowance	0.0	2.2	2.2
Personal Savings	6.5	0.0	6.5

income. Before attending the R.T.E. program none of the 197 students on file were receiving income from employment. Sixty-three percent received welfare or family benefits. Another 20 percent received financial support from their families, 6.6 percent were on a disability pension, 4.1 percent received Unemployment Insurance Benefits and a final 4.1 percent had personal savings. A more direct comparison can be obtained from statistics on the former R.T.E. students ($N = 44$) who responded to the follow-up questionnaire.

It is remarkable that, compared to results before the R.T.E. program, when none of the students on file had been working, after the R.T.E. program 35.5 percent were earning income through full- or part-time employment. The number receiving either welfare or family benefits dropped from 59 percent to 42 percent. In comparison, Kearns et al.'s (1987) study in Hamilton, Ontario, reported that 78 percent of participants received either welfare or family benefits; whereas 72 percent of O'Loughlin et al's (1989) Montreal participants relied on government benefits.

Not apparent from these statistics is the fact that those R.T.E. former students who went on to pursue further full- or part-time education are still, for the moment, primarily being financed through government assistance. However, when they complete their course work and find employment, the number receiving social assistance should decrease. The advantage to society of having individuals working rather than receiving social assistance is considerable (Walsh, 1982).

The jobs of most of those working at follow-up were primarily in the unskilled (74%) and trade/skilled areas (18.5%), as it was when many of the students entered the R.T.E. program. While, at first, the fact that more students were not working in skilled jobs may appear to be a failing, two factors must be considered.

First, most beginning R.T.E. students have not completed high school (71–75%). While the R.T.E. curriculum provides mathematics and English courses, these are for review and are offered in the hope that students will feel more comfortable being in an educational environment. The R.T.E. program has provided the bridge for some students to complete high school through upgrading courses, but many do not advance their formal schooling. Even with a high school degree, most students would be eligible only for unskilled or semi-skilled jobs. Half of the previous R.T.E. students who responded to the follow-up survey (46%) had taken further educational courses, including high school upgrading, community college, or university classes. Fifteen percent of these respondents were students at the time of completing the follow-up questionnaire (not including others who were part-time students in addition to working). In total, 50 percent of the previous R.T.E. students were either working or were students.

Second, the ongoing difficulties related to a chronic psychiatric condition cannot be discounted. For many R.T.E. program graduates, simply having a job, be it full- or part-time, is a major accomplishment. Weissman, Prusoff, Thompson, Harding, and Meyers (1978) cited an example of a young man with schizophrenia who had a college degree but was working full-time and regularly at an unskilled and low-paying job. He was doing well at the job and felt successful. However, his family felt that he was not living up to their expectations because of his education and ability. One might question whose criterion should be considered to judge how successfully the young man is functioning. Weissman and colleagues contend that individuals' progress must be considered in the context of their psychiatric disability and personal aspirations, rather than on the basis of their educational qualifications.

Student Satisfaction with the R.T.E. Program (Objective 6)

Students were asked to respond to three questions regarding their satisfaction with the R.T.E. program. Both recent and previous R.T.E. students reported almost identical satisfaction with the program. A majority of students (65%) felt that all or most of their needs had been met. Eighty-two percent stated that they were very or mostly satisfied with the program and 89 percent that they would most likely recommend the program if a friend were in need of similar help. This is a clear positive endorsement of the R.T.E. program from its alumni.

SUMMARY AND CONCLUSIONS

As they enter the R.T.E. program, students are experiencing severe difficulty with social adjustment—moreso than the reported normative information on psychiatrically disabled clients living in the community (Weissman & Bothwell, 1976). R.T.E. students fit the description of "young adult chronic patients" who experience more difficulty coping in the community than previous groups of the psychiatrically disabled (Sheets et al., 1982). The evaluation measures utilized in the present study were chosen to correspond with the key objectives of R.T.E.

students and staff.

This study demonstrated significant increases in self-esteem as students progressed through the program. The group of previous students demonstrated significantly higher levels of self-esteem than the group of students entering the R.T.E. program.

The study found significant increases in social adjustment in both students who were progressing through the program, and in a comparison of students at the start of R.T.E. and previous students. The follow-up responses showed significantly healthier scores than the population of students referred to R.T.E. on all objectives: self-esteem, social adjustment, and satisfaction with life domains. The students made friends in the program, an important accomplishment. Staff ratings confirmed that the students' level of functioning significantly increased during the program.

Over 50 percent of previous students were either working or continuing their education at follow-up. Although the jobs were often unskilled and both part- as well as full-time, 35 percent of these follow-up participants were earning income from employment, whereas none were working at the start of the R.T.E. program. Forty-six percent of students had taken further educational courses subsequent to attending the R.T.E. program, including high school upgrading, community college, or university classes.

Two research design limitations prevent an unequivocal endorsement of the program on the basis of this study. The lack of a comparison group with which to contrast the current students as they progressed through the program leaves open the possibility that individual scores may have improved without participation in the R.T.E. program. However, the fact that chosen measures had demonstrated test-retest reliability (that is, scores do not improve simply because one responds to the test a second time) adds reassurance that the improvement in scores is because of participation in the program. The consistency of the improvement between the different measures and in comparing both the students' view and the staff's perception of the students, adds further weight to the validity of the obtained results.

The second limitation, that the 39 percent of former R.T.E. students who responded to the follow-up questionnaire were likely biased in favor of better-functioning individuals, is more difficult to dismiss. In comparing the general characteristics of those who responded to those who did not, respondents were more likely to have graduated from the program and had higher levels of education before they attended the R.T.E. program, although no major differences in diagnosis or previous work experience were noted. On the basis of these characteristics, respondents who completed the follow-up questionnaire were already a somewhat more successful group upon entry to the R.T.E. program. Therefore, in interpreting the results from the respondents of the follow-up questionnaire, it should be remembered that these represent some of the most successful R.T.E. students.

Having acknowledged these limitations, the study results support the contention that the program objectives are significantly achieved by many of those students who attend the R.T.E. program and who successfully adapt to its format and expectations. Compared to other rehabilitation options for young psychiatric clients, such as day treatment and sheltered workshops, the R.T.E. program is structured, and it demands the ability to attend regularly and to interact with other students and counselors, and the ability to concentrate on school work. One of its main advantages for those who can function at this level is that it closely approximates the potential next step, education or employment. For many of its students, the R.T.E. program acts as a bridge to other programs and opportunities that continue to support their successful reintegration into the community.

REFERENCES

AHMED, S., VALLIANT, P., & SWINDLE, D. (1985). Psychometric properties of Coopersmith Self-Esteem Inventory. *Perceptual and Motor Skills, 61,* 1235-1241.

ANDREWS, F., & WITHEY, S. (1976). *Social indicators of well-being: Americans' perception of life quality.* New York: Plenum Press.

ANTHONY, W., BUELL, G., SHARRATT, S., & ALTHOFF, M. (1972). Psychiatric aftercare clinic effectiveness as a function of patient demographic characteristics. *Journal of Consulting and Clinical Psychology, 41,* 116-119.

ANTHONY, W., COHEN, M. & VITALO, R. (1978). The measurement of rehabilitation outcome. *Schizophrenia Bulletin, 4,* 365-383.

BAKER, F., & INTAGLIATA, J. (1982). Quality of life in the evaluation of community support systems. *Evaluation and Program Planning, 5,* 69-79.

BEARD, J., MALAMUD, T., & ROSSMAN, E. (1978). Psychiatric rehabilitation and long-term rehospitalization rates: The findings of two research studies. *Schizophrenia Bulletin, 4,* 622-635.

CARTER, D., & NEWMAN, F. (1976). *A client-oriented system of mental health service delivery and program management: A workbook and guide (MH Statistical Series C, No. 12).* Rockville, MD: National Institute of Mental Health.

COOPERSMITH, S. (1988). *Coopersmith Self-Esteem Inventories.* Palo Alto, CA: Consulting Psychologists Press.

EDWARDS, D., YARVIS, R., MUELLER, D., ZINGALE, H., & WAGMAN, W. (1978). Test-taking stability of adjustment scales: Can we assess patient deterioration? *Evaluation Quarterly, 2,* 275-291.

FARKAS, M., & ANTHONY, W. (1989). *Psychiatric rehabilitation programs: Putting theory into practice.* Baltimore, MD: John Hopkins University Press.

FISCHER, L., GOERING, P., LANCEE, W., & WASYLENKI, D. (1981). *Psychiatric aftercare in Metropolitan Toronto.* Report prepared for Ontario Ministry of Health.

GREEN, R., & GRACELY, E. (1987). Selecting a rating scale for evaluating services to the chronically mentally ill. *Community Mental Health Journal, 23,* 91-102.

GRINNELL, R.M., JR., & STOTHERS, M. (1988). Utilizing research designs. In R.M. Grinnell, Jr. (Ed.), *Social work research and evaluation* (pp. 199-239, 3rd ed.). Itasca, IL: Peacock.

KEARNS, R., TAYLOR, S., & DEAR, M. (1987). Coping and satisfaction among the chronically mentally disabled. *Canadian Journal of Community Mental Health, 6,* 13-24.

KROWINSKI, W., & FITT, D. (1978). A model for evaluating mental health programs: The functional baseline system. *Administration in Mental Health, 6,* 22-41.

LEHMAN, A. (1983). The effects of psychiatric symptoms on quality of life assessments among the chronically mentally ill. *Evaluation and Program Planning, 3,* 143-151.

NEWMAN, F. (1980). Global scales: Strengths, uses and problems of global scales as an evaluation instrument. *Evaluation and Program Planning, 3,* 257-268.

O'LOUGHLIN, J., LAURENDEAU, M., & GAGNON, G. (1989). English synopsis: An evaluation of a volunteer visitor program for socially isolated adults with chronic mental-health problems. *Canadian Journal of Community Mental Health, 8,* 48-52.

SCHULBERG, H., & BROMET, E. (1981). Strategies for evaluating the outcome of community services for the chronically mentally ill. *American Journal of Psychiatry, 138,* 930-935.

SHEETS, J., PREVOST, J,. & REIHMAN, J. (1982). Young adult chronic patients: Three hypothesized subgroups. *Hospital and Community Psychiatry, 33,* 197-203.

TEST, M. (1981). Effective community treatment of the chronically mentally ill: What is necessary? *Journal of Social Issues, 37,* 71-87.

WALSH, R. (1982). A psycho-educational approach to community intervention with ex-mental patients. *Canadian Journal of Community Mental Health, 1,* 76-84.

WARNER, J., BERMAN, J., WEYANT, J., CIARLO, J. (1983). Assessing mental health program effectiveness: A comparison of three client follow-up methods. *Evaluation Review, 7,* 635-658.

WEISSMAN, M., & BOTHWELL, S. (1976). Assessment of social adjustment by patient self-report. *Archives of General Psychiatry, 33,* 1111-1115.

WEISSMAN, M., PRUSOFF, B., THOMPSON, D., HARDING, P. & MEYERS, J. (1978). Social adjustment by self-report in a community sample and in psychiatric outpatients. *Journal of Nervous and Mental Disease, 166,* 317-326.

WILLER, B., & BIGGIN, P. (1976). Comparison of rehospitalized and nonrehospitalized psychiatric patients on community adjustment: Self assessment guide. *Psychiatry, 39,* 239-244.

Donna M. Phillips
Joseph P. Hornick

Study **H**

An Evaluation of the Psychological Component of a Treatment Program for Homeless Alcoholic Men

FEW STUDIES of homeless male alcoholics include a systematic assessment of their personalities. One such study (Blumberg, Shipley, & Shandler, 1973) found the group had a high degree of social pathology, which would be a severe hindrance to their being accepted as members of a larger community. They also found the men were significantly depressed, and experienced much dissatisfaction with themselves.

Holloway (1970) found the homeless male alcoholic to have an inability to cope with small problems and minor inconveniences, resentment and hatred toward parents, and a longing for affection and sympathy. In summary, this population appears to be psychologically unhealthy, especially in terms of depression and sociopathy.

These studies measured the psychological health of homeless alcoholic men in general. There is an even greater lack of literature that considers the impact of treatment programs on this population's psychological health. It must be emphasized that this research example is only presenting the results of the psychological component (one of three) of the treatment program for a community house for homeless alcoholic men.

PURPOSE OF STUDY

A comprehensive study was initially conducted to test the effectiveness of several aspects of a community house for homeless alcoholic men. Program objectives included improving residents' physical, psychological, and social functioning. These three program components were each evaluated using three separate instruments.

The purpose of this sample evaluation study is to briefly report the findings related to only the program's psychological health component. As existing literature in the area indicates homeless alcoholic men are psychologically less healthy than the general population, it is predicted that residents' psychological health will improve over the course of their stay in the community house.

PROGRAM DESCRIPTION

The community house evaluated in this study is a long-term residence designed to help homeless destitute men. However, as more than 90% of its residents have self-identified alcohol problems, the program has been tailored to meet the needs of homeless alcoholic men. (To protect the anonymity of the agency under evaluation, it will be referred to as the "House.")

The program is based on the premise that, by offering the men a place to live where they are treated with respect and are given support, responsibility, and access to available resources, they will have the opportunity to become responsible and contributing members of society.

The program under evaluation is run by a private, voluntary, nonprofit organization. The services are provided to homeless men of any religion, race, or background. Although most of the residents have chronic drug and/or alcohol problems, this is not a requirement of admission to the program.

The House consists of two adjacent residences with accommodations for 20 men. It has consistently operated at full capacity. The House has four paid staff: a director, and one evening, one night, and one weekend supervisor. The staff perform a number of duties, including: (a) designing and implementing plans for each resident's rehabilitation, (b) giving attention to residents' physical health problems, (c) supervising residents' work programs, (d) arranging social activities, (e) providing informal counseling, (f) arranging referrals to outside agencies, (g) maintaining records, and (h) enforcing house rules. These duties are performed in an environment where a minimum number of rules are in existence. The residents are expected to be responsible for, and deal with, the consequences of their actions.

Figure H-1 on the following page outlines the House's general goals and

Goals:

(1) To help the residents achieve personal fulfilment.
(2) To help the residents become responsible, contributing members of society.

Objectives:	**Activities:**
1.0 To improve psychological functioning.	- provide supportive, home-like atmosphere with minimal rules
1.1 To decrease depression anxiety, guilt, resentment, suspiciousness, psychological inadequacy, and insecurity.	- refer to outside agencies, groups for counseling
	- provide information, counseling, and the opportunity for mutual support

FIGURE H-1 PROGRAM GOALS, PSYCHOLOGICAL HEALTH OBJECTIVES, AND ACTIVITIES

specific psychological health objectives. The column on the right delineates the activities performed by program staff as they attempt to meet these objectives.

METHODOLOGY

This section presents the study's research design, sample, and the measuring instrument that was used to measure the dependent variable.

Research Design

A one-group pretest-posttest design was used to test the participants' movement toward improved psychological health. A standardized measuring instrument was self-administered once ($N = 22$), then again six weeks later ($N = 9$) to evaluate pretest-posttest differences.

Additional analyses compared the psychological profiles of program successes and program failures. Nine participants were characterized as program successes and the remaining thirteen were identified as program failures. An unplanned discharge, characterized by a return to drinking, was identified as a type of program failure. The assignment of participants to "success" and "failure" groups enabled a comparative analysis between those who stayed sober and in the program for an extended period of time (at least 3 months), and those who were unable to stay sober and "dropped out" of the program. This 3-month period of time was chosen as an indicator of program success based on previous research (Katz, 1986; Orford & Hawker, 1974; Rubington, 1970).

Sample and Measuring Instrument

All residents were asked to participate, and all who agreed did so voluntarily. The response rate to the pretesting was consistently 80 percent.

Due to admission criteria of the program, no participants were under 18 years of age, female, or showing signs of severe mental illness or mental incompetence. They had to be capable of climbing stairs. Thus, no severely physically disabled participants took part. Most participants had no other place to live when they requested admission to the House. A few were not destitute in this sense, but they stated they needed a sober environment. The two primary problems identified on the participants' admission were homelessness and alcoholism.

The high rate of sample attrition posed a problem, which is typical in studies of homeless, transient men. Of the 22 participants interviewed, 9 remained at the House for over 6 weeks and thus could be posttested.

Data were collected by the use of a standardized measuring instrument—the Clinical Analysis Questionnaire (CAQ) (Krug & Cattel, 1980). The CAQ questionnaire consists of 272 multiple choice questions which respondents answer about themselves. The CAQ is an instrument that simultaneously measures normal and pathological trait levels and provides a multidimensional profile of the individual. It consists of 28 scales: 16 measure normal personality traits; 7 measure primary manifestations of depression; and 5 measure traits from the MMPI pool. In addition to the 28 primary scales, it is possible to calculate second-order scores. By combining the primary scale scores in certain ways, these second-order scores indicate patterns such as Extroversion, Anxiety, Neuroticism, etc. Figure H-2 outlines the 37 CAQ scales.

FINDINGS AND DISCUSSION

This section presents the study's findings in two broad areas: (1) the comparison of pretest and posttest data, and (2) a comparison of program successes and failures.

Comparison of Pretest and Posttest Data

Due to sample attrition the sample size in the pretest-posttest data, analysis was greatly reduced from 22 to nine participants. A six-week treatment period

Normal Personality Traits	Clinical Factors	Second-Order Factors
A: Warmth	D1: Hypochondriasis	Ex: Extroversion
B: Intelligence	D2: Suicidal depression	Ax: Anxiety
C: Emotional stability	D3: Agitation	Ct: Tough poise
E: Dominance	D4: Anxious depression	In: Independence
F: Impulsivity	D5: Low energy level	Se: Superego
G: Conformity	D6: Guilt & resentment	So: Socialization
H: Boldness	D7: Boredom & withdrawal	D: Depression
I: Sensitivity	Pa: Paranoia	P: Psychoticism
L: Suspiciousness	Pp: Psychopathic deviation	Ne: Neuroticism
M: Imagination	Sc: Schizophrenia	
N: Shrewdness		
O: Insecurity		
Q2: Self-sufficiency		
Q4: Tension		
Q3: Self-discipline		

FIGURE H-2 THE CAQ SCALES

was established, although all participants were in the program for a longer period of time. Results indicate that the group of nine participants progressed in terms of their psychological functioning.

Table H-1 shows that participants' mean posttest scores differ notably from their mean pretest scores on 10 of the 37 CAQ scales. These differences indicate that, at time two, participants were somewhat more dependent (I+, M+), bored (D7+), and tended to be more realistic (Sc-), less sociopathic (Se+), and less depressed (D-) than at time one. They also suggest participants were more mindful of rules (N+, Q3+), although they tended to avoid people more (D3-), and that they were better able to keep their emotions in order (N+, Q3+) and were less apt to have negative feelings of self-worth (Ps-) (Krug & Cattel, 1980).

These changes indicate that the program was successful in decreasing participants' levels of deviance, and in increasing their levels of self-worth. In doing so, the program tended to constrain their independence, which is not unusual in any semi-instructional program. This may have been the only way to positively affect the sociopathy but, once dependent on the program, participants become bored and restless.

Regardless of changes made during the six-week period of the evaluation study, participants' overall psychological profiles remained abnormal, showing high levels of suicidal disgust, anxious depression, guilt and resentment, paranoia, schizophrenia, and general psychosis. This group of men showed a need for

TABLE H-1 PARTICIPANTS' MEAN PRETEST AND POSTTEST CAQ SCORES

CAQ Factors	Pretest	Posttest	Difference	*t*	*p*[1]
Normal sensitivity (I)	5.9	6.7	-.78	1.6	.06
Imagination (M)	5.1	6.3	-1.22	2.2	.03
Shrewdness (N)	6.4	7.4	-1.00	2.0	.04
Self-discipline (Q3)	3.4	4.4	-1.00	1.6	.07
Clinical agitation (D3)	3.7	2.8	.89	1.8	.05
Boredom & withdrawal (D7)	5.6	6.1	-.56	1.2	.12
Schizophrenia (Sc)	9.2	8.8	.44	1.8	.05
Psychological inadequacy (Ps)	8.2	7.4	.78	1.5	.07
Superego strength (Se)	3.7	4.5	-.58	1.4	.09
Depression (D)	7.3	6.7	.59	1.2	.10

[1] One-tailed test

mental health assessment and treatment, as is consistent with previous studies (Blumberg, Shipley, & Shandler, 1973; Holloway, 1970).

Comparison of Program Successes and Failures

Participants were assigned to a "success" group or a "failure" group. Assignment to these groups was based on whether the participant stayed in the program or dropped out, as is described in the methodology section of this report.

No statistically significant differences were found between the successes and failures on the CAQ, although clinically relevant differences were evident on five of the CAQ personality scales (i.e., the suspiciousness, insecurity, tension, quilt and resentment, and anxiety scales). These differing scores on the CAQ scales indicate that the failures were more suspicious, insecure, tense, resentful, and anxious than the successes (Krug & Cattell, 1980). These differing personality traits could explain why a failure (a program dropout) may be more suspecting and less tolerant of a program such as this one, especially in view of his inability to accept criticism.

LIMITATIONS

A major weakness limiting the methodology of this study is the lack of a control or a comparison group. The transient nature of the homeless alcoholic population prevented the formation of a control group, and the lack of a similar program in the Calgary area prevented the formation of a comparison group.

The small sample size ($N = 9$) was a major study limitation. This resulted from both the small program size (the House has room for 20 men) and sample attrition. Further, having a small sample size made it difficult to achieve statistical significance in data analyses.

Forming aggregate CAQ profiles from individual cases resulted in regression toward the mean, causing a minimization of variation. This increased the need to carefully observe and report major trends that were not statistically significant.

Ideally, baseline data should have been collected on all the participants upon their admission to the program, and measurement should have been repeated at six-week intervals throughout their stay. This was not possible due to time limitations.

Participants were the only data source in the study. This has a weakening effect on the methodology, which should be supported by another source such as assessment by a psychologist (Blumburg, Shipley, & Shandler, 1973).

In summary, the major methodological limitations were: lack of a control or comparison group, small sample size, lack of baseline data collected on participants' admission to the program, and data being collected from a single source. These limitations should be considered while viewing the study's results and conclusions.

SUMMARY AND RECOMMENDATIONS

The purpose of this evaluation study was to test the effectiveness of a psychological heath component of a community residence for homeless alcoholic men. The program consisted of a homelike residence supervised by four staff members who provided day and night assistance and informal counseling.

The participants who remained in the program longer than three months and graduated from it ($N = 9$) showed a prolonged improvement in major aspects of their psychological functioning, although their overall level of functioning remained poor. The other client group, the dropouts, could not be posttested. However, Clinical Analysis Questionnaire results showed the dropouts to be more suspicious, insecure, resentful, and generally less tolerant of structured programs than the graduates.

The findings and conclusions of this study have led to a number of recommendations. These recommendations have relevance to both program development and evaluation research in this area. The four recommendations relevant to program development for homeless alcoholic men are:

1. The mental health assessment procedure of applicants to the program should be more rigorous and more clearly defined. This would enable proper screening and referral of those men in need of specific mental health counseling.
2. Program residents should be regularly referred for mental health counseling.
3. Planned activities should be made available for residents, in order to

avoid boredom and withdrawal.

4. Future development should include a final program phase that offers a more autonomous living situation for program graduates who may be somewhat dependent on the program.

In terms of the recommendations for future research in this area, further use of the Clinical Analysis Questionnaire to measure the psychological functioning of homeless alcoholic men should be encouraged. In addition, further evaluation research on programs for homeless alcoholic men is needed, especially research that utilizes control groups and multiple data sources. Lastly, follow-up studies of programs are recommended, to further explore the long-term effects of treatment on homeless alcoholic men.

REFERENCES

BAHR, H. (1969). Lifetime affiliation patterns of elderly and late-onset heavy drinkers on skid row. *Quarterly Journal of Studies on Alcohol, 30*, 645-656.

BAHR, H. (1973). *Skid Row: An introduction to disaffiliation*. New York: Oxford University Press.

BLUMBERG, L., SHIPLEY, T., & SHANDLER, I. (1973). *Skid Row and its alternatives*. Philadelphia, PA: Temple University Press.

COOK, T. (1975). *Vagrant alcoholics*. London, England: Routledge & Kegan Paul.

HOLLOWAY, J. (1970). *They can't fit in*. London, England: Blackfriars Press.

KATZ, L. (1966). The Salvation Army men's social service center results. *Studies on Alcohol, 27*, 636-647.

KRUG, S.E., & CATTELL, R.B. (1980). *Clinical analysis questionnaire manual*. Champaign, IL: Institute for Personality and Ability Testing, Inc.

ORFORD, J., & HAWKER, A. (1974). An investigation of an alcoholism rehabilitation halfway house: The complex question of client motivation. *British Journal of Addictions, 69*, 315-323.

RUBINGTON, E. (1970). Referral, past treatment contacts, and length of stay in a halfway house. *Quarterly Journal of Studies on Alcohol, 31*, 659-668.

Karen J. Suk
Michael A. Rothery

Study I

How Mothers Support Their Pregnant and Parenting Teenage Daughters

IN SPITE OF DECLINING BIRTH RATES, the impact of pregnancy and parenting on adolescent women is a major cause for concern. Although teenage pregnancy is not a new phenomenon, the number of adolescents opting to parent their children has dramatically increased. These teenage mothers are at risk for a variety of physical, social, educational, and economic problems, including unstable partner relationships, difficulties with child-rearing, high school non-completion, lack of skills, and unemployment (Seaborn-Thompson, 1986; Wise & Grossman, 1980). Other problems associated with teen parenthood are isolation, conflict with peers, families, and community agencies, damage to self-esteem and personal effectiveness, and a high risk of depression (Barth, Schinke, & Maxwell, 1985; Seaborn-Thompson, 1986; Sherman & Donovan, 1991; Unger & Wandersman, 1988).

Social support, the affective and material resources provided through one's social network, has consistently been shown to have a buffering effect on the many negative consequences associated with adolescent parenting (Barth,

Schinke, & Maxwell, 1985; Seaborn-Thompson, 1986; Unger & Wandersman, 1988). Social support has been correlated with fewer pregnancy-related complications, and has benefits for the health of the child and the mother's educational and occupational future. The provision of support during the course of a teenage pregnancy can promote positive interpersonal functioning, can reduce the strain of pregnancy and teenage motherhood, and is associated with better mental health. High social support is associated with positive self-regard and lowered stress, which, in turn, is thought to improve maternal attitudes and behavior (Barth, Schinke & Maxwell, 1985; Turner, Grindstaff, & Phillips, 1990). Barrera (1981) reports that pregnant adolescents' satisfaction with the support they receive appears to be a good predictor of emotional symptomatology, especially depression.

Pregnant and parenting adolescents use a range of people for support: friends, the fathers of their babies, and, of course, their families. The data reported in this article focus on the last potential source of support, specifically the teens' mothers. Teenage women are at a developmental stage where their relationships with their mothers are likely to be important, and both clinical and research evidence suggests that this is an important potentially supportive relationship to understand when considering the teenage mother's resources.

RESEARCH QUESTIONS

The research questions guiding this study were:

1. What kinds of social support do pregnant and parenting adolescents receive from their mothers?
2. Does the type and level of social support teens receive from their mothers appear to change after the birth of the baby—i.e., do pregnant and parenting teens differ in this respect?

METHOD

Sample Selection

Forty-four research participants (20 pregnant, 24 parenting) were recruited from a school-based Pregnant and Parenting Adolescent Program serving a western Canadian city. Notices outlining the purpose of the study were circulated to the professionals involved with the adolescents, along with a request for volunteers. All potential subjects were approached individually, either after having indicated an interest in participating or if their social worker suggested their names, and informed consents were obtained. All subjects were interviewed individually, in their homes or the school setting.

Sample Characteristics

The average age of the sample was 18 years. Eighty-five percent of the pregnant adolescents lived with their parent(s), compared to 20.8 percent of the parenting adolescent mothers. Forty-six percent of the parenting adolescents lived independently, compared to none of the pregnant adolescents interviewed.

Operationalization

The instrument utilized in this study was the Arizona Social Support Interview Schedule (ASSIS), designed by Barrera (1981). The ASSIS provides a method for subjects to identify individuals who provide a range of different types of support (or "support functions"): (1) material aid (e.g., goods, financial help); (2) physical assistance (e.g., help with the practicalities of life such as transportation, child care); (3) intimate interaction; (4) advice or guidance; (5) feedback; and (6) social participation. In addition, the ASSIS identifies those social network members who are both a source of support and a source of interpersonal conflict. Because "social participation" is much more relevant to relationships with friends than parents, it will not be included in the findings for this article.

The ASSIS was chosen because the types of support it measures and its ability to assess levels of conflict associated with supportive relationships are congruent with what the researcher considered theoretically relevant to the population studied. Also, the ASSIS measures support in two important but different ways: (1) Does the subject *perceive* that she receives a particular kind of support through a particular relationship, and (2) Can she report *actually* having received such support in the month prior to the interview?

Limitations

Because participation in the study was voluntary, no information could be gained respecting those who chose not to participate. The cross-sectional design also did not allow for establishing the comparability of the two groups with respect to factors other than pregnancy or childbirth so it cannot be confidently stated that differences between the two groups are due primarily to their difference in status.

Also, since the sample was a nonrandom, availability sample, it is unclear as to how generalizable the results are. Clearly, the way family relationships are used for support under different circumstances varies culturally, and applying conclusions from this research to culturally diverse groups should be undertaken very tentatively, if at all.

RESULTS

Relationship of Sample to Their Mothers

The numbers of young women in the total sample who perceive that their mothers are a source of support is high for all five of the types of support included in the analysis; equally high is the number who perceive their relationship with their mothers as a potential source of conflict. The strong importance of mothers to teenage daughters as they become mothers themselves is therefore verified by our data. The relationship is obviously one that is meaningful and emotionally charged (positively and perhaps also negatively) for the majority of the sample.

There is a consistent discrepancy whereby the young women were able to report *actual* support provision less frequently than they indicated that their mothers were *perceived* as supportive. This may be, in part, valid—a young woman may know that her mother is available to provide material aid, for example, without having actually accessed help of that kind in the past month. Still, the strong discrepancy between perceived and actual support for functions like "intimate interaction" and "advice" is noteworthy, since when these characterize a relationship they tend to be an ongoing feature of it.

The findings also indicate that pregnant and parenting adolescents are very different in their reports of the support available to them from their mothers—pregnant adolescents reported receiving support from their mothers more frequently than did parenting adolescents, with reference to both *perceived* and *actual* supports. These differences are significant for four of the support types examined: intimate interaction, material aid, advice, and positive feedback. Interestingly, the perceived potential for conflict was also significantly less for parenting adolescents, although actual reported frequency of conflictual involvement was not (a difference exists in a congruent direction, but it is not statistically significant).

DISCUSSION

Teenage pregnancy often represents a crisis for the individual woman and her family (Dunst, Vance, & Cooper, 1986). Teenage pregnancy has been viewed at times as an opportunity for a family to reduce role ambiguity during times of transition; also the crisis of teenage pregnancy often serves to draw families together (Buchholz & Gol, 1986). It has also been hypothesized that pregnancy temporarily raises the status of the young woman in her family (Buchholz & Gol, 1986). The pregnancy seems to represent a time of high support from family members for the adolescent that may or may not have been present earlier.

Crnic and Greenberg (1987) highlight the importance of intimate support as it relates to parents' general life satisfaction when their babies were one, four, and eight months old. The lack of any meaningful intimate support perceived by

TABLE I-1 SUPPORT FROM MOTHERS

Type of Support	Total Sample (%) $N = 44$	Pregnant (%) $n = 20$	Parents (%) $n = 24$	χ^2 Value
Material Aid				
Perceived	72	90	58	5.5[a]
Actual	50	75	29	9.2[b]
Physical				
Perceived	55	65	46	1.6
Actual	50	65	38	3.3
Intimate				
Perceived	53	75	33	7.6[a]
Actual	39	65	17	10.8[b]
Advice				
Perceived	64	80	50	4.2[a]
Actual	50	60	42	1.5
Feedback				
Perceived	59	80	42	6.6[a]
Actual	52	75	33	7.6[a]
Conflict				
Perceived	64	80	50	4.2[a]
Actual	52	65	42	2.4

[a] = statistically significant at $p \leq .05$
[b] = statistically significant at $p \leq .01$

parenting adolescents from their mothers in this sample is disconcerting, especially for those adolescents who do not experience a great deal of support from other sources. Some researchers such as Seaborn-Thompson (1986) have referred to the first six months of the baby's life as the "honeymoon" period for the adolescent mother and her child, where the infants are relatively less demanding and family support for the young mother is at its maximum. Seaborn-Thompson (1986) suggests that family support often decreases just as the child is becoming more demanding.

Reasons for this change may include an effort by the young mother to reduce feelings of indebtedness, by no longer accepting a needed benefit or by slowly distancing herself from those who provide the most help. Also, mothers of the teens may tire of providing aid when their daughters' ability to reciprocate is constrained. An imbalance in supportive exchanges, over an extended period of time, is almost certain to threaten or at least strain even close relationships

(Schumaker & Brownell, 1984).

The differing reports of support from mothers by pregnant and parenting adolescents in this study generate many more questions for future research studies. If support from mothers decreases over time, one may ask what the impact of this on the young mother will be. What causes the support from mothers to decrease for so many teenage mothers? Does the continued need for support by their daughters lead to a type of burnout on the mothers' part? Do the support needs of parenting adolescents change over time, in such a way that it is more difficult for their families to support them? Is the process of providing and receiving support affected by other relationships, such as a relationship with a boyfriend or friends? Are these young women trying to become independent and therefore feeling reluctant to depend on their mothers?

If part of the struggle for these young women is due to the developmental stage they are in, the presence of conflict with their mothers may not be surprising. However, the parenting adolescents in this sample experienced no significantly more or less *actual* conflict with their mothers than the pregnant adolescents did, in spite of the fact that the pregnant adolescents *perceived* their mothers more often as a potential source of interpersonal conflict. Again this generates more questions for further research. What is the meaning of the conflict to both the mothers and the daughters in this sample? Is mother-daughter conflict an inherent part of such relationships during adolescence, regardless of the pregnancy and early child-rearing of these young women? Is the high number of adolescent parents who live away from home the result of the conflict experienced with their mothers and families during pregnancy?

Although the presence of interpersonal conflict with mothers figured largely in this sample, its meaning or impact on the young mother, the child, and the grandmother cannot be determined. Qualitative research, which could examine the meaning of the relationship to the different individuals, would greatly enhance our understanding of the impact of relationships that are both supportive and at times stress producing.

Finally, much interest has been generated in the past several years in examining social support as a process, and in including at least two perspectives of supportive exchanges within the research design (Pierce, Sarason, & Sarason, 1990; Schumaker & Brownell, 1984). The impact of teenage pregnancy and parenting on the mothers of these young women and their perception of how it has affected their relationships with their daughters would clearly enhance our understanding, not only of social support as an exchange process, but of the impact of such a life event on mother-daughter relationships.

REFERENCES

BARRERA, M. JR. (1981). Social support in the adjustment of pregnant adolescents. In B.H. Gottlieb (Ed.), *Social networks and social support* (pp. 11-42). Newbury Park, CA: Sage.

BARTH, R.P., SCHINKE, S.P., & MAXWELL, J.S. (1985). Coping skills training for school age mothers. *Journal of Social Service Research, 8*, 75-94.

BUCHHOLZ, E.S., & GOL, B. (1986). More than playing house: a developmental perspective on the strengths in teenage motherhood. *American Journal of Orthopsychiatry, 56*, 347-359.

CRNIC, K., & GREENBERG, M. (1987). Maternal stress, social support and coping: Influences on the early mother-infant relationship. In C.F.Z. Boukydis (Ed.), *Research on support for parents and infants in the postnatal period* (pp. 25-40). Norwood, NJ: Ablex Publishing.

DUNST, C.J., VANCE, S.D., & COOPER, C.S. (1986). A social systems perspective of adolescent pregnancy: determinants of parent and parent child behaviour. *Infant Mental Health Journal, 7*, 34-48.

PIERCE, G.R., SARASON, B.R., & SARASON, I.G. (1990). Integrating social support perspectives, working models, personal relationships and situational factors. In S. Duck & R.C. Silverman (Eds.), *Personal relationships and social support* (pp.173-189). London: Sage.

SCHUMAKER, S.A., & BROWNELL, A. (1984). Towards a theory of social support: Closing conceptual gaps. *Journal of Social Issues, 40*, 11-36.

SEABORN-THOMPSON, M.S. (1986). The influence of supportive relations on the psychological well-being of teenage mothers. *Social Forces, 64*, 1006-1024.

SHERMAN, B.R., & DONOVAN, B.R. (1991). Relationship of perceived maternal acceptance-rejection in childhood and social support networks of pregnant adolescents. *American Journal of Orthopsychiatry, 61*, 103-113.

TURNER, R.J., GRINDSTAFF, C.F., & PHILLIPS, N. (1990). Social support and outcome in teenage pregnancy. *Journal of Health and Social Behaviour, 31*, 43-57.

UNGER, D.G., & WANDERSMAN, P. (1988). The relation of family and partner support to the adjustment of adolescent mothers. *Child Development, 59*, 1056-1060.

WISE, S., & GROSSMAN, F.K. (1980). Adolescent mothers and their infants: Psychological factors in early attachment and interaction. *American Journal of Orthopsychiatry, 50*, 454-468.

Barbara Thomlison
Michael A. Rothery

Study J

What Clients Can Tell Us About the Helping Process

THE GRINNELL (1997) TEXT argues that both quantitative and qualitative research methods have a contribution to make to the advancement of social work knowledge. Where the researcher's interest is in understanding subtleties about social work relationships or the subjective experience of clients and workers involved in the helping process, qualitative research may be the method of choice. This is because it has evolved as an approach intended to gather information about the complex meanings that events have for people without prejudging how they should be conceptualized and measured.

Our study employed a qualitative approach in an effort to better understand what it is like to be a social worker's client. More specifically, we examine the subjective experience of four women receiving social services from social workers in a child protection agency.

LITERATURE REVIEW

While some qualitative researchers recommend against reviewing the literature about a problem at least until after data are gathered and analyzed, others recommend flexibility in this regard (Miles & Huberman, 1984). The present study took the more conservative approach of reviewing other related research before approaching clients to be interviewed. Four earlier qualitative inquiries that focused on client's perceptions and the process of helping were found.

Mayer and Timms (1970) examined working class women's experiences with a voluntary family service agency, and documented a problem with incongruence between clients' and workers' goals. Whereas clients came to the agency seeking concrete assistance, workers' agendas emphasized insight therapy.

Maluccio (1979) examined workers' and clients' expectations about each other. Qualities of the client that workers value positively include sincerity, openness, responsiveness, ability to risk, and capacity to establish relationships. Clients characterize the ideal worker as someone who is warm, accepting, understanding, involved, natural, genuine, competent, and able to share.

Forman (1982) conducted an ethnographic study of two impoverished women which challenged common myths and stereotypes regarding single motherhood (that they are crisis prone and that this characterizes their parenting, for example).

Corby (1988) conducted a four-year study of the social workers investigating families suspected of child abuse. While the worker-client relationship was generally perceived as helpful, Corby found that clients were poorly informed regarding how workers perceived them. Also, the views of these involuntary clients were frequently discounted, and a power imbalance whereby the worker had primary control of the helping process was often apparent.

RESEARCH QUESTION

As in the four studies introduced above, the focus of the present study was on the social work relationship. Specifically, we were interested in what clients of a child protection agency experienced in their relationship with their social workers.[1]

STUDY PARTICIPANTS

A large urban child protection agency was approached, and management agreed to let the study proceed at that site following a review of the proposed methods, ethical considerations, and potential benefits. A letter introducing the study was sent to all child protection workers in the agency; of those who volunteered their assistance, two workers were selected who facilitated contact with two clients each. The four client research participants chosen in this way were women who had been involved with the agency for a minimum of two years. Three had children in foster care, one had placed a child for adoption, and two had been in foster care themselves as children.

DATA COLLECTION

Prior to each interview, we made a practice of writing notes in a field work journal describing our own experiences, ideas, thoughts and observations for each situation. The field work journal included many aspects of meeting, interviewing, and leaving the participants, and served as an important supplement to the data from the interviews themselves.

An inquiry interview was employed, using a modification of Spradley's (1979) ethnographic interview format, which relies on descriptive questioning. No specific interview schedule was developed, though participants were approached with a general focus and goal in mind, which was to have them recall and describe ideas, images, thoughts, and experiences regarding child protection social workers.

The interviews were held in the clients' homes, and began with introductions and setting up audio recording equipment (for which prior approval had been obtained). The question that launched the formal data collection was a general one: "Can you tell me about your experience with social workers?"

Analytic questions, which seek an explanation for events were avoided; instead, clients were asked to provide a detailed *description* of their experiences of social workers. For example, rather than asking a client what they found "helpful," we asked the clients to recall specific social worker activities, and how these were experienced when they occurred.

As the participants began identifying experiences or issues that were of interest to them, they would be asked for considerable amounts of descriptive detail about the events or issues and about their own reactions to them. For example, when the participants commented that they could tell at first contact what a worker would be like, they were encouraged to elaborate on that through various probes:

"What do you mean by that?"

"What are some of the things you see that tell you what a worker will be like?"

"Can you give me an example of when you first met a worker and knew instinctively what he or she would be like?"

"What exactly did you notice that seemed important?"

"How did this affect you?"

Pursuing issues in this way, developing a number of detailed examples for each, was a demanding process. Interviews lasted about three hours, and produced a formidable volume of data.

DATA REDUCTION AND ANALYSIS

A complete audiotape was made of each interview and was subsequently transcribed. The transcripts were analyzed using well-established qualitative data processing methods (Kirk & Miller, 1986; Lincoln & Guba, 1981).

Unitizing

The first step in data reduction was unitizing, or breaking information down into the smallest meaningful units of information that could stand by themselves—a "small piece of news" as experienced by the client. Typical examples were: "You need a shoulder to cry on," or "Some workers want to know everything about you."

Each transcript was read numerous times, with units being highlighted and marginal notes made about them without regard for patterns or themes. Subsequently the units and notes related to them were transcribed onto index cards (one card per unit for a total of 412 cards).

Analytical Memos

The notes associated with units were essentially analytical memos, or comments written by us to capture their thoughts about the data. These could be initial analytical impressions as to what the unit may be an example of: "Client is adopting professional jargon" or "Client observes worker's style of dress as an indicator of potential difficulty." Notes might also be questions that flag units requiring further thought: "What does this mean?" or "Is this important?" Alternatively, notes could record developing thoughts about how units relate to one another, or to observations recorded earlier in the field work journal.

Categorization

The next important step in the analysis was to classify the units into categories. Cards that appeared to belong together were sorted into batches. These preliminary decisions were then evaluated, pushing ourselves to specify similarities and differences clearly: Why did units in one batch belong together, and what was it that differentiated one batch (category) from another?

TABLE J-1 SUMMARY CATEGORIES FROM CLIENT INTERVIEWS

Client Motivation	Worker Empathy	Worker Authority	Trust
Self-determination	Support	Authority over parent	Need for trust
Women's history	Genuineness	Authority over child	
Child's situation	Friendship	Judgmental	
Parent–child care situation	Advocacy		

Resorting

The quest for clarity about similarities and differences resulted in extensive resorting. Categories were combined when this could be done without losing information (the ability to make essential distinctions). The quest for clarity also led to a conceptual understanding about what the categories meant, or about the underlying logic that suggested clustering units in particular ways.

Identification of Themes

Whereas the initial sorting of the cards produced well over 30 categories, the process of clarification and resorting reduced these to 12. Just as units had been grouped into categories, these categories could be grouped, on the basis of similarities and differences, under four general unifying themes (as presented in Table J-1), which will be discussed further in the section on Findings, below.

Some brief examples may help to clarify the analysis, though they will vastly oversimplify a long and difficult process. The participant statement "you need a shoulder to cry on" was identified as a meaning unit. When it was grouped together with similar units, a category labeled "support" was established that consisted of all comments by clients indicating that they looked to the worker for emotional support. Units similar to the comment "I ask her about her holiday...we talk back and forth" were eventually grouped together into a "friendship" category. These two categories, "support" and "friendship," along with two additional kindred categories ("genuineness" and "advocacy") were ultimately themselves grouped together under a general theme—a category of categories labeled "Worker Empathy"—as it became clear to us that the importance of workers' sympathetic understanding and support was a theme that ran through all four groupings.

FINDINGS

Twelve categories and four general themes (presented in Table J-1) were derived from the original 412 units. Client Motivation, Worker Empathy, and Worker Authority emerged as key aspects of the worker-client relationship. Trust seemed highly related to the other themes, but captured something in addition—a quality of the clients' belief systems respecting their workers.

Client Motivation

An unexpected finding in the study was the importance clients gave to their own sense of motivation. The importance of motivation as perceived by the social worker or therapist is well documented (Maluccio, 1979). However, statements regarding the client's awareness of the amount of control they have over their situation are rare.

All participants in this study emphasized their own desire for service as a key ingredient in the worker-client relationship. This theme comprised four different categories: self-determination, women's history of problems, child's situation and problems, and parent–child care situation.

Self-Determination

All clients unanimously reported that their own willingness to get service was central to a successful relationship with the worker. Although these women had not been voluntarily involved with child welfare services, all four discussed how they felt they had either initiated contact, or at least had "explained to (the worker) what the problem was." Clients also felt that they could have had a different worker if they had wanted to: "I'm picky about what worker I get." Some informants talked about how they started to like a worker because "she wasn't pushy" or because she had "given me a choice...(about her) coming around." Generally, clients disliked workers who were too "nosy" or too "bossy." "If I'm going to do something I'm going to do it in my own time." "Don't tell me when to do it." The crucial importance of the client's willingness to participate is best expressed by one woman: "It has to come from both sides and it cannot all come from the worker's side and you turn around and reject everything."

Women's History of Problems

Within the first few minutes of each interview, all informants made at least one statement about their own background in relation to their present involvement with the agency. Comments included historical, positive and negative accounts of involvement with the agency (two clients had negative childhood memories about being in the agency, another had her first child removed by child welfare). Clients commented about the circumstances that existed when they first became involved with child protection: "I was used to getting punches"; "I was having problems with medication"; "I didn't even have a place to live."

Although clients felt their own backgrounds were an important factor, all four commented on not liking new workers because it meant going over their past, and complained that some workers were too "nosy."

Child's Situation

Discussion about their children's problems usually surfaced later in the interview in the context of talking about what they did with their workers, or what they had wanted their workers to do. Two women had children who had been sexually assaulted and they had expected and received individual help for their daughters, "She goes to the agency for art therapy...it helps her out...she's terrified of men."

The clients also made it clear that child protective services was involved primarily because of the "children's problems," with little ownership of the situation.

Parent–Child Care Situation

Two clients discussed their children's difficult behavior; one parent was frustrated by a worker's attempts to work with her son in their home, "I know it won't work, he needs to be put in care."

Worker Empathy

In describing the workers, informants referred to qualities of support, genuineness, friendship, and advocacy, all of which connected to a generally empathic style on the worker's part.

Support

Clients found workers supportive if they expressed interest, paying "attention to the kids...(as well as) the mother," or by inquiring about someone's health, and by making themselves available after hours. Self-disclosure also was experienced supportively, and workers who shared some aspects of their own lives were appreciated. Sharing personal thoughts and feelings is the skill clients identify as having the strongest association with satisfaction in their relationship to their worker.

Genuineness

Along with the worker's sharing of self, all clients identified worker genuineness as crucial to establishing a good relationship. Clients were cautious about a worker who was "phoney" and two talked about how some workers seem too "textbooked." One woman compared the "unnatural worker to a poor mechanic who may work for hours and still not know what was wrong."

Friendship

The women enjoyed informal friendly conversations, "I ask her about her holiday...we talk back and forth." Because informants often described the ideal worker-client relationship as like a friendship, they were also asked if there were differences between the two. Two of the clients reported that the major differences were that with friends you could "go to parties, go drinking and have fights." A third informant talked about how she preferred workers who dressed informally and did not look rigid "like a school principal," but she also drew a line between informality and friendship: "We don't go out for coffee."

Friendship often tied in with another important theme: consistency. Clients did not like dealing with new and unknown workers: "I don't like talking to a total stranger. They bring up your whole past...A worker you've had for a while, whatever your problem is today, she talks about the problem today."

Advocacy

Clients valued advocacy functions and successfully securing resources as a positive worker behavior. "Your worker's there for you...if any mother is having problems with their kid, call the children's aid. If you need a break or something, children's aid is more than happy before you hit your kid to help you out. They are there for you." "They can get you housing and things." "Say someone needed an operation on their mouth or something, their teeth were all screwed up and dental assistance didn't cover it and you had a children's aid worker and you told her it doesn't cover it and all that—she would help you out and pay for the bill."

Worker Authority

An important theme throughout all client interviews was the perception of power and authority possessed by the workers, with three categories being apparent: authority over the parent, authority over the child, and authority as expressed in a judgmental attitude. In each of these categories, informants discriminated carefully between justified and unjustified uses of authority.

Authority Over the Parent

For the woman who had previously lost one child to child welfare, the way workers exercised continued authority in relation to her was crucial: "They gave me a chance...they could have took my kid away from me, but they didn't, they gave that chance." However, other comments from participants were not always positive: "They're sneaky...if they had a chance to come in and take your child they would."

Informants clearly sanctioned some exercise of authority in that they expected workers to intervene if necessary: "If people are beating their kids, they deserve to have their kids taken away." Three of the women talked about how they had sent friends to child protective services, and how they had also reported abuse cases to child protection: "If I turn around and see that the baby or any child is being treated unjustly call me the stoolie."

Authority Over the Child

Many units indicated that clients saw workers as having authority and responsibility in relation to their children, and often the exercise of this authority was seen as one of the ways that workers can be useful. One client expressed a disliking of workers who "sucked up to my kid," and appreciation for a worker who was "strict and got things done." Another recounted how when her child got out of control she called the worker, who stepped in and was able to enforce limits. Even in her absence, the worker acts as a useful symbol of authority: "I think she (a teenage daughter) knows that the worker won't put up with just anything, and this makes her think a bit more..."

One parent sees the worker as a more benign alternative to other authorities who could enter her child's life: "If the children's aide takes you and you're a little kid, they put you in a foster home, they won't put in jail."

Authority Expressed Judgmentally

Clients were acutely aware of the status difference between workers and themselves: "They're usually well dressed and they've got a good education." One client reported satisfaction with the fact that "my house could be a pig pen, they don't care. They're here to see my family, not to see my house."

Clients did not like it when workers were overbearing or critical about circumstances that were not directly relevant to the children, and feeling judged in a superficial way by some workers was an important theme. One client complained about "their eyes (being) all over the place," another talked about how "I got nervous, they watched me how I bathed him, they watched me how I fed him...they were gawking right at me." Clients particularly disliked workers who advised how to look after children when the workers had no children.

Trust

A predominant theme in all of the interviews was the presence or lack of mutual trust in the client-worker relationship. Trust appeared to be a delicate balance between clients' willingness to get service, workers' ability to express caring and warmth, and the sense clients have of the worker's skill and readiness to use authority constructively.

Without trust the social work relationship becomes adversarial. One client who described a majority of negative experiences with child protective services concluded her interview by talking about being able to work with the agency: "But you know, you have to be really trusting them and I don't."

Clients regarded trust as a reciprocal thing. While they emphasized the importance of being able to feel that their workers trusted them and were prepared to "give me a chance," they also needed to trust their workers: "You take this big step, share something with one of the workers that you have expectations that (they will) help or something" and "are not going to blab what you tell them in confidence."

DISCUSSION

Qualitative researchers have evolved different methods for assuring that the information they obtain and the analysis that grows out of that information are credible or valid. In this case, the involvement of two researchers, both with extensive child protection experience, allowed for a degree of consensual validity to be achieved. Also, the field work journal was used as a second source of data and assisted us in corroborating observations. In addition, all interviews and analyses were compared with four of Maluccio's transcripts and his final coding matrix (Maluccio, 1979).

A step that is increasingly advocated in qualitative research to assure validity was also taken in this case. Clients were provided with a draft of categories and a summary of the findings, their comments were sought regarding the accuracy of the findings, and adjustments were made to accurately reflect those comments.

The findings of this study are consistent with others in the literature regarding clients' perceptions of their relationship with the worker and the helping process. For example, Mayer and Timms (1970), and Maluccio (1979) share our finding regarding the primary role played by empathy.

Conclusions from this study, as with much qualitative research, are not intended to be generalized, because they are not based on a representative group of informants. However, the study met its purpose by generating an improved understanding of the social work relationship as it is experienced by four clients.

The clients in this study consider that empathy, motivation, and authority are issues that affect their ability to establish a trusting relationship with their social workers. Whether these factors are similarly important to large groups of clients, and identifying the predictable ways they interact to contribute to the development of effective relationships, would be excellent considerations for future research by quantitative as well as qualitative scholars.

REFERENCES

CORBY, B. (1988). *Working with child abuse: Social work practice and the child abuse system.* Philadelphia: Milton Keynes. Open University Press.

FORMAN, R.Z. (1982). *Let us now praise obscure women.* Washington, DC: University Press of America.

GRINNELL, R.M., JR. (Ed.). (1997). *Social work research and evaluation: Quantitative and qualitative approaches* (5th ed.). Itasca, IL: Peacock.

KIRK, J., & MILLER, M. (1986). *Reliability and validity in qualitative research.* Newbury Park, CA: Sage.

LINCOLN, Y.S., & GUBA, E.G. (1981). *Effective evaluation.* San Francisco, CA: Jossey Bass.

MALUCCIO, A.N. (1979). *Learning from clients.* New York: Free Press.

MAYER, J. E., & TIMMS, N. (1970). *The client speaks: Working class impressions of casework.* New York: Atherton Press.

MILES, M.B., & HUBERMAN, A.M. (1984). *Qualitative data analysis: A sourcebook of new methods.* Newbury Park, CA: Sage.

SPRADLEY, J. (1979). *The ethnographic interview.* New York: Holt, Rinehart & Winston.

ENDNOTE

1. The researchers in this study were the senior author and a colleague, Mr. Nico Trocmé.

Allan Edward Barsky

Study K

Neutrality in Child Protection Mediation

THE RAPID GROWTH OF MEDIATION in fields as diverse as divorce mediation and commercial dispute resolution has raised the interest of a growing number of child welfare service providers and scholars interested in finding a more constructive process for developing collaborative service plans with families and youth (Mayer, 1987). Several jurisdictions have already introduced mediators at various levels of the child protection system (Barsky, 1995a; Oran, Creamer, & Libow, 1984; Thoennes, 1994; Savoury, Beals, & Parks, 1995).

Mediation is proposed by some advocates as a more effective method of engaging families in treatment (Bernstein, Campbell, & Sookraj, 1993). Others argue that it could provide major time and cost savings by avoiding protracted court hearings (Morden, 1989). Yet others maintain that mediation provides a basis for empowering families and ensuring that child protection services proceed in a manner that is least intrusive to families and children (Regehr, 1994; Wildgoose, 1987).

Most writings to date have focused either on developing a rationale for using mediation in child protection (Eddy, 1992; Palmer, 1989; Wildgoose, 1987) or on evaluation of various programs (Campbell & Rodenburgh, 1994; Center for Policy Research, 1992; Golten, 1986; Mayer, 1984; Smith, Maresca, Duffy, Banelis, Handelman, & Dale, 1992; Wildgoose & Maresca, 1994). However, there has been insufficient work describing the process of child protection mediation, and analyzing ways in which mediation can be integrated into child protection services.

Accordingly, this study was designed to provide an in-depth understanding of the process of mediation in child protection, and to identify the essential aspects that contribute to developing more effective working relationships with child welfare clients. This paper focuses on neutrality, one of the primary aspects of child protection "CP" mediation identified in the larger study (Barsky, 1995a).

This study is distinct from prior studies because it entails the use of extensive interviews with family members, as well as with professionals involved in mediation and other CP processes. An analysis of their experiences contributes to the child welfare and mediation literature: (1) by beginning to determine the critical experiences of parties involved in the different processes, (2) by developing a framework delineating the essential aspects of the mediation process that are unique to mediation, and (3) by identifying mediative skills and strategies that can be employed in other areas of child protection services.

DESIGN AND METHODS

In order to develop a better understanding of the dynamics of child protection mediation, this study used naturalistic inquiry methods (Denzin & Lincoln, 1994). A series of exploratory "long interviews" (McCracken, 1988) were conducted with 17 adult family members, mediators, and child protection workers ("CPWs") who had been directly involved in five mediation cases. The primary focus of these interviews was to have research participants discuss what they felt were the critical issues in their experiences with mediation. The researcher also conducted six pre-mediation interviews, and six additional interviews with family members and CPWs from three nonmediation comparison cases. The experiences of the research participants in the pre-mediation interviews and in the nonmediation cases provided the contrast points used in identifying the essential aspects of mediation (Spradley, 1979).

Sample

Mediation cases were sampled on the basis of availability and willingness to participate, from a pool of approximately 30 mediation cases seen by the Center for Child and Family Mediation in Metropolitan Toronto. The Center offers mediation to families from Toronto who are involved in the child protection system. Out of this catchment population, all subjects had to meet the following minimum criteria in order to be eligible for mediation:

- The physical safety of the child was assured (i.e., the child was not in any immediate danger).
- The case involved a legitimate child protection concern (suspicions, evidence, or potential for neglect/abuse), and the question of whether a child was in need of protection was not in issue.
- All parties' participation in the process was voluntary.
- All parties to the actual negotiations were competent to negotiate for themselves (i.e., absence of any condition that rendered the party unable to understand the process, to bargain, or to make his/her interests known; the implications for mediation of the existence of an uncontrolled mental illness, significant retardation, language impediment, substance abuse, etc. were assessed on a case-by-case basis).
- There was an absence of any family violence so severe as to render any of the parties incapable of negotiating due to intimidation.
- There were no outstanding criminal charges related to the issues to be mediated.
- There were no ongoing family assessments. (Barsky, 1992)

Although it was not possible (due to client confidentiality) to directly collect data on the nonstudy cases, the study cases had a similar profile to cases described in a prior evaluation of the Center (Wildgoose & Maresca, 1994). The study cases involved a range of child protection issues including neglect, abuse, wardship, access, and supervision. Parties involved in this research study included CPWs, parents, grandparents, extended family members, and foster parents.

The number of mediation sessions in the study sample ranged from three to eight, similar to the average number of sessions used by the Center. The study sample included both cases that settled and cases that did not settle in mediation; however, the levels of conflict in some of the nonstudy cases that did not settle may have been higher than the levels of conflict in the study sample.

None of the cases proceeded to trial following mediation, whereas the Center has had cases that have had to go to trial. Given this limitation, it may be inappropriate to generalize from this study about cases that cannot be resolved in mediation and need to be tried in court. Although the nature and size of the sample do mean that any generalization of the results of this study must be made with caution, the main purposes of this study—to explore the experiences of parties involved in child protection mediation and to explore whether they are unique to this process—were not compromised by the nature of the sample that was actually drawn.

In terms of demographics of research participants, most families involved in both the mediation and nonmediation cases were headed by a single mother who was either on social assistance or earning less than $30,000 per annum. All but one family had either one or two children. These demographics are consistent with the general population of families involved in child protection mediation in Toronto.

The sample of nonmediated cases was drawn purposively on a case-by-case basis by having CPWs from the mediation sample identify matching cases from their own caseloads. Selection was done to ensure that the comparison cases matched the mediation cases in terms of demographic profiles, type and severity of maltreatment, placement status, and level of involvement by participants in the case-planning process. In terms of ethnicity, families in the mediation sample included people from European, African, and mixed Euro-African families. All of the families in the nonmediation sample came from Euro-Canadian backgrounds.

Matching for ethnicity was not prioritized, because both mediators and child protection workers suggested that the most important factor to consider was the type of intervention used in the nonmediation cases. Some types of interventions in the child protection process engender philosophies related to those which underpin mediation: e.g., solution-focused therapy, case conferencing, and plan of care meetings (Tjaden, 1994; Bernstein, Campbell & Sookraj, 1993). Accordingly, in order to explore whether mediation is qualitatively different from other child protection processes, the investigator tried to select comparison cases in which mediation-like interventions were employed.

Data Collection

Semi-structured interviews were conducted with family members, CPWs, and mediators one interviewee at a time (except in one family, where the parents asked to be interviewed together so that they would be more at ease). Each interview was 50 to 90 minutes in duration and was conducted at a location of convenience to the interviewee. Question guides were used to ensure that all relevant questions and topics were raised. Interviews were conducted flexibly in order to focus the study on the participants' perspectives on mediation and the child protection process, rather than limit the study's preconceived problem areas. Questions for the interview guide were developed from the following sources:

- Research studies on CP mediation from the Denver/Boulder project (Mayer, 1987; Pearson, Thoennes, Mayer, & Golten, 1986).
- Pilot research studies on CP mediation completed in Toronto (Morden, 1989; Smith et al., 1992).
- Research studies on child protection cases without mediation (Shulman, 1991).

Additional data were obtained from mediation case files and data being collected for evaluative research on the Center (Morden, 1989). These data helped to supplement and check data gathered in the qualitative interviews.

Ethical Issues

Because this research study dealt with human research participants, the proposal underwent the ethics review procedure required by the University of Toronto School of Graduate Studies. The following ethical guidelines were established and followed:

- Participation in both the mediation and the research study components was strictly voluntary. Participants were permitted to withdraw from the research study, without obligation to provide justification (in one situation where there was initial consent to participate, consent was later withdrawn and information from that case was excluded from the research study).
- No one was denied mediation on the basis that he or she refused to participate in the research study component.
- The researcher did not have access to confidential information concerning any child protection cases, unless and until consents had been received from all of the relevant parties (especially, the parents and the child protection agency).
- The researcher took all reasonable measures to limit access to the data, even in coded form, on a need-to-know basis. Transcription of tapes was done by the primary researcher and one typist. Names and other identifying information in the tapes were altered in the written transcripts to protect the identities of the participants. The researcher stored all of the data in his private office.
- Participants were given notice that anonymity could not be absolutely guaranteed, because research records do not have privileged status under the law and, while it was unlikely, could be subpoenaed for a court trial. As a precondition of participation in the research study, participants were asked to sign an agreement not to call the researcher or any of his documentation for use in any further child protection proceedings.
- Identifying information was separated from the research data, and no identifying information was included in any published material resulting from this study.
- Once the final thesis and oral review were successfully completed, all tapes were erased.

Data Analysis

The interviews were audiotaped and transcribed. In a situation where a parent asked not to be taped, written notes were used to develop a transcript. Each interview was read, reread, and analyzed as it was completed, rather than waiting to analyze all of the interviews together. Key themes and patterns from the interviewees' perspectives were identified from the transcripts (Lincoln & Guba, 1985; Taylor & Bogden, 1984). The interview guides were altered for subsequent interviews in order to further explore important topics and perspectives raised by interviewees that were not originally identified by the researcher. McCracken's five-stage model for data analysis was employed (McCracken, 1988). The transcribed texts were processed for analysis with the *Ethnograph* computer software package (Seidel & Clark, 1984).

Four different types of comparisons were made between interviews:

- First, each interview was compared to an interview of another party from the same child protection case (e.g., a parent's interview could be compared to interviews of the mediator and the CPW on the case, etc.). Different participants in the same mediation or child protection process provided different perspectives and experiences.
- Second, interviews from one case were compared to interviews from other cases, but from the same group of cases (i.e., another mediation case or another nonmediation case).
- Third, interviews from pre-mediation were compared to interviews from post-mediation.
- Finally, interviews from one group of cases were compared to interviews from the other group of cases (e.g., mediation cases compared to nonmediation cases).

Coincidences and contrasts in the data were noted in memoranda that were generated at each stage of the analysis.

Lincoln & Guba's (1985) method for establishing trustworthiness was used throughout the study. "Credibility," "transferability," "dependability," and "confirmability" (the qualitative research equivalents of internal validity, external validity, reliability, and objectivity) were each considered.

The researcher operationalized credibility through the use of the following techniques:

- **Triangulation of data**: Cross-checking data and interpretations through the use of multiple data sources, methods, investigators, or theories. The primary sources used for this purpose included data collected from different participants (mediators, CPWs, parents, etc.), through qualitative interviews, evaluative instruments, and case progress notes. In addition, one mediation case was audiotaped in its entirety, allowing for triangulation in this case. Multiple researchers could have been used for the purposes of triangulation, but they are not necessary if there are other sources. Since the researcher's dissertation was intended to be an independent piece of research, multiple researchers were not used. The following analysis, however, does triangulate data in terms of checking whether facts collected are consistent with theory and findings in the literature.

- **Member checking**: Correcting, verifying, and challenging the soundness of the researcher's findings, constructions, and interpretations with the persons who participated in the original interviews.
- **Peer debriefing**: An external check employed by systematically talking through research experiences, findings, and decisions (for the purposes of catharsis, challenge, design of next steps, and legitimization) with non-involved professional peers. Consultation with mediators from the Center and with the thesis committee were used on an ongoing basis, as they were most familiar with the topics under study. The researcher has also presented this research study at a number of professional conferences, and has solicited feedback from peers in other jurisdictions across North America and Australia.
- **Negative case analysis:** A process of refining working hypotheses (to try to account for all known cases, without exception or with only a reasonable level of exceptions) as more and more data become available.
- **Referential adequacy:** Checking preliminary findings and interpretations against the transcripts and other raw data.
- **Reflexive journals:** The use of reflexive journals that display the researcher's mind processes, philosophical position, and bases of decision about the inquiry. (Lincoln & Guba, 1985)

Two other methods for ensuring credibility—prolonged engagement and persistent observation—were not used, due to pragmatic considerations. Given the level of personal, emotional, and legal concerns in CP cases, prolonged engagement and persistent observation would be too intrusive and too disruptive of the child protection process to warrant their use. Some difficulties with trust and openness were identified in some of the research interviews, which may have been alleviated if the researcher had had a longer period engagement.

In particular, some of the professionals were hesitant to say anything that could be interpreted as shedding a negative light on any of their colleagues (e.g., questioning competence or clinical orientation). Some parents and workers also tended to cast themselves in a positive light (e.g., in terms of responsibility for the conflict between the family and the child protection system).

Each of these tendencies was understandable from the participants' perspectives. Other researchers have decided not to interview family members, because of the "reluctance of many to be candid or critical... concerned about being cooperative" (Center for Policy Research, 1992, pp. 13-14). Since the purpose of the present research study was to gain an understanding of mediation from the participants' perspectives, interviewing family members was essential. In order to take these concerns into account, the following guidelines were followed in interviewing and analyzing the data:

- The researcher reassured the participants that their anonymity would be maintained. One concession that this required was that the researcher could not provide fully detailed descriptions of each case in writing up

this analysis. Data had to be separated from each individual case, so that people from within the child protection system could not identify who said what.
- Questions implying judgment—such as whether mediation or another intervention is "good" or "bad"—were avoided.
- In analyzing the data, an evaluation of the effectiveness of mediation or other interventions was not inferred.

In terms of *transferability*, a "thick description" is required in order to enable someone interested in this research study to make an informed judgment about the transferability of the knowledge (Lincoln & Guba, 1985). The depth of description in the findings section is intended to fulfill this requirement. The description of the research sample above can also be used in order to assess the transferability of conclusions from this research study. Finally, the reader may be referred to other CP mediation research that has been written up by the Center (Morden, 1989; Wildgoose & Maresca, 1994), or to literature that describes similar models (e.g., Campbell & Rodenburgh, 1994; Hogan, 1993). The Project Report by Wildgoose and Maresca (1994) provides a detailed description of the program and also provides 23 individual case summaries.

Throughout the process of inquiry, the researcher maintained thorough files stored on computer and on paper. This audit trail included the following:

- Proposal, ethics review, and comprehensive paper (identifying literature, the researcher's understanding of the literature, the initial course of action, methods, questions and consent forms).
- Audiotapes of the interviews (erased upon completion of the author's dissertation).
- Transcriptions of the audiotapes, with identifying information removed.
- Memoranda and notes on cases, interviews, and dissertation committee meetings (including successive stages of coding and development of themes, reflective memoranda, tentative hypotheses, and notes of how decisions were made concerning data collection).
- Coded interviews using the *Ethnograph*.
- Searches of specific themes.
- Successive drafts of the analysis and findings.

Mediator files that have been reviewed for the purposes of triangulation would not be available to the auditor since this includes identifying information for which the parties have not given consent to be viewed by an external auditor.

Retention of this audit trail allows for *dependability* to be checked through the use of an "auditor" to examine whether the process of inquiry was carried out in a way that is consistent with good professional practice. The audit trail also enabled a check for *confirmability* by examining whether the products (the findings, interpretations, and recommendations) were internally consistent and supported by the raw data (the taped and transcribed interviews). The transparency of method and systematic record keeping used in this study allow for the analysis to be followed and replicated (Denzin & Lincoln, 1994; Lincoln & Guba, 1985).

Data collected from the eight cases comprised 26 interviews (not including member checks). At an average of 22 pages of transcript per interview, the 26 interviews produced approximately 550 pages of transcript. During the initial stage of analysis, the researcher attempted to hit as many themes as the participants' data indicated. This resulted in a broad base of 92 themes. Many of these themes overlapped, and some of them did not prove to be significant in later analysis. However, since the purpose of the study was to look at mediation from the participants' perspectives, it was beneficial to start with a broad identification of themes. While the number of initial themes was difficult to manage, as soon as the process of distilling themes begins, there is greater chance of misconstruing the meanings of the primary data and losing some of the distinctions. Reduction was necessary in order to allow for meaningful discussion and conceptualization of the participants' experiences.

The initial themes were loosely categorized into nine pools: (1) Intentions and Concerns of the Parties, (2) Mediation Interventions, (3) Dynamics between the Parties, (4) Appropriateness for Mediation, (5) Comparisons Made by the Parties, (6) Roles of the Parties, (7) Factors Affecting Decisions, (8) Outcomes, and (9) Impact of the Research Study. These pools provided a framework for the full write-up of this study (Barsky, 1995a).

The next stage of analysis led to the identification of the so-called "essential aspects" of the mediation process. These themes were derived in part from the aspects of mediation that mediation participants identified as being most important. There were also certain recurring themes that the parties did not specifically state were the most important, but which emerged implicitly as defining features of their experiences in the mediation process. One of the difficulties in this process was to try to separate out themes that the interviewer may have suggested through the use of leading questions. For this purpose, it was useful to look at the early portions of the interview where the interviewer asked more general questions.

Eventually, ten distinct essential elements were discerned: alliance, bringing parties together, facilitating communication, keeping peace, developing options, enhancing understanding, focusing the parties, contracting, neutrality, and fairness. These themes do not encompass all of the original themes, but do cover a broad spectrum. In order for the analysis to be manageable, similar themes were regrouped into more general themes. For example, a number of narrower themes from the Mediation Interventions grouping (e.g., clarify, share information) were placed into a broader theme, facilitating communication. The written analysis of facilitating communication reflects its components, as identified in the initial labeling process. The analysis continued by drawing contrasts and comparisons among the original data, the development of themes and information from the literature.

FINDINGS

As noted above, ten essential aspects of mediation were identified in the original research study (Barsky, 1995a). For the purposes of illustration, the following discussion focuses on just one of these aspects—neutrality. For ease of reference, the first initial of each participant's pseudonym corresponds with the first initial of the participant's role: P = Parent, C = Child, W = Worker, M = Mediator, and G = Grandparent.

Mediators, family members, and CPWs each described the mediator as a "neutral" or "impartial" third party. All three groups tended to rate mediator neutrality as a very important element of the mediation process. Upon exploring further what these parties meant by "neutrality," four themes emerged: not siding; absence of preexisting bias; absence of decision-making authority; and no stake in a specific type of outcome.

One of the most consistent themes across cases and parties was the understanding that a mediator could be neutral by *not siding with one party more than any other*. Family members provided the following three examples of how the mediator would treat everybody equally, giving everyone the same opportunity to speak and listening to all sides:

> [The mediator] never sided with us, or not really sided with us and not sided with Children's Aid workers. She always tried to keep it into a medium... At the beginning of every meeting she would say, "Okay, well, I am not here to take your side or your side. I will sit and listen to both sides..."

> Melanie would go talk to the [foster] family, come talk to us, but she was really on nobody's side, so it was just a matter of listening...

> [Mediators need to be] nonbiased and represent both sides equally...

These types of sentiments were mirrored by CPWs, who spoke of the mediator's asking all parties for their points of view and giving everyone's input the same treatment.

> Martha had the ability to treat everybody as equal around the table, to give no one person's ideas or voice more than the others. So it becomes presented more on an equal footing. And everybody got their fair air time. Everyone's opinion got heard...

> A neutral person, someone that sort of will work for both parties, doesn't work for one side or the other.

> Mindy's neutrality was... appearing to give everyone equal footing and to consider everybody in the decisions, asking everybody's opinions about a decision. [Mindy was] moving us along, but not appearing to come down on one side or the other.

The mediators were also conscious of how aligning or even appearing to align with one side would compromise their neutrality. If they met individually with one party, then they would be sure to meet individually with all of the parties. The mediators generally held the mediation sessions at their own offices, rather than at the CPW's office or at the family's home, so as to avoid the appearance of siding with one party. They also tried to ensure that everybody's voice was heard within the mediation sessions.

Absence of a preexisting bias was a second concept identified by some of the family members, CPWs, and mediators as one of the components of neutrality. One uncle suggested that the mediator was able to treat the parties as equals because of the fact that the mediator had no prior history with the family:

> We went to somebody who knew nothing about the case, because she met with people and heard their perceptions, and then came to the table to talk to us as equal partners.

Neutrality in this sense meant that the parties did not see the mediators as being partial to a certain type of outcome.

Since most of the cases dealt with by the Center were already in court, the CPWs were generally parties to the court action. In contrast, the mediators had no standing in the court proceedings. One mediator suggested that not being a party to the action was critical to her neutrality.

CPWs in particular believed that one of the reasons that a mediator may be perceived as more neutral (as compared to a CPW) was the fact that the mediator had no prior history with the family. Although CPWs attempted to be open-minded and unbiased about how to resolve conflicts with the family, some CPWs acknowledged that they sometimes became entrenched in a particular position.

Some of the mediators also agreed that CPWs may become locked into a position, making it difficult for them to negotiate a new arrangement with the family. In two mediation cases, certain family members perceived that the CPW had aligned with other family members. Therefore, even though the primary conflict was between various family members, the CPWs were not seen by the family as neutral mediators. A similar situation occurred in a nonmediation case where the CPW attempted to mediate between a mother and two sets of grandparents. One of the grandmothers felt that the CPW was biased against her, making it difficult for her to accept the CPW in a mediator's role.

In some cases, CPWs and parents had asked the mediators specifically about their affiliations. Family members and their lawyers were particularly interested in whether the mediator was employed by the child protection agency, the court, or other government sources. Some family members were satisfied with mediator neutrality if the mediator were not employed by the protection agency; others believed that all government agencies were the same and questioned whether the mediator was really any different from someone from the protection agency:

> I think [my mother, Genny] does believe mediation is the same process as Children's Aid... She has nothing against Melanie, but it's the same process, dealing with the same people, the same government people you're dealing with. It's just that somebody else is there as a mediator.

The concerns that family members had about the affiliations of their mediator were similar to concerns that they had about judges. In one case, the worker noted that the mother questioned the judge's neutrality: "Patricia doesn't fully trust a judge, and to this day thinks that a judge works for the Children's Aid." Over the course of mediation, Patricia developed an understanding about the mediator's independence from the protection agency. However, she continued to doubt the judge's neutrality.

In four mediation cases, family members believed that the protection agency had betrayed them in the past. Regardless of the worker's attempts to show the family good faith, the family members could not see the CPW as neutral. To the extent that a mediator could demonstrate that she was not part of the agency, the family believed that the mediator would not be biased in the agency's favor.

Accordingly, there was a sense among family members that if the mediator were not directly connected with the agency, then the mediator could be accepted as more neutral. Family members who understood that the mediator was not bound by the same regulations as the protection agency also seemed to have more faith in the neutrality of the mediator:

> Wendy... has her regulations and guidelines that she has to follow. By her explaining anything to me, I would have a little bit of doubt as to the sincerity of it because of her regulations, whereas Melanie has no involvement. So whatever she's going to do is going to be better for everybody involved. So, I would tend to not question as much what she says...

Some CPWs knew the mediators from prior cases where the mediators had acted as lawyers for one of the parties. As long as the mediator had not acted in the same case, this did not tend to cause grave concerns about the mediator's neutrality from the family's perspective. In one case where the CPW knew the mediator from when she worked as a lawyer for the agency, the CPW initially found it hard to see the mediator as neutral. The CPW expected that the mediator would tend to side with her. However, when the mediator really treated the family in a neutral manner, this invoked strong feelings for the CPW. The CPW believed the father was a pedophile. When the mediator treated him with respect and without judgment, the CPW found this hard to accept. The CPW thought, "Oh my God. How can she believe him." The mediator was attempting to demonstrate that she was hearing what the father said. When the mediator did not challenge his statements, the CPW felt this indicated that she was believing what he was saying. The CPW eventually understood that the mediator needed to respond this way in order to maintain neutrality.

Both CPWs and mediators suggested that critical to mediator neutrality was the fact that mediators *did not have any decision-making authority:*

> CPW: Maureen was not there making the decision... And that's where my role is different, because I have to make a decision and she doesn't.

Whereas CPWs have the mandate and power to remove children from their homes, initiate a child protection hearing, and make recommendations to the court, mediators have no legitimate power to impose decisions on the parties and have no direct reporting obligations to the court. This concern was not as apparent from the responses of family members. The concern, however, was implicit in their references to wanting someone who was not biased and did not take sides. For family members, their explicit concern was not so much about a person having decision-making power, but whether the person with power was biased or sided against them.

According to one mediator, family members entering the mediation process often "don't know the mediator from Adam." Most of them are unfamiliar with the mediation profession, as well as with the mediator personally. As a matter of practice, the mediators explained to all of the parties that they did not have the power to impose decisions upon them:

> One of the things that I do is I tell them that I'm not an employee of the Children's Aid Society, so that I'm not connected with that organization. And then I tell them that I don't make any decisions. You know, that I'm not going to do a report. I'm not going to talk to anybody else, you know, outside of research, about the case. I don't get to make any decisions. And if they, at any point, think that it's not working, they can walk without consequence. I'm not the one that they should be convincing.

The CPW in a nonmediation case confirmed that one of the characteristics that makes a mediator neutral is that mediators do not have the mandate or power to advance a particular outcome:

> Well, I had the authority that I could, you know, I mean the court makes the final decision, but I think we really make the final decision as to whether or not the kids go home. In terms of assessment, we advise the court. So Paul knew I had the authority. So I think that's the major difference. You know, mediators are neutral. We're not neutral. We're certainly fighting for those kids, to get the best that they can in terms of planning and care... [Paul] sees me as having power and authority, definitely.

In one case, Wilma noted that while her supportive role was amenable to neutrality, she also had an authoritative role that ran counter to neutrality. In that role, she was required to make decisions that would have an impact on the family:

> Through Patricia's eyes, the mediator is someone who's separate, not part of the agency. You know, and through her eyes the agency is supposed to be biased against her... Although we try to wear two hats, I mean I try to be the supportive worker, but I also have to be the protection worker, and that's the double hats, the authoritarian figure and the supportive one, right? When the authoritarian figure comes out, which usually happens when you go to court, the client can't see you as supportive, and really you're not supportive to what they want, so that's where the mediator comes in. Because they can be in the middle... And that's where my role is different.

> Because I have to make a decision, and she doesn't. I could be wrong. You know, that's where my lack of experience with mediation comes in.

The final keystone of neutrality was whether the mediator had a *stake in a specific outcome*. This concern was also identified most specifically by mediators and CPWs. One CPW referred to the fact that a mediator has nothing to win or lose in the situation. Similarly, the mediators tended to agree that a mediator had no stake in the outcome of the mediation other than trying to ensure that no one thinks (at the end of the process) that the mediator took sides. The mediators were concerned about the process being fair, but had no vested interest.

One CPW suggested that once CPWs adopt a certain position, maintaining that position may become a vested interest. She suggested that mediators were neutral because they never had to decide whose position was more credible or better for the child:

> I think sometimes we get entrenched in our positions and have a hard time thinking that something could be different. Sometimes we get what feels like very far along in the court process, and we become entrenched. And whether that be the Official Guardian or the Children's Aid, I think it makes it hard for that person to act as the mediator... I think sometimes while we do an awful lot of mediation, knowing or not knowing that it's in court, and also that there are other resources and all sorts of things. I think when it gets into where people are really entrenched in positions, then I think we, whether it's clients or lawyers, people don't see us as being able to be the mediator, because we have a very vested interest. And here comes somebody who has no vested interest. Maybe that's what I was trying to get at when I was talking about the neutrality. *Mindy had no vested interest, except wanting to try to help us work this out. But she had no vested interest in one opinion being better than the other, or more credible or better for the child.* And so I think that's what makes the difference. (emphasis added)

Wanda said she expected a mediator to be an "objective person" to help them work through their dispute. She defined "objective" as follows:

> Somebody who's listening to both sides and, and has nothing to win or lose in the whole situation. They can just reflect on what is being said. And, and point out different areas that maybe neither [side has seen before], 'cause I'm involved and maybe Patricia's involved...

In Case 6, the parties specifically wanted a mediator to meet with the child, Charles, "as a neutral person, not as someone with a vested interest." Previously, the family had heard different messages from the foster parents and various workers about what Charles wanted. The family did not trust what they were saying. The family believed that when the foster mother asked Charles whether he wanted to spend time with his uncles, she may have influenced what Charles said because she did not want Charles to spend time with them. The family also believed that the CPW wanted to keep the foster mother happy. The family had more faith in having the mediator convey Charles' wishes, because the mediator did not have a stake in a particular outcome:

> In this case, one of my specific roles was going to be to meet with Charles as a neutral person, not as someone with a vested interest or any interest really in what he had to say. Up until this point they were hearing things from the worker, Wendy, and from the foster mother, Barb, and they weren't hearing things, and which wasn't necessarily consistent with what they were, had been hearing in the past from Charles directly. And so I think, yes, in this case, it was a little bit more important than even the other cases to establish, reinforce my position of neutrality.

Melanie suggested that the only stake that she had as a mediator was to try to ensure that the parties felt that the process was fair to each of them:

> I have a stake as the mediator in ensuring that nobody thinks that I'm taking sides. That's my biggest stake... You want to be able to put out options for people, so that they know what's possible and even to stimulate brainstorming. You know, I'll throw out three, you throw out three, you throw out three sort of thing. So that's the stake that I have — not alienating anybody, and making sure that everybody feels that it's fair. You know, if somebody walks out feeling that it was unfair or that they were coerced, then to me, I have failed. They can walk out without an agreement; that happens all the time. There's nothing that says it always has to work. Maybe it's better that they don't walk out with an agreement, but if anybody walks out feeling that it was unfair, that's when I think I've failed as a mediator.

The definitions of neutrality provided by the parties are generally consistent with definitions in the literature. A proposed set of national standards for court-connected mediation programs in the United States, for instance, defined impartiality as freedom from favoritism or bias either by appearance, word or by action, and a commitment to serve all of the parties as opposed to a single party. This definition covers three of the four categories of neutrality identified in the current research study: absence of preexisting bias, having no stake in the outcome, and not siding with one party.

The fourth category of neutrality, the absence of decision-making authority, is not generally included in definitions of neutrality. Mediators are generally assumed not to have decision-making authority, aside from the issue of neutrality. In the context of CP cases, the issue of decision-making authority has different connotations than in other fields of mediation. Professionals mandated under the child protection system are generally charged with the responsibility for assessing risks to children and taking appropriate measures to redress them. Child protection mediators are an exception. They are not mandated to make decisions regarding protection concerns. The parties involved in this study viewed this absence of decision-making responsibility as contributing to the neutrality of the mediator.

By refraining from expressing opinions and from making decisions, the mediators avoided any sort of alignment with the position of one party or the other. Further, this helped to ensure that the parties saw the role of a mediator as different from that of the CPW. This also differentiated them from the role of a judge. Although judges may be neutral in term of having no preexisting bias, they do have decision-making authority and they are bound by legal principles.

Two other aspects of neutrality were identified that did not fit into the four categories. One CPW said that neutrality required that the mediator establish ground rules and follow through on them. Another CPW said the neutrality required that the mediator be up front about the issues that needed to be dealt with. Although these are not generally ideas associated with the concept of neutrality, they are dynamics that help parties to gain and maintain trust with the mediator.

LIMITATIONS

While this in-depth qualitative study produced an unexpected wealth of material on the processes of mediation in child welfare settings, several limitations in the design of the study must be carefully considered before drawing conclusions from the findings. As with many small sample naturalistic studies, caution should be used in generalizing the findings beyond the study sample. The study was carried out in only one agency using a specific pilot mediation model. In addition the sample was not systematically drawn and did not appear to include some of the higher conflict cases seen in the program.

A second important limitation with the study is the small number of pre-mediation interviews. Although pre-mediation interviews run the risk of influencing the process itself, they provided an interesting contrast point for the analysis.

Finally, identification of a matched comparison group proved to be more difficult than anticipated. The investigators and participants had difficulty coming to agreement about what would constitute an equivalent nonmediated process, and at what point in the process should the interviews take place. Finding an equivalent group was particularly difficult given that the mediation program was a pilot program benefiting from the effects of a novel, voluntary, and well-staffed demonstration program.

CONCLUSIONS

Child protection mediation is a peculiar use of mediation, given that one of the clients is a professional who traditionally assumes a mediation role in her own work. When suspicions of child abuse or neglect are brought to the attention of a child protection agency, the assigned worker is mandated to investigate and intervene in order to ensure that the child is not at risk. In order to achieve these ends, the worker can draw on a range of generalist social work roles: enabler, broker, advocate, activist, mediator, negotiator, educator, initiator, coordinator and group facilitator (Zastrow, 1995). According to Zastrow (1995):

> The mediator role involves intervention in disputes between parties to help them find compromises, reconcile differences, or reach mutually satisfactory agreements... A mediator remains neutral, not siding with either party in the dispute. Mediators make sure they understand the positions of the parties. They help clarify positions, recognize miscommunication, and help the parties present their cases clearly. (p. 19)

In the context of child protection, a worker could mediate between disputing family members about how they will share responsibility for a child's needs. Similarly, a worker could mediate between parents and foster parents about how and when the parents will spend time with the child. But is a child protection worker truly able to function as a neutral third party? For CP mediation to have value as a distinct intervention, it needs to be defined in a way that is different from just "good clinical practice" by CPWs. Otherwise, a CPW could fulfill the role, making the use of an independent mediator redundant (Barsky, 1995b). One of the major findings from the present research study was that neutrality does differentiate the role of a mediator from the role of a CPW.

If neutrality means having someone who listens to all sides and who can view a situation with an open mind, then the question arises about whether a CPW could be neutral in these respects. CPWs who have received sufficient training ought to be able to listen to all sides and treat everyone's views with equal respect. In fact, these are generally accepted standards for professional social workers. CPWs may become locked in a certain position or may become overidentified with one client to the exclusion of others. However, if a CPW does lose this sense of neutrality, the agency can assign a new (more neutral) worker to try to work things out. The worker does not necessarily have to be from outside of the agency. In fact, changing workers for this purpose was used in at least two of the research cases.

Of the four themes that comprise neutrality, the two that separate mediators from CPWs are the concepts of "absence of authority" and "having no stake in a particular outcome." The role of a mediator can be distinguished from that of a CPW by virtue of the fact that the mediator has responsibility for establishing a collaborative problem-solving process, without incurring the task of determining the best substantive outcome (Mayer, 1989). The mediator helps the parties develop their own mutual understanding about what needs to be done for the safety and welfare of the children.

In contrast, CPWs are mandated to carry out the provisions of the child protection legislation. While they must first try to resolve protection issues on a consensual basis, they are vested with the authority and power to secure the protection of children on a nonvoluntary basis. They also have the authority to make recommendations to the court with regard to ongoing intervention on a nonvoluntary basis. This creates a tendency for workers and clients to act as partisans in negotiating with one another:

> Each has a different definition of the problem and different loyalties, commitments and investments in outcome. (Murdach, 1980, p. 458)

Neutrality is bound by perception. Many people have preconceived ideas about CPWs. Even if CPWs strive to be open minded, flexible and non-judgmental, they have great difficulty overcoming preconceptions of family members that contradict these efforts. Although some family members who participated in the research study originally viewed mediators with suspicion, family members tended to trust mediators as neutral parties within the first or second session. Because mediators were able to secure the trust of parties in ways unavailable to CPWs, mediators were able to move the parties to consensus in situations where collaboration and agreement had previously eluded the parties.

The differences between mediation and other child protection processes do not suggest that mediation is an inherently better process in all situations. For instance, mediators were able to build trust in some cases because family members saw them as independent of the child protection system. However, in some of the nonmediation cases, family members did not necessarily want to work with an independent professional. The CPW may have built up a positive working relationship through strategies unavailable to mediators (e.g., advocacy for the family with other systems; familiarity through intensive work over a longer period of time; provision of concrete services; and building trust by following through on successive agreements).

Further, some family members wanted an intervenor who would make decisions. They wanted clear-cut solutions more than participation in the decision-making process. In some cases that had gone to court over an extended period, family members were frustrated by the lack of finality. Mediation does not necessarily conclude with an agreement. If the parties do not want agreement or if agreement is not possible, then mediation is not their optimal choice.

The fact that neutrality is an essential aspect of CP mediation has significant implications for research and practice. Further study is needed to identify the limits of neutrality:

- What are the mediator's obligations in a situation where treating both parties equally would allow the more powerful party (usually the CPW) take unfair advantage of the other party?
- What are the mediator's obligations in a situation where the mediator believes that the parties are coming to an agreement that will put a child at undue risk of abuse or neglect?

For CP mediators, this research study identifies four components of neutrality to take into account: not siding; absence of preexisting bias; absence of decision-making authority; and no stake in a specific type of outcome. Each of these elements contributes to the mediator's ability to establish trust with the parties, which subsequently helps them work toward a consensual resolution of their conflict.

Although the present research study was not intended to evaluate the effectiveness of CP mediation, research participants tended to volunteer positive feedback on their experiences in mediation. In particular, mediation helped them resolve issues without going to court, helped build a more positive relationship between family members and the agency, and gave all parties a sense of being heard and treated fairly. CP mediation is not a panacea, as noted by the frustration of some parties in cases that did not settle. However, given the efficacy of mediation in this small sample of cases, further study is warranted.

REFERENCES

BARSKY, A.E. (1992). Mediation in child protection cases: Managing mandate, authority and power, with self-determination, choice and autonomy. Comprehensive doctoral paper. University of Toronto, Faculty of Social Work.

BARSKY, A.E. (1995a). Essential aspects of mediation in child protection cases. Doctoral dissertation, University of Toronto Faculty of Social Work, Toronto.

BARSKY, A.E. (1995b). Mediation in child protection cases. In H.H. Irving & M. Benjamin (Eds.), *Family mediation: Contemporary issues* (pp. 377-406). Newbury Park, CA: Sage.

BERNSTEIN, M., CAMPBELL, J., & SOOKRAJ, N. (1993). *Transforming child welfare services in the 90's.* Unpublished paper, Catholic Children's Aid Society of Metropolitan Toronto.

CAMPBELL, J., & RODENBURGH, M. (1994). *Mediation pilot project evaluation.* Unpublished program evaluation, Ministry of Social Services, Victoria, BC.

CENTER FOR POLICY RESEARCH, DENVER. (1992). *Alternatives to adjudication in child abuse and neglect cases.* Alexandria, VA: State Justice Institute.

DENZIN, N.K., & LINCOLN, Y.S. (Eds.). (1994). *Handbook of qualitative research.* Newbury Park, CA: Sage.

EDDY, W.A. (1992). *Mediation in San Diego's Dependency Court: A balancing solution for a system under fire?* Unpublished paper, University of San Diego School of Law.

GOLTEN, M.M. (1986). *Child Protection Mediation Project.* Final report. Denver: CDR Associates.

HOGAN, J. (1993, July). Mediating child welfare cases. Paper presented at the Academy of Family Mediators Conference, Washington, DC.

LINCOLN, Y.S., & GUBA, E.G. (1985). *Naturalistic inquiry.* Newbury Park, CA: Sage.

MAYER, B. (Ed.). (1984). *Child Protection Project Manual.* Denver: CDR Associates.

MAYER, B. (1987). *Mediation and compliance in child protection.* Unpublished doctoral dissertation, University of Denver.

MAYER, B. (1989). Mediation in child protection cases: The impact of third party intervention on compliance attitudes. *Mediation Quarterly, 24,* 89-106.

MCCRACKEN, G. (1988). *The long interview.* Newbury Park, CA: Sage.

MORDEN, P. (1989). *Child Protection Mediation Demonstration Project.* Research proposal, Children's Aid Society Foundation of Metropolitan Toronto.

MURDACH, A.D. (1980, November). Bargaining and persuasion with non-voluntary clients. *Social Work,* 458-461.

ORAN, H., CREAMER, J., & LIBOW, J. (1984). *Dependence Mediation Court Project: The first seven months* (Evaluation Report). Los Angeles: Supreme Court.

PALMER, S.E. (1989). Mediation in child protection cases: An alternative to the adversarial system. *Child Welfare, 68,* 21-31.

PEARSON, J., THOENNES, N., MAYER, B., & GOLTEN, M.M. (1986). Mediation of child welfare cases. *Family Law Quarterly, 20*, 303-320.

REGEHR, C. (1994). The use of empowerment in child custody mediation. *Family Mediation Quarterly, 11*, 361-372.

SAVOURY, G.R., BEALS, H.L., & PARKS, J.M. (1995). Mediation in child protection: Facilitating the resolution of disputes. *Child Welfare, 74*, 743-762.

SEIDEL, J.V., & CLARK, J.A. (1984). *The Ethnograph:* A computer program for the analysis of qualitative data. *Qualitative Sociology, 7*, 110-125.

SHULMAN, L. (1991). *Interactional social work practice: Toward an empirical theory.* Itasca, IL: Peacock.

SMITH, R., MARESCA, J., DUFFY, M., BANELIS, N., HANDELMAN, C., & DALE, N. (1992). *Mediation in child protection: Limited or limitless possibilities.* Unpublished report, Demonstration Project of the Children's Aid Society of Metropolitan Toronto.

SPRADLEY, J.P. (1979). *The ethnographic interview.* New York: Holt, Rinehart & Winston.

TAYLOR, S.J., & BOGDAN, R. (1984). *Introduction to qualitative research methods* (2nd ed.). New York: John Wiley.

THOENNES, N. (1994). Child protection mediation in the juvenile court. *The Judge's Journal, 33,* 14-19, 40-43.

TJADEN, P.G. (1994). Dispute resolution in child protection cases. *Negotiation Journal, 10*, 373-390.

WILDGOOSE, J. (1987). Alternative dispute resolution of child protection cases. *Canadian Journal of Family Law, 6,* 61-84.

WILDGOOSE, J., & MARESCA, J. (1994). *Report on the Centre for Child and Family Mediation, Toronto.* Kitchener, ON: Network-Interaction for Conflict Resolution.

ZASTROW, C. (1995). *The practice of social work* (5th ed.). Belmont, CA: Wadsworth.

For a better understanding of the statistical terms contained in this Glossary, please refer to: Robert W. Weinbach and Richard M. Grinnell, Jr. (1998). *Statistics for Social Workers* (4th ed.). White Plains, New York: Longman.

PART III

Glossary

Absolute frequency distribution A simple table that displays the frequencies for the values of a variable.

Abstracting/indexing services Providers of specialized reference tools that make it possible to find information quickly and easily, usually through subject headings and/or author approaches.

Abstracts Reference materials consisting of citations and brief descriptive summaries from quantitative and qualitative research studies.

Acceptance region The outcome of any statistical test that leads to the rejection, or nonrejection, of the null hypothesis.

Accountability A system of responsibility in which program administrators account for all program activities by answering to the demands of a program's stakeholders and by justifying the program's expenditures to the satisfaction of its stakeholders.

Aggregated case-level evaluation designs The collection of a number of case-level evaluations to determine the degree to which a program objective has been met.

Aggregate-level data Derived from micro-level data, aggregate-level data are grouped so that the characteristics of individual units of analysis are no longer identifiable; for example, the variable, "gross national income" is an aggregation of data about individual incomes.

Alternate-forms method A method for establishing reliability of a measuring instrument by administering, in succession, equivalent forms of the same instrument to the same group of research participants.

Alternative hypothesis See Rival Hypothesis.

Alternative world view Insight into another culture; information derived directly from cultural minorities and not based on majority values and perceptions of "normal" behavior.

Analysis of covariance A statistical method used to compensate for possible beginning inequivalencies of the dependent variable(s) between two or more groups in order to eliminate rival hypotheses; a method of statistical control through which scores on the dependent variable are adjusted according to scores on a second variable.

Analysis of variance A statistical test that determines the statistical significance between the means of two or more groups; referred to as "ANOVA."

Analytic generalization The type of generalizability associated with case studies; the research findings of case studies are not assumed to fit another case no matter how apparently similar; rather, research findings are tested to see if they do in fact fit; used as working hypotheses to test practice principles.

Analytical memos Notes made by the researcher in reference to qualitative data that raise questions or make comments about meaning units and categories identified in a transcript.

Annual report A detailed account or statement describing a program's processes and results over a given year; usually produced at the end of a fiscal year.

ANOVA Abbreviation for "analysis of variance."

Antecedent variable A variable that precedes the introduction of one or more dependent variables.

Antiquarianism An interest in past events without reference to their importance or significance for the present; the reverse of presentism.

***A* phase** In case-level evaluation designs, a phase (*A* Phase) in which the baseline measurement of the target problem is established before the intervention (*B* Phase) is implemented.

Applied research approach A search for practical and applied research results that can be applied in actual social work practice situations; complementry to the pure research approach.

A priori probability The probability of a future event calculated from prior knowledge of the number of possible outcomes of the future event and their frequencies.

Area probability sampling A form of cluster sampling which uses a three-stage process to provide the means to carry out a research study when no comprehensive list of the population can be compiled.

Arithmetic mean See Mean.

Assessment-related case study A type of case study that generates knowledge about specific clients and their situations; focuses on the perspectives of the study's participants.

Audit trail The documentation of critical steps in a qualitative research study that allows for an independent reviewer to examine and verify the steps in the research process and the conclusions of the research study.

Authority The reliance on authority figures to tell us what is true; one of the five ways of knowing.

Availability sampling See Convenience Sampling.

Axes Straight horizontal and vertical lines in a graph upon which values of a measurement, or the corresponding frequencies, are plotted.

Back-translation The process of translating an original document into a second language, then having an independent translator conduct a subsequent translation of the first translation back into the language of origin; the second translation is then compared with the original document for equivalency.

Bar graph A graphical technique of descriptive statistics that uses the heights of separated bars to show how often each score occurs; has spaces between the bars to represent nominal level data.

Baseline A period of time, usually three or four data collection periods, in which the level of the client's target problem is measured while no intervention is carried out; designated as the *A* phase in case-level evaluation designs.

Between-group differences Usually contrasted to differences within groups, differences between groups are considered large only if they are large in comparison to within-group differences.

Between research methods approach Triangulation by using different research methods available in *both* the qualitative and the quantitative research approaches in a single research study.

Bias Not neutral; an inclination to some form of prejudice or preconceived position.

Biased sample A sample unintentionally selected in such a way that some members of the population are more likely than others to be picked for sample membership.

Bimodal distribution A frequency distribution with two modes having equal frequencies.

Binary variable A dichotomous variable whose values are 0 (reflecting *absence* of the variable) and 1 (reflecting *presence* of the variable).

Binomial effect size display (BESD) A technique for interpreting the *r* value in a meta-analysis by converting it into a 2 by 2 table displaying magnitude of effect.

Biography Tells the story of one individual's life, often suggesting what the person's influence was on social, political, or intellectual developments of the times.

Bivariate analysis A statistical analysis of the relationship between two, but not more than two, variables.

***B* phase** In case-level evaluation designs, the intervention phase, which may, or may not, include simultaneous measurements.

Case The basic unit of social work practice, whether it be an individual, a couple, a family, an agency, a community, a county, a state, or a country.

Case-level evaluation designs Designs in which data are collected about a single client system—an individual, group, or community—in order to evaluate the outcome of an intervention for the client system; a form of appraisal that monitors change for individual clients; designs in which data are collected about a single client system—an individual, group, or community—in order to evaluate the outcome of an intervention for the client system; also called single-system research designs.

Case study Using research approaches to investigate a research question or hypothesis relating to a specific case; used to develop theory and test hypotheses; an in-depth form of research in which data are gathered and analyzed about an individual unit of analysis, person, city, event, society, etc.; it allows more intensive analysis of specific details; the disadvantage is that it is hard to use the results to generalize to other cases.

Categories Groupings of related meaning units that are given one name; used to organize, summarize, and interpret qualitative data; categories in a qualitative study can change throughout the data analysis process, and the number of categories in a given study depends upon the breadth and depth the researcher aims for in the analysis.

Category In a qualitative data analysis, an aggregate of meaning units that share a common feature.

Category saturation The point in qualitative data analysis when all identified meaning units fit easily into the existing categorization scheme and no new categories emerge; the point at which first-level coding ends.

Causality A relationship of cause and effect; the effect will invariably occur when the cause is present.

Causal relationship A relationship between two variables for which we can state that the presence of, or absence of, one variable determines the presence of, or absence of, the other variable.

CD-ROM sources Computerized retrieval systems that allow searching for indexes and abstracts stored on compact computer discs (CDs).

Cell A single compartment in a statistical table.

Census data Data from the survey of an entire population in contrast to a survey of a sample.

Central tendency A "typical" value for a variable within any data set; a statistic that reflects a middle value within a statistical array.

Chance The probability of an event occurring due to some random variation.

Chi-square table See Cross-Tabulation Table.

Chi-square test A nonparametric statistic that allows us to decide whether observed frequencies are essentially equal to, or significantly different from, expected frequencies.

Citation A brief identification of a reference which includes name of author(s), title, source, page numbers, and year of publication.

Classical experimental design An explanatory research design with randomly assigned experimental and control groups in which the dependent variable is measured before and after the treatment (the independent variable) for both groups, but only the experimental group receives the treatment (the dependent variable).

Client system *An* individual client, *a* couple, *a* family, *a* group, *an* organization, or *a* community that can be studied with case- and program-level evaluation designs and with quantitative and qualitative research approaches.

Closed-ended questions Items in a measuring instrument that require respondents to select one of several response categories provided; also known as fixed alternative questions.

Cluster analysis A statistical procedure that groups together measuring instruments that appear to measure the same constructs.

Cluster diagram An illustration of a conceptual classification scheme where the researcher draws and labels circles for each theme that emerges from the data; the circles are organized in a way to depict the relationships between themes.

Cluster sampling A multistage probability sampling procedure in which the population is divided into groups (or clusters) and the groups, rather than the individuals, are selected for inclusion in the sample.

Code The label assigned to a category or theme in a qualitative data analysis; shortened versions of the actual category or theme label; used as markers in a qualitative data analysis; usually no longer than eight characters in length and can use a combination of letters, symbols, and numbers.

Codebook A device used to organize qualitative data by applying labels and descriptions that draw distinctions between different parts of the data that have been collected.

Coding (1) In data analysis, translating data from respondents onto a form that can be read by a computer; (2) In qualitative research, marking the text with codes for content categories.

Coding frame A specific framework that delineates what data are to be coded and how they are to be coded in order to prepare them for analyses.

Coding sheets In a literature review, a sheet used to record for each research study the complete reference, research design, measuring instrument(s), population and sample, outcomes, and other significant features of the study.

Cohort study A longitudinal survey design that uses successive random samples to monitor how the characteristics of a specific group of people, who share certain characteristics or experiences (cohorts), change over time.

Collaterals Professionals or staff members who serve as indigenous observers in the data collection process.

Collective biographies Studies of the characteristics of groups of people who lived during a past period and had some major factor in common.

Collectivist culture Societies that stress interdependence and seek the welfare and survival of the group above that of the individual; collectivist cultures are characterized by a readiness to be influenced by others, preference for conformity, and cooperation in relationships.

Comparative rating scale A rating scale in which respondents are asked to compare an individual person, concept, or situation, to others.

Comparative research design The study of more than one event, group, or society to isolate explanatory factors; there are two basic strategies in comparative research: (1) the study of elements that differ in many ways but that have some major factor in common, and (2) the study of elements that are highly similar but different in some important aspect, such as modern industrialized nations that have different health insurance systems.

Comparison group A nonexperimental group to which research participants have not been randomly assigned for purposes of comparison with the experimental group. Not to be confused with control group.

Comparison group posttest-only design A descriptive research design with two groups, experimental and comparison, in which the dependent variable is measured once for both groups, and only the experimental group receives the treatment (the independent variable).

Comparison group pretest-posttest design A descriptive research design with two groups, experimental and comparison, in which the dependent variable is measured before and after the treatment for both groups, but only the experimental group receives the treatment.

Compensation Attempts by researchers to compensate for the lack of treatment for control group members by administering it to them; a threat to internal validity.

Compensatory rivalry Motivation of control group members to compete with experimental group members; a threat to internal validity.

Complete observer A term describing one of four possible research roles on a continuum of participant observation research; the complete observer acts simply as an observer and does not participate in the events at hand.

Complete participant The complete participant is at the far end of the continuum from the complete observer in participant observation research; this research role is characterized by total involvement.

Completeness One of the four criteria for evaluating research hypotheses.

Comprehensive qualitative review A nonstatistical synthesis of representative research studies relevant to a research problem, question, or hypothesis.

Computerized retrieval systems Systems in which abstracts, indexes, and subject bibliographies are incorporated in computerized data bases to facilitate information retrieval.

Concept An understanding, an idea, or a mental image; a way of viewing and categorizing objects, processes, relations, and events.

Conceptual classification system The strategy for conceiving how units of qualitative data relate to each other; the method used to depict patterns that emerge from the various coding levels in qualitative data.

Conceptual framework A frame of reference that serves to guide a research study and is developed from theories, findings from a variety of other research studies, and the author's personal experiences and values.

Conceptual validity See Construct Validity.

Conceptualization The process of selecting the specific concepts to include in quantitative and qualitative research studies.

Concomitant variation The situation in which two variables vary together; research participants who differ with respect to Variable *X* will also differ with respect to Variable *Y*.

Concurrent validity A form of criterion validity that is concerned with the ability of a measuring instrument to predict accurately an individual's status by comparing concurrent ratings (or scores) on one or more measuring instruments.

Confidence interval The range of sampling mean values within which the population mean is likely to fall; the scores (or cases) in a population distribution, typically 95 percent, that are included between the limits of tolerable error, typically 5 percent.

Confidence limits Upper and lower boundaries of confidence intervals.

Confidentiality An ethical consideration in research whereby anonymity of research participants is safeguarded by ensuring that raw data are not seen by anyone other than the research team and that data presented have no identifying marks.

Confounding variable A variable operating in a specific situation in such a way that its effects cannot be separated; the effects of an extraneous variable thus confound the interpretation of a research study's findings.

Consistency Holding steadfast to the same principles and procedures in the qualitative data analysis process.

Constant A concept that does not vary and does not change; a characteristic that has the same value for all research participants or events in a research study.

Constant comparison A technique used to categorize qualitative data; it begins after the complete set of data has been examined and meaning units identified; each unit is classified as similar or different from the others; similar meaning units are lumped into the same category and classified by the same code.

Constant error Systematic error in measurement; error due to factors that consistently or systematically affect the variable being measured and that are concerned with the relatively stable qualities of respondents to a measuring instrument.

Construct See Concept.

Construct validity The degree to which a measuring instrument successfully measures a theoretical construct; the degree to which explanatory concepts account for variance in the scores of an instrument; also referred to as conceptual validity in meta-analyses.

Content analysis A data collection method in which communications are analyzed in a systematic, objective, and quantitative manner to produce new data.

Content validity The extent to which the content of a measuring instrument reflects the concept that is being measured and in fact measures that concept and not another.

Contextual detail The particulars of the environment in which the case (or unit of analysis) is embedded; provides a basis for understanding and interpreting case study data and results.

Contingency table See Cross-Tabulation Table.

Continuous random variable A random variable that theoretically assumes any value between two points on a measurement scale.

Contradictory evidence Identifying themes and categories that raise questions about the conclusions reached at the end of qualitative data analysis; outliers or extreme cases that are inconsistent or contradict the conclusions drawn from qualitative data; also called negative evidence.

Contributing partner A social work role in which the social worker joins forces with others who perform different roles in quantitative and qualitative research studies.

Control group A group of randomly assigned research participants in a research study who do not receive the experimental treatment and are used for comparison purposes. Not to be confused with comparison group.

Control variable A variable, other than the independent variable(s) of primary interest, whose effects we can determine; an intervening variable that has been controlled for in the study's research design.

Convenience sampling A nonprobability sampling procedure which relies on the closest and most available research participants to constitute a sample.

Convergent validity The degree to which different measures of a construct yield similar results, or converge.

Correlated groups *t*-test A hypothesis-testing procedure used to decide whether two given dependent samples could have occurred by chance; sometimes referred to as dependent *t*-tests.

Correlated variables Variables whose values are associated; values of one variable tend to be associated in a systematic way with values in the others.

Correlational analyses Statistical methods that allow us to discover, describe, and measure the strength and direction of associations between and among variables.

Correlation coefficient A single number that indicates both the strength and direction of the relationship between two ordinal, interval, or ratio level variables; correlation coefficients have values between +1 and −1, with positive values indicating positive relationships and negative values indicating negative relationships.

Correlation matrix A table used to display the correlations among three or more pairs of variables.

Cost-benefit analysis An analytical procedure that not only determines the costs of the program itself; but also considers the monetary benefits of the program's effects.

Cost-effectiveness analysis An analytical procedure that assesses the costs of the program itself, the monetary benefits of the program's effects are not assessed.

Covariance See Analysis of Covariance.

Covariate The measure used in an analysis of covariance for adjusting the scores of the dependent variable.

Cover letter A letter to respondents or research participants that is written under the official letterhead of the sponsoring organization and describes the research study and its purpose.

Credibility The trustworthiness of both the steps taken in qualitative data analysis and the conclusions reached.

Criterion validity The degree to which the scores obtained on a measuring instrument are comparable to scores from an external criterion believed to measure the same concept.

Criterion variable The variable whose values are predicted from measurements of the predictor variable.

Critical region A set of outcomes of a statistical test that leads to the rejection of the null hypothesis.

Critical value A value of a test statistic that demarcates the region of rejection and is thus used as a criterion for statistical significance in hypothesis testing.

Cross-cultural comparisons Research studies that include culture as a major variable; studies that compare two or more diverse cultural groups.

Cross-sectional research design A survey research design in which data are collected to indicate characteristics of a sample or population at a particular moment in time.

Cross-tabulation table A simple table showing the joint frequency distribution of two or more nominal level variables.

Cultural encapsulation The assumption that differences between groups represent some deficit or pathology.

Culturally equivalent Similarity in the meaning of a construct between two cultures.

Cultural relativity The belief that human thought and action can be judged only from the perspective of the culture out of which they have grown.

Cumulative frequency distribution A frequency distribution that gives the number of scores occurring at or below each value of a variable.

Cumulative frequency polygon A frequency polygon that shows how often scores occur at or below each value of a variable.

Cumulative percentage distribution A table that shows what percentage of scores occur at or below each value of a variable.

Curvilinear correlation A relationship between two variables that, if displayed using a scattergram, would form one or more curves.

Cut-and-paste method A method of analyzing qualitative data whereby the researcher cuts segments of the typed transcript and sorts these cuttings into relevant groupings; it can be done manually or with computer assistance.

Data The numbers, words, or scores, generated by quantitative and qualitative research studies; the word "data" is plural.

Data analyses The process of turning data into information; the process of reviewing, summarizing, and organizing isolated facts (data) such that they formulate a meaningful response to a research question.

Data archive A place where many data sets are stored and from which data can be accessed.

Data coding Translating data from one language or format into another, usually to make it readable for a computer.

Data collection method Procedures specifying techniques to be employed, measuring instruments to be utilized, and activities to be conducted in implementing a quantitative or qualitative research study.

Data set A collection of related data items, such as the answers given by respondents to all the questions in a survey.

Data source The provider of the data, whether it be primary—the original source, or secondary—an intermediary between the research participant and the researcher analyzing the data.

Datum Singular of data.

Decision-making rule A statement that we use (in testing a hypothesis) to choose between the null hypothesis; indicates the range(s) of values of the observed statistic that leads to the rejection of the null hypothesis.

Deduction A conclusion about a specific case(s) based on the assumption that it shares a characteristic with an entire class of similar cases.

Deductive reasoning Forming a theory, making a deduction from the theory, and testing this deduction, or hypothesis, against reality; in research, applied to theory in order to arrive at a hypothesis that can be tested; A method of reasoning whereby a conclusion about specific cases is reached based on the assumption that they share characteristics with an entire class of similar cases.

Degrees of freedom A characteristic of the sample statistic that determines the appropriate sampling distribution; the number of ways in which the data are free to vary.

Demand needs When needs are defined by only those individuals who indicate that they feel or perceive the need themselves.

Demographic data Vital and social facts that describe a sample or a population.

Demoralization Feelings of deprivation among control group members which may cause them to drop out of a research study; a threat to internal validity.

Dependability The soundness of both the steps taken in a qualitative data analysis and the conclusions reached.

Dependent events Events that influence the probability of occurrence of each other.

Dependent variable A variable that is dependent on, or caused by, another variable; an outcome variable, which is not manipulated directly but is measured to determine if the independent variable has had an effect.

Derived scores Raw scores of research participants, or groups, converted in such a way that meaningful comparisons with other individuals, or groups, are possible.

Descriptive research Research studies undertaken to increase precision in the definition of knowledge in a problem area where less is known than at the explanatory level; situated in the middle of the knowledge continuum.

Descriptive statistics Methods used for summarizing and describing data in a clear and precise manner.

Design bias Any effect that systematically distorts the outcome of a research study so that the study's results are not representative of the phenomenon under investigation.

Determinism A contention in quantitative research studies that only an event that is true over time and place and that will occur independent of beliefs about it (a predetermined event) permits the generalization of a study's findings; one of the four main limitations of the quantitative research approach.

Deterministic causation When a particular effect appears, the associated cause is always present; no other variables influence the relationship between cause and effect; the link between an independent variable that brings about the occurrence of the dependent variable exists every time.

Deviation from the mean The distance of a single score from the mean of the distribution from which the scores come.

Deviation score The difference between the mean of a distribution and an individual score of that distribution.

Dichotomous variable A variable that can take on only one of two values.

Differential scale A questionnaire-type scale in which respondents are asked to consider questions representing different positions along a continuum and select those with which they agree.

Differential selection A potential lack of equivalency among preformed groups of research participants; a threat to internal validity.

Diffusion of treatments Problems that may occur when experimental and control group members talk to each other about a research study; a threat to internal validity.

***d* index** A measure of effect size in a meta-analysis.

Directional hypothesis See One-Tailed Hypotheses.

Directional test See One-Tailed Hypotheses.

Direct observation An obtrusive data collection method in which the focus is entirely on the behaviors of a group, or persons, being observed.

Direct observation notes These are the first level of field notes, usually chronologically organized, and they contain a detailed description of what was seen and heard; they may also include summary notes made after an interview.

Direct relationship A relationship between two variables such that high values of one variable are found with high values of the second variable, and vice versa.

Discrete variable A variable that assumes only a finite number of values.

Discriminant validity The degree to which a construct can be empirically differentiated, or discriminated from, other constructs.

Distribution The pattern of frequency of occurrence of scores.

Divergent validity The extent to which a measuring instrument differs from other instruments that measure unrelated constructs.

Dominant–less dominant research model A model combining qualitative and quantitative research approaches in a single study where one approach stands out as having the major role in the research design; the other approach has a minor or complementary role.

Double-barreled question A question in a measuring instrument that contains two questions in one, usually joined by an *and* or an *or*.

Dummy variable A variable created by converting a qualitative variable into a binary variable.

Duration recording A method of data collection that includes direct observation of the target problem and recording of the length of time each occurrence lasts within a specified observation period.

Ecological fallacy An error of reasoning committed by coming to conclusions about individuals based only on data about groups.

Edge coding Adding a series of blank lines on the right side of the response category in a measuring instrument to aid in processing the data.

Effect size In meta-analyses, the most widely used measure of the dependent variable; the effect size statistic provides a measure of the magnitude of the relationship found between the variables of interest and allows for the computation of summary statistics that apply to the analysis of all the studies considered as a whole.

Empirical Knowledge derived from the five ways of knowing.

Error of central tendency A measurement error due to the tendency of observers to rate respondents in the middle of a variable's value range, rather than consistently too high or too low.

Error of measurement See Measurement Error.

Ethical research project The systematic inquiry into a problem area in an effort to discover new knowledge or test existing ideas; the research study is conducted in accordance with professional standards.

Ethics in research Quantitative and qualitative data that are collected and analyzed with careful attention to their accuracy, fidelity to logic, and respect for the feelings and rights of research participants; one of the four criteria for evaluating research problem areas *and* formulating research questions out of the problem areas.

Ethnicity A term that implies a common ancestry and cultural heritage and encompasses customs, values, beliefs, and behaviors.

Ethnocentricity A person makes assumptions about normal behavior that are based on his or her own cultural framework without taking cultural relativity into account; the failure to acknowledge alternative world views.

Ethnograph A computer software program that is designed for qualitative data analysis.

Ethnographic A form of content analysis used to document and explain the communication of meaning, as well as to verify theoretical relationships; any of several methods of describing social or cultural life based on direct, systematic observation, such as becoming a participant in a social system.

Ethnography The systematic study of human cultures and the similarities and dissimilarities between them.

Ethnomethodology Pioneered by Harold Garfinkel, this method of research focuses on the common sense understanding of social life held by ordinary people (the ethos), usually as discovered through participant observation; often the observer's own methods of making sense of the situation become the object of investigation.

Evaluation A form of appraisal using valid and reliable research methods; there are numerous types of evaluations geared to produce data which in turn produce information that helps in the decision-making process; data from evaluations are used to develop quality programs and services.

Evaluative research designs Case- and program-level research designs that apply various research designs and data collection methods to find out if an intervention (or treatment) worked at the case-level and if the social work program worked at the program-level.

Existing documents Physical records left over from the past.

Existing statistics Previously calculated numerical summaries of data that exist in the public domain.

Expected frequencies In a chi-square test, the frequencies of observations in different categories (cells) that would be most likely to appear if the null hypothesis were true.

Experience and intuition Learning what is true through personal past experiences and intuition; two of the five ways of knowing.

Experiment A research study in which we have control over the levels of the independent variable and over the assignment of research participants, or objects, to different experimental conditions.

Experimental designs (1) Explanatory research designs or "ideal experiments;" (2) Case-level research designs that examine the question, "Did the client system improve because of social work intervention?"

Experimental group In an experimental research design, the group of research participants exposed to the manipulation of the independent variable; also referred to as a treatment group.

Explanatory research "Ideal" research studies undertaken to infer cause-effect and directional relationships in areas where a number of substantial research findings are already in place; situated at the top end of the knowledge continuum.

Exploratory research Research studies undertaken to gather data in areas of inquiry where very little is already known; situated at the lowest end of the knowledge continuum. See Nonexperimental Design.

External evaluation An evaluation that is conducted by someone who does not have any connection with the program; usually an evaluation that is requested by the agency's funding sources; this type of evaluation complements an in-house evaluation.

External validity The extent to which the findings of a research study can be generalized outside the specific research situation.

Extraneous variables See Rival Hypothesis.

Face validity The degree to which a measurement has self-evident meaning and measures what it appears to measure.

Factor analysis A statistical procedure in which construct validity is determined by reducing a large number of questions, or measuring instruments, to a smaller number by discovering which ones go together and what relationships exist between groups of factors.

Factorial experiments Experimental research designs that look at the separate effects and interactions of two or more independent variables at the same time.

Feasibility One of the four criteria for evaluating research problem areas *and* formulating research questions out of the problem areas.

Feedback When data and information are returned to the persons who originally provided or collected them; used for informed decision making at the case- and program-levels; a basic principle underlying the design of evaluations.

Field notes A record, usually written, of events observed by a researcher; the notes are taken as the study proceeds and later they are used for analyses.

Field research Research conducted in a real-life setting, not in a laboratory; the researcher neither creates nor manipulates anything within the study, but observes it.

Field-tested The pilot of an instrument or research method in conditions equivalent to those that will be encountered in the research study.

File drawer problem (1) In literature searches or reviews, the difficulty in locating studies that have not been published or are not easily retrievable; (2) In meta-analyses, errors in effect size due to reliance on published articles showing statistical significance.

Firsthand data Data obtained from people who directly experience the problem being studied.

First-level coding A process of identifying meaning units in a transcript, organizing the meaning units into categories, and assigning names to the categories.

Flexibility The degree to which the design and procedures of a research study can be changed to adapt to contextual demands of the research setting.

Focus group interview A group of people brought together to talk about their lives and experiences in free-flowing, open-ended discussions which usually focus on a single topic.

Formative evaluation A type of evaluation that focuses on obtaining data that are helpful in planning the program and in improving its implementation and performance.

***F* ratio** The between-group estimates of the variance of the sampling distribution of the mean divided by the within-group's estimate.

Frequency Number of observations falling in a cell, or value category, of a specific variable.

Frequency distribution A table or graph that shows the number of times (frequency) with which different values of the variable occur in a group of observations.

Frequency polygon A graphic technique of descriptive statistics that uses the height of connected dots to show how often each score occurs.

Frequency recording A method of data collection by direct observations in which each occurrence of the target problem is recorded during a specified observation period.

Frequency table In its simplest form, a two-column table with one column listing values of a variable and the other column listing the frequency with which the different values occur within a group of observations.

***F* statistic** A statistic used to compare variances among three or more populations that have normal distributions; used in analysis of variance.

Fugitive data Informal information found outside regular publishing channels.

Gaining access A term used in qualitative research to describe the process of engagement and relationship development between the researcher and the research participants.

Generalizable explanation evaluation model An evaluation model whose proponents believe that many solutions are possible for any one social problem and that the effects of programs will differ under different conditions.

Generalizing results Extending or applying the findings of a research study to individuals or situations not directly involved in the original research study; the ability to extend or apply the findings of a research study to subjects or situations that were not directly investigated.

Goal Attainment Scale (GAS) A modified measurement scale used to evaluate case or program outcomes.

Government documents Printed documents issued by local, state, and federal governments; such documents include reports of legislative committee hearings and investigations, studies commissioned by legislative commissions and executive agencies, statistical compilations such as the census, the regular and special reports of executive agencies, and much more.

Grand tour questions Queries in which research participants are asked to provide wide-ranging background information; mainly used in qualitative research studies.

Graphic rating scale A rating scale that describes an attribute on a continuum from one extreme to the other, with points of the continuum ordered in equal intervals and then assigned values.

Grid A chart that lists both general and specific criteria for choosing a data collection method, as well as the possible data collection methods for a given study.

Grounded theory A final outcome of the qualitative research process which is reached when the insights are grounded on observations and the conclusions seem to be firm.

Grouped cumulative frequency distribution An extension of a grouped frequency distribution that shows how often scores occur at or below each interval.

Grouped frequency distribution A table or graph in which frequencies are not listed for each possible value of the variable; rather, frequencies are listed for each of a number of intervals on the measurement scale.

Grouped frequency histogram A histogram that shows how often scores occur at given intervals.

Grouped frequency polygon A frequency polygon that shows how often scores occur at given intervals.

Group evaluation designs Evaluation designs that are conducted with groups of cases for the purpose of assessing to what degree program objectives have been achieved.

Group research designs Research designs conducted with two or more groups of cases, or research participants, for the purpose of answering research questions or testing hypotheses.

Halo effect A measurement error due to the tendency of an observer to be influenced by a favorable trait(s) of a research participant(s).

Hawthorne effect Effects on research participants' behaviors or attitudes attributable to their knowledge that they are taking part in a research study; a reactive effect; a threat to external validity.

Heterogeneity of respondents The extent to which a research participant differs from other research participants.

Heuristic A theory used to stimulate creative thought and scientific activity.

Histogram A graphic representation of a frequency distribution in which the horizontal line represents values of a variable and the vertical line represents frequencies with which those values occur; a bar is constructed over each value of the variable (or the midpoint of each interval, if the data are grouped) and extended to the appropriate frequency.

Historical research The process by which we study the past; a method of inquiry that attempts to explain past events based on surviving remains.

History in research design The possibility that events not accounted for in a research design may alter the second and subsequent measurements of the dependent variable; a threat to internal validity.

Homogeneity of respondents The extent to which a research participant is similar to other research participants.

Horizontal axis The horizontal dimension of a two-dimensional graph; represents values of the independent variable in frequency distributions; sometimes called the *x*-axis or the abscissa.

Hypothesis A theory-based prediction of the expected results of a research study; a tentative explanation that a relationship between or among variables exists.

Hypothetico-deductive method A hypothesis-testing approach where a hypothesis is derived on the deductions based from a theory.

Ideographic research Research studies that focus on unique individuals or situations.

Implementation of a program The action of carrying out a program in the way that it was designed.

Independent groups *t*-test A statistical test that decides whether two given independent samples could have occurred by chance.

Independent variable A variable that is not dependent on another variable but is believed to cause or determine changes in the dependent variable; an antecedent variable that is directly manipulated in order to assess its effect on the dependent variable.

Index A group of individual measures that, when combined, are meant to indicate some more general characteristic.

Indigenous observers People who are naturally a part of the research participants' environment and who perform the data collection function; includes relevant others (e.g., family members, peers) and collaterals (e.g., social workers, staff members).

Indirect measures A substitute variable, or a collection of representative variables, used when there is no direct measurement of the variable of interest; also called a proxy variable.

Individual synthesis Analysis of published studies related to the subject under study.

Individualism A way of living that stresses independence, personal rather than group objectives, competition, and power in relationships; achievement measured through success of the individual as opposed to the group.

Inductive reasoning Building on specific observations of events, things, or processes to make inferences or more general statements; in research studies, applied to data collection and research results to make generalizations to see if they fit a theory; a method of reasoning whereby a conclusion is reached by building on specific observations of events, things, or processes to make inferences or more general statements.

Inferential statistics Statistical methods that make it possible to draw tentative conclusions about the population based on observations of a sample selected from that population and, furthermore, to make a probability statement about those conclusions to aid in their evaluation.

Information anxiety A feeling attributable to a lack of understanding of information, being overwhelmed by the amount of information to be accessed and understood, or not knowing if certain information exists.

Informed consent Signed statements obtained from research participants prior to the initiation of the research study to inform them what their participation entails and that they are free to decline participation.

In-house evaluation An evaluation that is conducted by someone who works within a program; usually an evaluation for the purpose of promoting better client services; also known as an internal evaluation; this type of evaluation complements an external evaluation.

Institutional review boards (IRBs) Boards set up by institutions in order to protect research participants and to ensure that ethical issues are recognized and responded to in the a study's research design and procedures.

Instrumentation Weaknesses of a measuring instrument, such as invalidity, unreliability, improper administrations, or mechanical breakdowns; a threat to internal validity.

Integration Combining evaluation and day-to-day practice activities to develop a complete approach to client service delivery; a basic principle underlying the design of evaluations.

Interaction effects Effects produced by the combination of two or more threats to internal validity.

Internal consistency The extent to which the scores on two comparable halves of the same measuring instrument are similar; inter-item consistency.

Internal validity The extent to which it can be demonstrated that the independent variable within a research study is the only cause of change in the dependent variable; overall soundness of the experimental procedures and measuring instruments.

Interobserver reliability The stability or consistency of observations made by two or more observers at one point in time.

Interpretive notes Notes on the researcher's interpretations of events which are kept separate from the record of the facts noted as direct observations.

Interquartile range A number that measures the variability of a data set; the distance between the 75th and 25th percentiles.

Interrater reliability The degree to which two or more independent observers, coders, or judges produce consistent results.

Interrupted time-series design An explanatory research design in which there is only one group of research participants and the dependent variable is measured repeatedly before and after treatment; used in case- and program evaluation designs.

Interval level of measurement The level of measurement with an arbitrarily chosen zero point that classifies its values on an equally spaced continuum.

Interval recording A method of data collection which involves a continuous direct observation of an individual during specified observation periods divided into equal time intervals.

Intervening variable See Rival Hypothesis.

Interview data Isolated facts that are gathered when research participants respond to carefully constructed research questions; data, which are in the form of words, are recorded by transcription.

Interview schedule A measuring instrument used to collect data in face-to-face and telephone interviews.

Interviewing A conversation with a purpose.

Intraobserver reliability The stability of observations made by a single observer at several points in time.

Intrusion into lives of research participants The understanding that specific data collection methods can have negative consequences for research participants; a criterion for selecting a data collection method.

Inverse relationship A relationship between two variables such that high values of one variable are found with low values of the other variable, and vice versa; sometimes referred to as a negative relationship or *negative correlation.*

Itemized rating scales A measuring instrument that presents a series of statements which respondents or observers rank in different positions on a specific attribute.

Journal A written record of the process of a qualitative research study. Journal entries are made on an ongoing basis throughout the study and include study procedures as well as the researcher's reactions to emerging issues and concerns during the data analysis process.

Key informants A subpopulation of research participants who seem to know much more about "the situation" than other research participants.

Knowledge base A body of knowledge and skills specific to a certain discipline.

Knowledge creator and disseminator A social work role in which the social worker actually carries out and disseminates the results of a quantitative and/or qualitative research study to generate knowledge for our profession.

Knowledge level continuum The range of knowledge levels, from exploratory to descriptive to explanatory, at which research studies can be conducted.

Latent content In a content analysis, the true meaning, depth, or intensity of a variable, or concept, under study.

Level of probability See Statistical Significance.

Levels of measurement The degree to which characteristics of a data set can be modeled mathematically; the higher the level of measurement, the more statistical methods that are applicable.

Limited review An existing literature synthesis that summarizes in narrative form the findings and implications of a few research studies.

Linear correlation A correlation between variables that if displayed using a scattergram would approximate a straight line.

Linear relationship A relationship between two variables whereby a straight line can be fitted satisfactorily to the points on the scattergram; the scatter of points will cluster elliptically around a straight line rather than around some type of curve.

Literature review See Literature Search and Review of the Literature.

Literature search In a meta-analysis, scanning books and journals for basic, up-to-date research articles on studies relevant to a research question or hypothesis; sufficiently thorough to maximize the chance of including all relevant sources. See Review of the Literature.

Logical consistency The requirement that all the steps within a quantitative research study must be logically related to one another.

Logical positivism A philosophy of science holding that the scientific method of inquiry is the only source of certain knowledge; in research, focuses on testing hypotheses deduced from theory.

Logistics In evaluation, refers to getting research participants to do what they are supposed to do, getting research instruments distributed and returned; in general, the activities that insure that procedural tasks of a research or evaluation study are carried out.

Longitudinal case study An exploratory research design in which there is only one group of research participants and the dependent variable is measured more than once.

Longitudinal design A survey research design in which a measuring instrument(s) is administered to a sample of research participants repeatedly over time; used to detect dynamic processes such as opinion change.

Magnitude recording A direct-observation method of soliciting and recording data on amount, level, or degree of the target problem during each occurrence.

Management information system (MIS) System in which computer technology is used to process, store, retrieve, and analyze data collected routinely in such processes as social service delivery.

Manifest content Content of a communication that is obvious and clearly evident.

Manipulable solution evaluation model An evaluation model whose proponents believe that the greatest priority is to serve the public interest, not the interests of its stakeholders who have vested interests in the program being evaluated; closely resembles an outcome evaluation.

Mann-Whitney *U* test A nonparametric hypothesis-testing procedure used to decide whether two given independent samples would have arisen by chance from identically distributed populations; a statistical test for comparing two populations based on independent random samples from each.

Marginals The count of frequencies with which certain responses occur; in a cross-tabulation table, the row and column totals.

Matched pairs test A statistical test for the comparison of two population means.

Matching A random assignment technique that assigns research participants to two or more groups so that the experimental and control groups are approximately equivalent in pretest scores or other characteristics, or so that all differences except the experimental condition are eliminated.

Matrix A two-dimensional grid, in which pairs of categories or themes are examined for similarities and differences; a "+" symbol is used to show agreement between categories and a "–" symbol is used to show categories that are at odds with each other.

Maturation Unplanned change in research participants due to mental, physical, or other processes operating over time; a threat to internal validity.

Mean Average score for a group of scores within any given data set.

Mean deviation Measure of variability that is literally the mean (absolute value) of the deviations about the mean.

Meaning units In a qualitative data analysis, a discrete segment of a transcript that can stand alone as a single idea; can consist of a single word, a partial or complete sentence, a paragraph, or more; used as the basic building blocks for developing categories.

Measure of central tendency A single number that describes the location, or relative magnitude, of a typical score within a sample or population; the mode, median, and mean are examples of central tendency.

Measure of variability A single number that describes how spread out a group of scores is within a sample or population; the range, variance, and standard deviation are examples of variability.

Measurement The assignment of labels or numerals to the properties or attributes of observations, events, or objects according to specific rules.

Measurement error Any variation in measurement that cannot be attributed to the variable being measured; variability in responses produced by individual differences and other extraneous variables.

Measuring instrument Any instrument used to measure a variable(s).

Median A measure of central tendency defined as the point on a measurement scale where 50 percent of the observations fall above it and 50 percent of the observations fall below it.

Member checking A process of obtaining feedback and comments from research participants on interpretations and conclusions made from the qualitative data they provided; asking research participants to confirm or refute the conclusions made.

Meta-analysis A research method in which mathematical procedures are applied to the quantitative findings of studies located in a literature search to produce new summary statistics and to describe the findings for a meta-analysis.

Methodology The procedures and rules that detail how a single research study is conducted.

Micro-level data Data derived from individual units of analysis, whether these data sources are individuals, families, corporations, etc.; for example, age and years of formal schooling are two variables requiring micro-level data.

Missing data Data not available for a research participant about whom other data are available, such as when a respondent fails to answer one of the questions in a survey.

Missing links When two categories or themes seem to be related, but not directly so, it may be that a third variable connects the two.

Mixed research model A model combining aspects of qualitative and quantitative research approaches within all (or many) of the methodological steps contained within a single research study.

Mode A measure of central tendency; the most frequently occurring value in a distribution of scores.

Monitoring approach to evaluation Evaluation that aims to provide ongoing feedback so that a program can be improved while it is still underway; it contributes to the continuous development and improvement of a human service program; this approach complements the project approach to evaluation.

Mortality Loss of research participants through normal attrition over time in an experimental design that requires retesting; a threat to internal validity.

Multicultural research Representation of diverse cultural factors in the subjects of study; such diversity variables may include religion, race, ethnicity, language preference, gender, etc.

Multigroup posttest-only design An exploratory research design in which there is more than one group of research participants and the dependent variable is measured only once for each group.

Multiple-baseline design A case-level evaluation design with more than one baseline period and intervention phase which allows the causal inferences regarding the relationship between a treatment intervention and its effect on clients' target problems and which helps control for extraneous variables. See Interrupted Time-Series Design.

Multiple-group design An experimental research design with one control group and several experimental groups.

Multiple-treatment interference Effects of the results of a first treatment on the results of second and subsequent treatments; a threat to external validity.

Multistage probability sampling Probability sampling procedures used when a comprehensive list of the population does not exist and it is not possible to construct one.

Multivariate (1) A relationship involving two or more variables; (2) A hypothesis stating an assertion about two or more variables and how they relate to one another.

Multivariate analysis A statistical analysis of the relationship among three or more variables.

Mutually exclusive events In applications of probability theory, two or more events that cannot both happen on a single trial; on a single flip of a coin, for example, the events "heads" and "tails" are mutually exclusive.

Narrowband measuring instrument Measuring instruments that focus on a single, or a few, variables.

Nationality A term that refers to country of origin.

Naturalist A person who studies the facts of nature as they occur under natural conditions.

Needs assessment Program-level evaluation activities that aim to assess the feasibility for establishing or continuing a particular social service program; an evaluation that aims to assess the need for a human service by verifying that a social problem exists within a specific client population to an extent that warrants services.

Negative case sampling Purposefully selecting research participants based on the fact that they have different characteristics than previous cases.

Negative relationship The situation in correlational analysis where high values of one variable tend to be associated with low values of another, and vice versa.

Negative skew A descriptive term applied to frequency distributions with many high values and few extremely low values.

Nominal level of measurement The level of measurement that classifies variables by assigning names or categories that are mutually exclusive and exhaustive.

Nondirectional test See Two-Tailed Hypotheses.

Nonexperimental design A research design at the exploratory, or lowest level, of the knowledge continuum; also called preexperimental.

Nonoccurrence data In the structured-observation method of data collection, a recording of only those time intervals in which the target problem did not occur.

Nonparametric tests Refers to statistical tests of hypotheses about population probability distributions, but not about specific parameters of the distributions.

Nonprobability sampling Sampling procedures in which all of the persons, events, or objects in the sampling frame have an unknown, and usually different, probability of being included in a sample.

Nonreactive Methods of research that do not allow the research participants to know that they are being studied; thus, they do not alter their responses for the benefit of the researcher.

Nonresponse The rate of nonresponse in survey research is calculated by dividing the total number of respondents by the total number in the sample, minus any units verified as ineligible.

Nonsampling errors Errors in a research study's results that are not due to the sampling procedures.

Norm In measurement, an average or set group standard of achievement that can be used to interpret individual scores; normative data describing statistical properties of a measuring instrument such as means and standard deviations.

Normal curve A symmetrical curve that graphically represents a standard distribution of scores.

Normal distribution A symmetrical, bell-shaped curve that often arises when a trait is composed of a large number of random, independent factors; the curve possesses a specific mathematical formula.

Normalization group The population sample to which a measuring instrument under development is administered in order to establish norms; also called the norm group.

Normative needs When needs are defined by comparing the objective living conditions of a target population with what society—or, at least, that segment of society concerned with helping the target population—deems acceptable or desirable from a humanitarian standpoint.

Null hypothesis A statement concerning one or more parameters that is subjected to a statistical test; a statement that there is no relationship between the two variables of interest.

Numbers The basic data unit of analysis used in quantitative research studies.

Objectivity A research stance where a study is carried out and its data are examined and interpreted without distortion by personal feelings or biases.

Observer One of four roles on a continuum of participation in participant observation research; the level of involvement of the observer participant is lower than the complete participant and higher than the participant observer.

Obtrusive data collection methods Direct data collection methods that can influence the variables under study or the responses of research participants; data collection methods that produce reactive effects.

Occurrence data In the structured-observation method of data collection, a recording of the first occurrence of the target problem during each time interval.

One-group posttest-only design An exploratory research design in which the dependent variable is measured only once.

One-group pretest-posttest design A descriptive research design in which the dependent variable is measured twice—before and after treatment.

One-sample *t*-test A hypothesis-testing procedure used to decide whether the results from a given sample could have occurred by chance.

One-stage probability sampling Probability sampling procedures in which the selection of a sample that is drawn from a specific population is completed in a single process.

One-tailed hypotheses Statements that predict specific relationships between independent and dependent variables.

On-line sources Computerized literary retrieval systems that provide printouts of indexes and abstracts.

Open-ended questions Unstructured questions in which the response categories are not specified or detailed.

Operational definition Explicit specification of a variable in such a way that its measurement is possible.

Operationalization The process of developing operational definitions of the variables that are contained within the concepts of a quantitative and/or qualitative research study.

Ordinal level of measurement The level of measurement that classifies variables by rank-ordering them from high to low or from most to least.

Ordinate See Vertical Axis.

Origin The point of a graph at which the abscissa and ordinate intersect.

Outcome The effect of the manipulation of the independent variable on the dependent variable; the end product of a treatment intervention.

Outcome measure The criterion or basis for measuring effects of the independent variable or change in the dependent variable.

Outcome-oriented case study A type of case study that investigates whether client outcomes were in fact achieved.

Outside observers Trained observers who are not a part of the research participants' environment and who are brought in to record data.

Paired observations An observation on two variables, where the intent is to examine the relationship between them.

Panel research study A longitudinal survey design in which the same group of research participants (the panel) is followed over time by surveying them on successive occasions.

Parameter A characteristic of a population determined from observations on every member of the population.

Parametric tests Statistical methods for estimating parameters or testing hypotheses about population parameters.

Participant observation An obtrusive data collection method where the researcher, or the observer, participates in the life of those being observed; both an obtrusive data collection method and a research approach, this method is characterized by the one doing the study undertaking roles that involve establishing and maintaining ongoing relationships with research participants who are often in the field settings, and observing and participating with the research participants over time.

Participant observer The participant observer is one of four roles on a continuum of participation in participant observation research; the level of involvement of the participant observer is higher than the complete observer and lower than the observer participant.

Pearson's product-moment correlation coefficient A correlation coefficient that specifies the strength and direction of a relation between two interval- or ratio-level variables.

Percent Synonymous with "in 100" or the number of cases out of 100.

Percentage distribution A table that displays the percentage of cases that were found to have each of the respective measurements of a variable.

Percentile A point on the measurement scale below which a specified percentage of the group's observations fall; the 20th percentile, for instance, is the value that has 20 percent of the observations below it.

Percentile rank A transformed score that tells us the percentage of scores failing at or below a given score.

Perfect relationship A relationship between two variables such that the value of one variable is known if the value of the other variable is specified.

Permanent product recording A method of data collection in which the occurrence of the target problem is determined by observing the permanent product or record of the target problem.

Pie chart A graph that displays the frequency distribution of a variable as portions of a circle reflecting percentages of the whole.

Pilot study See Pretest (2).

Population An entire set, or universe, of people, objects, or events of concern to a research study, from which a sample is drawn.

Positive relationship The situation in correlational analyses that exists when high values of the first variable tend to be associated with high values of the second variable.

Positive skew A descriptive term applied to frequency distributions with many low values and a few extremely high values; on a frequency polygon graph, positive skew produces a "tail" in the direction of the positive values.

Positively skewed distribution See Positive Skew.

Positivism See Logical Positivism.

Posttest Measurement of the dependent variable after the introduction of the independent variable.

Potential for testing One of the four criteria for evaluating research hypotheses.

Practitioner/researcher A social worker who guides practice through the use of research findings; collects data throughout an intervention using research methods, skills, and tools; disseminates practice findings.

Pragmatists Researchers who believe that both qualitative and quantitative research approaches can be integrated in a single research study.

Prediction The estimation of scores on one variable from data about one or more other variables.

Predictive validity A form of criterion validity that is concerned with the ability of a measuring instrument to predict future performance or status on the basis of present performance or status.

Predictor variable The variable that, it is believed, allows us to improve our ability to predict values of the criterion variable.

Preexposure Tasks to be carried out in advance of a research study to sensitize the researcher to the culture of interest; these tasks may include participation in cultural experiences, intercultural sharing, case studies, ethnic literature reviews, value statement exercises, etc.

Preliminary plan for data analysis A strategy for analyzing qualitative data that is outlined in the beginning stages of a qualitative research study; the plan has two general steps: (1) previewing the data, and (2) outlining what to record in the researcher's journal.

Presentism Applying current thinking and concepts to interpretations of past events or intentions.

Pretest (1) Measurement of the dependent variable prior to the introduction of the independent variable; (2) Administration of a measuring instrument to a group of people who will not be included in the study to determine difficulties the research participants may have in answering questions and the general impression given by the instrument; also called a pilot study.

Pretest-treatment interaction Effects that a pretest has on the responses of research participants to the introduction of the independent variable or the experimental treatment; a threat to external validity.

Previous research Research studies that have already been completed and published; they provide information about data collection methods used to investigate research questions that are similar to our own; a criterion for selecting a data collection method.

Primary data Data in its original form, as collected from the research participants; a primary data source is one that puts as few intermediaries as possible between the production and the study of the data.

Primary language The preferred language of the research participants.

Primary reference source A report of a research study by the person who conducted the study; usually an article in a professional journal.

Principle of unlikely successive coincidences The principle applied in experimental case-level evaluation designs to demonstrate that there was more than one coincidence in which improvement in a target problem began only after a given treatment was initiated.

Probabilistic causation When the presumed cause is present, the associated outcome may or may not be present; the link between an independent variable that brings about the occurrence of the dependent variable exists most (but not all) of the time.

Probability sampling Sampling procedures in which every member of the designated population has a known probability of being selected for the sample.

Problem area In social work research, a general expressed difficulty about which something researchable is unknown; not to be confused with research question.

Problem-solving process A generic method with specified phases for solving problems; also described as the scientific method.

Process-oriented case study A type of case study that illuminates the micro-steps of intervention that lead to client outcomes; describes how programs and interventions work and gives insight to the "black box" of intervention.

Professional standards Rules for making judgments about evaluation activity that are established by a group of persons who have advanced education and usually have the same occupation.

Program An organized set of political, administrative, and clinical activities that function to fulfill some social purpose.

Program development The constant effort to improve program services to better achieve outcomes; a basic principle underlying the design of evaluations.

Program efficiency Assessment of a program's outcome in relation to the costs of obtaining the outcome.

Program evaluation A form of appraisal, using valid and reliable research methods, that examines the processes or outcomes of an organization that exists to fulfill some social purpose.

Program goal A statement defining the intent of a program that cannot be directly evaluated; it can, however, be evaluated indirectly by the program's objectives which are derived from the program goal; not to be confused with program objectives.

Program-level evaluation A form of appraisal that monitors change for groups of clients and organizational performance.

Program objectives A statement that clearly and exactly specifies the expected change, or intended result, for individuals receiving program services; qualities of well-chosen objectives are meaningfulness, specificity, measurability, and directionality; not to be confused with program goal.

Program participation The philosophy and structure of a program that will support or supplant the successful implementation of a research study within an existing social service program; a criterion for selecting a data collection method.

Program process The coordination of administrative and clinical activities that are designed to achieve a program's goal.

Program results A report on how effective a program is at meeting its stated objectives.

Project approach to evaluation Evaluation that aims to assess a completed or finished program; this approach complements the monitoring approach.

Proportion A fraction of one.

Proxy An indirect measure of a variable that a researcher wants to study; it is often used when the variable of inquiry is difficult to measure or observe directly.

Pure research approach A search for theoretical results that can be utilized to develop theory and expand our profession's knowledge bases; complementary to the applied research approach.

Purists Researchers who believe that qualitative and quantitative research approaches should never be mixed.

Purpose statement A declaration of words that clearly describes a research study's intent.

Purposive sampling A nonprobability sampling procedure in which research participants with particular characteristics are purposely selected for inclusion in a research sample; also known as judgmental or theoretical sampling.

***p* value** The level of probability for a test of statistical significance; a measure of the relationship between the independent and dependent variables.

Qualitative data Data that measure a quality or kind; when referring to variables, qualitative is another term for categorical or nominal variable values; when speaking of kinds of research, qualitative refers to studies of subjects that are hard to quantify; qualitative research produces descriptive data based on spoken or written words and observable behaviors.

Qualitative research approach Research studies that focus on the facts of nature as they occur under natural conditions and emphasize qualitative description and generalization; a process of discovery sensitive to holistic and ecological issues; a research approach that is complementry to the quantitative research approach.

Quantification In measurement, the reduction of data to numerical form in order to analyze them by way of mathematical or statistical techniques.

Quantitative data Data that measure a quantity or amount.

Quantitative research approach A research approach to discover relationships and facts that are generalizable; research that is "independent" of subjective beliefs, feelings, wishes, and values; a research approach that is complementry to the qualitative research approach.

Quasi-experiment A research design at the descriptive level of the knowledge continuum that resembles an "ideal" experiment but does not allow for random selection or assignment of research participants to groups and often does not control for rival hypotheses.

Questionnaire-type scale A type of measuring instrument in which multiple responses are usually combined to form a single overall score for a respondent.

Quota sampling A nonprobability sampling procedure in which the relevant characteristics of the sample are identified, the proportion of these characteristics in the population is determined, and research participants are selected from each category until the predetermined proportion (quota) has been achieved.

Race A variable based on physical attributes that can be subdivided into the Caucasoid, Negroid, and Mongoloid races.

Random assignment The process of assigning individuals to experimental or control groups so that the groups are equivalent; also referred to as randomization.

Random error Variable error in measurement; error due to unknown or uncontrolled factors that affect the variable being measured and the process of measurement in an inconsistent fashion.

Randomized cross-sectional survey design A descriptive research design in which there is only one group, the dependent variable is measured only once, the research participants are randomly selected from the population, and there is no independent variable.

Randomized longitudinal survey design A descriptive research design in which there is only one group, the dependent variable is measured more than once, and research participants are randomly selected from the population before each treatment.

Randomized one-group posttest-only design A descriptive research design in which there is only one group, the dependent variable is measured only once, and research participants are randomly selected from the population.

Randomized posttest-only control group design An explanatory research design in which there are two or more randomly assigned groups, the control group does not receive treatment, and the experimental groups receive different treatments.

Random numbers table A computer-generated or published table of numbers in which each number has an equal chance of appearing in each position in the table.

Random sampling An unbiased selection process conducted so that all members of a population have an equal chance of being selected to participate in a research study.

Range Difference between the largest and smallest numbers within an array.

Rank-order scale A comparative rating scale in which the rater is asked to rank specific individuals in relation to one another on some characteristic.

Rating scale A type of measuring instrument in which responses are rated on a continuum or in an ordered set of categories, with numerical values assigned to each point or category.

Ratio level of measurement The level of measurement that has a nonarbitrary, fixed zero point and classifies the values of a variable on an equally spaced continuum.

Raw scores Scores derived from administration of a measuring instrument to research participants or groups.

Reactive effect (1) An effect on outcome measures due to the research participants' awareness that they are being observed or interviewed; a threat to external and internal validity; (2) Alteration of the variables being measured or the respondents' performance on the measuring instrument due to administration of the instrument.

Reactivity The belief that things being observed or measured are affected by the fact that they are being observed or measured; one of the four main limitations of the quantitative research approach.

Reassessment A step in qualitative data analysis where the researcher interrupts the data analysis process to reaffirm the rules used to decide which meaning units are placed within different categories.

Recoding Developing and applying new variable value labels to a variable that has previously been coded; usually, recoding is done to make variables from one or more data sets comparable.

Reductionism In the quantitative research approach, the operationalization of concepts by reducing them to common measurable variables; one of the four main limitations of the quantitative research approach.

Regression analysis A variation of a correlational analysis that makes possible prediction of the value of one variable from observations on another variable.

Rejection level Set of values of a statistical test that indicates rejection of the null hypothesis; a probability associated with the test of a hypothesis using statistical techniques that determine whether or not the null hypothesis is rejected; probability of rejecting the null hypothesis when it is true.

Relative frequency distribution A table or graph that shows observation categories and the proportion of the group that falls within each value category—that is, the relative frequency of each category.

Relevancy One of the four criteria for evaluating research problem areas *and* formulating research questions out of the problem areas.

Reliability (1) The degree of accuracy, precision, or consistency in results of a measuring instrument, including the ability to produce the same results when the same variable is measured more than once or repeated applications of the same test on the same individual produce the same measurement; (2) The degree to which individual differences on scores or in data are due either to true differences or to errors in measurement.

Reliability coefficient A statistical representation of the relationship or correlation between two sets of scores.

Replication Repetition of the same research procedures by a second researcher for the purpose of determining if earlier results can be confirmed.

Research consumer A social work role reflecting the ethical obligation to base interventions on the most up-to-date research knowledge available.

Research design The entire plan of a quantitative and/or qualitative research study from problem conceptualization to the dissemination of findings.

Research hypothesis A statement about a study's research question that predicts the existence of a particular relationship between the independent and dependent variables; can be used in both the quantitative and qualitative approaches to research.

Research method The use of quantitative and qualitative research approaches to find out what is true; one of the five ways of knowing.

Research participants People utilized in research studies; also called subjects or cases.

Research question A specific research question that is formulated directly out of the general research problem area; answered by the qualitative and/or quantitative research approach; not to be confused with problem area.

Researchability The extent to which a research problem is in fact researchable and the problem can be resolved through the consideration of data derived from a research study; one of the four criteria for evaluating research problem areas *and* formulating research questions out of the problem areas.

Researcher bias The tendency of researchers to find results they expect to find; a threat to external validity.

Resources The costs associated with collecting data in any given research study; includes materials and supplies, equipment rental, transportation, training staff, and staff time; a criterion for selecting a data collection method.

Response categories Possible responses assigned to each question in a standardized measuring instrument, with a lower value generally indicating a low level of the variable being measured and a larger value indicating a higher level.

Response rate The total number of responses obtained from potential research participants to a measuring instrument divided by the total number of responses requested, usually expressed in the form of a percentage.

Response set Personal style; the tendency of research participants to respond to a measuring instrument in a particular way, regardless of the questions asked, or the tendency of observers or interviewers to react in certain ways; a source of constant error.

Review of the literature (1) A search of the professional literature to provide background knowledge of what has already been examined or tested in a specific problem area; (2) Use of any information source, such as a computerized data base, to locate existing data or information on a research problem, question, or hypothesis.

Rival hypothesis A hypothesis that is a plausible alternative to the research hypothesis and might explain the results as well or better; a hypothesis involving extraneous or intervening variables other than the independent variable in the research hypothesis; also referred to as an alternative hypothesis.

Robust results Results from a research study that are capable of standing up to further studies and that together constitute the aims of science.

Rules of correspondence A characteristic of measurement stipulating that numerals or symbols are assigned to properties of individuals, objects, or events according to specified rules.

***r* value** The correlation coefficient; a measure of association between two variables; also called Pearson's *r* or Pearson's product-moment correlation.

Sample A subset of a population of individuals, objects, or events chosen to participate in or to be considered in a research study.

Sampling error (1) The degree of difference that can be expected between the sample and the population from which it was drawn; (2) A mistake in a research study's results that is due to sampling procedures.

Sampling frame A listing of units (people, objects, or events) in a population from which a sample is drawn.

Sampling plan A method of selecting members of a population for inclusion in a research study, using procedures that make it possible to draw inferences about the population from the sample statistics.

Sampling theory The logic of using methods to ensure that a sample and a population are similar in all relevant characteristics.

Scale A measuring instrument composed of several items that are logically or empirically structured to measure a construct.

Scattergram A graphic representation of the relationship between two interval- or ratio-level variables.

Science Knowledge that has been obtained and tested through use of quantitative and qualitative research studies.

Scientific community A group that shares the same general norms for both research activity and acceptance of scientific findings and explanations.

Scientific determinism See Determinism.

Scientific method A generic method with specified steps for solving problems; the principles and procedures used in the systematic pursuit of knowledge.

Scope of a study The extent to which a problem area is covered in a single research study; a criterion for selecting a data collection method.

Score A numerical value assigned to an observation; also called data.

Search statement A preliminary search statement developed by the researcher prior to a literature search and which contains terms that can be combined to elicit specific data.

Secondary analysis An unobtrusive data collection method in which available data that predate the formulation of a research study are used to answer the research question or test the hypothesis.

Secondary data Data that predate the formulation of the research study and which are used to answer the research question or test the hypothesis.

Secondary data sources A data source that provides nonoriginal, secondhand, data.

Secondary reference source A source related to a primary source or sources, such as a critique of a particular source item or a literature review, bibliography, or commentary on several items.

Secondhand data Data obtained from people who are indirectly connected to the problem being studied.

Selection-treatment interaction The relationship between the manner of selecting research participants and their response to the independent variable; a threat to external validity.

Self-anchored scales A rating scale in which research participants rate themselves on a continuum of values, according to their own referents for each point.

Self-disclosure Shared communication about oneself, including one's behaviors, beliefs, and attitudes.

Semantic differential scale A modified measurement scale in which research participants rate their perceptions of the variable under study along three dimensions—evaluation, potency, and activity.

Semi-interquartile range Half the interquartile range.

Sequential triangulation When two distinct and separate phases of a research study are conducted and the results of the first phase are considered essential for planning the second phase; research questions in Phase 1 are answered before research questions in Phase 2 are formulated.

Service recipients People who use human services—individuals, couples, families, groups, organizations, and communities; also known as clients or consumers; a stakeholder group in evaluation.

Simple random sampling A one-stage probability sampling procedure in which members of a population are selected one at a time, without a chance of being selected again, until the desired sample size is obtained.

Simultaneous triangulation When the results of a quantitative and qualitative research question are answered at the same time; results to the qualitative research questions, for example, are reported separately and do not necessarily relate to, or confirm, the results from the quantitative phase.

Situationalists Researchers who assert that certain research approaches (qualitative or quantitative) are appropriate for specific situations.

Situation-specific variable A variable that may be observable only in certain environments and under certain circumstances, or with particular people.

Size of a study The number of people, places, or systems that are included in a single research study; a criterion for selecting a data collection method.

Skewed distribution A distribution in which more observations fall on one side of the mean than on the other side.

Skewness A quality of the distribution of a set of data dealing with whether the data are (or are not) symmetrically distributed around a central point.

Snowball sampling A nonprobability sampling procedure in which individuals selected for inclusion in a sample are asked to identify other individuals from the population who might be included; useful to locate people with divergent points of view.

Social desirability (1) A response set in which research participants tend to answer questions in a way that they perceive as giving favorable impressions of themselves; (2) The inclination of data providers to report data that present a socially desirable impression of themselves or their reference groups. Also referred to as impression management.

Social work research Scientific inquiry in which qualitative and quantitative research approaches are used to answer research questions and create new, generally applicable knowledge in the field of social work.

Socially acceptable response Bias in an answer that comes from research participants trying to answer questions as they think a "good" person should, rather than in a way that reveals what they actually believe or feel.

Socioeconomic variables Any one of several measures of social rank usually including income, education, and occupational prestige; abbreviated "SES."

Solomon four-group design An explanatory research design with four randomly assigned groups, two experimental and two control; the dependent variable is measured before and after treatment for one experimental and one control group, but only after treatment for the other two groups, and only experimental groups receive the treatment.

Specificity One of the four criteria for evaluating research hypotheses.

Split-half method A method for establishing the reliability of a measuring instrument by dividing it into comparable halves and comparing the scores between the two halves.

Spot-check recording A method of data collection that involves direct observation of the target problem at specified intervals rather than continuously.

Spurious relationship Occurring by chance; not a "real" relationship.

Stakeholder A person or group of people having a direct or indirect interest in the results of an evaluation.

Stakeholder service evaluation model Proponents of this evaluation model believe that program evaluations will be more likely to be utilized, and thus have a greater impact on social problems, when they are tailored to the needs of stakeholders; in this model, the purpose of program evaluation is not to generalize findings to other sites, but rather to restrict the evaluation effort to a particular program.

Standard deviation A measure that denotes the average deviation of scores about the mean and thus reflects the amount of variability in the data set.

Standard distribution See Normal Curve.

Standard error of the mean A measure, derived by dividing the standard deviation of the population mean by the square root of the sample size, which denotes the precision of estimate from the sample mean to the population mean.

Standard score A score stated in units of standard deviation from the mean of the distribution.

Standardized measuring instrument A professionally developed measuring instrument that provides for uniform administration and scoring and generates normative data against which later results can be evaluated.

Statistic A single number that can be used to summarize, analyze, or evaluate a group of observations; the product of a statistical test.

Statistical regression The tendency for extremely high or low scores to regress, or shift, toward the average (mean) score on subsequent tests; a threat to internal validity.

Statistical significance Significance of a relationship between two or more variables in a statistical sense; statistically significant results are usually at the .05 level.

Statistically significant Judged too unlikely to have occurred by chance. A statistically significant relationship between variables is, most likely, a real relationship.

Statistics The branch of mathematics concerned with the collection and analysis of data using statistical techniques.

Stratified random sampling A one-stage probability sampling procedure in which a population is divided into two or more strata to be sampled separately, using simple random or systematic random sampling techniques.

Structured interview schedule A complete list of questions to be asked and spaces for recording the answers; the interview schedule is used by interviewers when questioning respondents.

Structured observation A data collection method in which people are observed in their natural environments using specified methods and measurement procedures. See Direct Observation.

Subscale A component of a scale that measures some part or aspect of a major construct; also composed of several items that are logically or empirically structured.

Summated scale A questionnaire-type scale in which research participants are asked to indicate the degree of their agreement or disagreement with a series of questions.

Summative evaluation A type of evaluation that examines the ultimate success of a program and assists with decisions about whether a program should be continued or chosen in the first place among alternative program options.

Survey research A data collection method that uses survey-type data collection measuring instruments to obtain opinions or answers from a population or sample of research participants in order to describe or study them as a group.

Symmetrical distribution A distribution in which, for every observation on one side of the mean, there is another observation at an equal distance on the other side of the mean.

Synthesis Undertaking the search for meaning in our sources of information at every step of the research process; combining parts such as data, concepts, and theories to arrive at a higher level of understanding.

Systematic To arrange the steps of a research study in a methodical way.

Systematic random sampling A one-stage probability sampling procedure in which every person at a designated interval in a specific population is selected to be included in a research study's sample.

Systematic error Measurement error that is consistent, not random.

Target population The group about which a researcher wants to draw conclusions, another term for a population about which one aims to make inferences.

Target problem (1) In case-level evaluation designs, the problems social workers seek to solve for their clients; (2) A measurable behavior, feeling, or cognition that is either a problem in itself or symptomatic of some other problem.

Temporal research design A research study that includes time as a major variable; the purpose of this design is to investigate change in the distribution of a variable or in relationships among variables over time; there are three types of temporal research designs: cohort, panel, and trend.

Temporal stability Consistency of responses to a measuring instrument over time; reliability of an instrument across forms and across administrations.

Testing effect The effect that taking a pretest might have on posttest scores; a threat to internal validity.

Test-retest reliability Reliability of a measuring instrument established through repeated administration to the same group of individuals.

Thematic notes In observational research, thematic notes are a record of emerging ideas, hypotheses, theories, and conjectures; thematic notes provide a place for the researcher to speculate and identify themes, make linkages between ideas and events, and articulate thoughts as they emerge in the field setting.

Theme In qualitative data analysis, a concept or idea that describes a single category or a grouping of categories; an abstract interpretation of qualitative data.

Theoretical framework A frame of reference that serves to guide a research study and is developed from theories, findings from a variety of other studies, and the researcher's personal experiences.

Theoretical sampling See Purposive Sampling.

Theory A reasoned set of propositions, derived from and supported by established data, which serves to explain a group of phenomena; a conjectural explanation that may, or may not, be supported by data generated from qualitative and quantitative research studies.

Time orientation An important cultural factor that considers whether one is future-, present-, or past-oriented; for instance, individuals who are "present-oriented" would not be as preoccupied with advance planning as those who are "future-oriented."

Time-series design See Interrupted Time-Series Design.

Tradition Traditional cultural beliefs that we accept—without question—as true; one of the five ways of knowing.

Transcript A written, printed, or typed copy of interview data or any other written material that have been gathered for a qualitative research study.

Transition statements Sentences used to indicate a change in direction or focus of questions in a measuring instrument.

Treatment group See Experimental Group.

Trend study A longitudinal study design in which data from surveys carried out at periodic intervals on samples drawn from a particular population are used to reveal trends over time.

Triangulation The idea of combining different research methods in all steps associated with a single research study; assumes that any bias inherent in one particular method will be neutralized when used in conjunction with other research methods; seeks convergence of a study's results; using more than one research method and source of data to study the same phenomena and to enhance validity; there are several types of triangulation, but the essence of the term is that multiple perspectives are compared; it can involve multiple data sources or multiple data analyzers; the hope is that the different perspectives will confirm each other, adding weight to the credibility and dependability of qualitative data analysis.

Triangulation of analysts Using multiple data analyzers to code a single segment of transcript and comparing the amount of agreement between analyzers; a method used to verify coding of qualitative data.

***t*-score** A standard score that has been transformed to a distribution with a mean of 50 and a standard deviation of 10.

***t*-test** A parametric hypothesis test that uses the t distribution to arrive at a decision; determines if there is a statistically significant difference between two means.

Two-phase research model A model combining qualitative and quantitative research approaches in a single study where each approach is conducted as a separate and distinct phase of the study.

Two-tailed hypotheses Statements that *do not* predict specific relationships between independent and dependent variables.

Unimodal A distribution with only one mode.

Unit of analysis A specific research participant (person, object, or event) or the sample or population relevant to the research question; the persons or things being studied; units of analysis in research are often persons, but may be groups, political parties, newspaper editorials, unions, hospitals, schools, etc.; a particular unit of analysis from which data are gathered is called a case.

Univariate A hypothesis or research design involving a single variable.

Univariate analysis Statistical analysis of the distribution of values of a single variable.

Universe See Population.

Unobtrusive methods Data collection methods that do not influence the variable under study or the responses of research participants; methods that avoid reactive effects.

Unstructured interviews A series of questions that allow flexibility for both the research participant and the interviewer to make changes during the process.

Validity (1) The extent to which a measuring instrument measures the variable it is supposed to measure and measures it accurately; (2) The degree to which an instrument is able to do what it is intended to do, in terms of both experimental procedures and measuring instruments (internal validity) and generalizability of results (external validity); (3) The degree to which scores on a measuring instrument correlate with measures of performance on some other criterion.

Variable A concept with characteristics that can take on different values.

Variability Dispersion of a distribution; the extent to which values differ among themselves; variability is not the name of a specific statistic; rather, it is the term applied to the characteristic of dispersion.

Variance Measure of variability that is the average value of the squares of the deviations from the mean of the scores in a distribution.

Verbatim recording Recording interview data word-for-word and including significant gestures, pauses, and expressions of persons in the interview.

Vertical axis The vertical dimension of a two-dimensional graph; it usually represents frequency in frequency distributions, relative frequency in relative frequency distributions, and cumulative proportion in cumulative proportion graphs.

Wideband measuring instrument Measuring instruments that measure more than one variable.

Within-group differences Refers to the amount of variation on any particular variable within a specific population or target group; it is often contrasted with comparisons between groups.

Within-methods research approach Triangulation by using different research methods available in *either* the qualitative *or* the quantitative research approaches in a single research study.

Words The basic data unit of analysis used in qualitative research studies.

Worker cooperation The actions and attitudes of program personnel when carrying out a research study within an existing social service program; a criterion for selecting a data collection method.

Working hypothesis An assertion about a relationship between two or more variables that may not be true but is plausible and worth examining.